Women's Sexuality After Childhood Incest

A Norton Professional Book

Women's Sexuality After Childhood Incest

Elaine Westerlund

W. W. NORTON & COMPANY • NEW YORK • LONDON

Printed in the United States of America.

First Edition

The text of this book was composed in Elante and Korinna. Composition by Bytheway Typesetting Services, Inc. Manufacturing by Haddon Craftsmen, Inc.

Library of Congress Cataloging-in-Publication Data

Westerlund, Elaine.
    Women's sexuality after childhood incest / Elaine Westerlund.
        p.   cm.
    "A Norton professional book"—Half t.p.
    Includes bibliographical references and index.
    ISBN 0-393-70141-7
    1. Incest victims—United States—Sexual behavior. 2. Incest victims—United States—Mental health. 3. Sex therapy—United States. 4. Adult child sexual abuse victims—United States.
    I. Title.
HQ72.U53W47   1992
362.7'6—dc20   92-5320   CIP

W.W. Norton & Company, Inc., 500 Fifth Avenue, New York, N.Y. 10110
W.W. Norton & Company, Ltd., 10 Coptic Street, London WC1A 1PU

1 2 3 4 5 6 7 8 9 0

To the brave women
who speak in these pages and
to the brave little girls they were

CONTENTS

PREFACE   ix

ACKNOWLEDGMENTS   xii

INTRODUCTION   3

  1. Myth and Reality   6

  2. The Study and the Participants   24

  3. The Incest and Its Impact   37

  4. Body Perception and Reproduction   52

  5. Sexual Preference and Sexual "Lifestyle"   61

  6. Sexual Functioning   74

  7. "Lucky" Women   88

8. "Uncomfortable" Women   103

9. "Damaged" Women   125

10. Treatment Recommendations: Cognitive and Behavioral   148

11. Treatment Recommendations: Physical and Educational   161

Epilogue   177

APPENDIX A   Methodology   181

APPENDIX B   Westerlund Incest Survivors Questionnaire   188

APPENDIX C   Interview Question   211

APPENDIX D   Interview Guide   212

APPENDIX E   Tables   214

APPENDIX F   Treatment and Self-Help Resources   224

APPENDIX G   Deep Muscle Relaxation Guide   227

REFERENCES   229

INDEX   235

PREFACE

THIS BOOK IRONICALLY OWES ITS EXISTENCE to three men in my family who unwittingly challenged me to produce it. I have lived what I write about here, and feel blessed and privileged to have conducted the study on which this book is based. It has been an incredibly enriching experience to have the women in these pages share their lives with me, and it has been gratifying to see this book develop from their words and my own.

The idea for this book was conceived in 1980 when I "uncovered" another "woman like me" and began reading what had been written about "us." At the time most of the literature annoyed me and some of it infuriated me, but I continued to read and soon discovered not only what had been written but also what remained to be written. And I decided "we" would all be better off if a survivor wrote about our sexuality than if "we" left it up to "them."

My feelings about "them" changed over time as more of "them" began listening to more of "us," and as the literature began reflecting that shift. But my interest in writing a book about sexuality in women with incest histories also grew.

As it turns out, the time is far more ripe today for this book than it was a decade ago. Now women are not only regularly mentioning the "unmentionable"; they are declaring that *nothing* is sacred—not even family—if their bodies are not sacred first. It was in that spirit that the women in these pages participated in the study on which this book is based. I am deeply grateful to them for trusting me with their childhood and their womanhood.

This study was not a simple one to participate in or to conduct. The research was very gradually developed between 1980 and 1984 during the early years of my work with Incest Resources, a nonprofit, self-help organization I cofounded in Cambridge, Massachusetts. During those years I was completing my graduate school coursework and was serving at various psychology internship sites in addition to working as a volunteer for Incest Resources. Designing the study, originally for my doctoral dissertation, was a project I could only work on in my "spare" time. In 1984 my son was born and "spare" time was all the harder to come by. The data collection was not carried out until late 1985 and early 1986. Data analysis and dissertation write-up were completed during late 1986 and early 1987.

It seemed a simple enough matter back in the spring of 1987 to put a book together incorporating the study findings and expanding upon the topic. Little did I know, with growing professional and personal commitments, that this would take an additional four years.

It was my intent, when I decided to do this book, to provide a single, comprehensive volume of knowledge accumulated over time on female sexuality after incest. The opening section of the book provides the reader with a full description of what was known and documented prior to the completion of this study. The Introduction reports on the incidence and prevalence of incest among U.S. females, the frequency of complaints regarding sexuality among such females, and the inadequacy of our knowledge on the subject at the time. Chapter 1 offers a review of the research literature prior to this study and a discussion of the myths and stereotypes that surrounded women with incest histories and their sexuality when the study was undertaken.

The second section of the book gives an overview of the study and the women who participated in it, including their past- and then-present lives. Chapter 2 describes the research, including the study sample, the questionnaire, the interviews, the participants, and the study limitations. Chapter 3 presents the women's experiences of incest, including their responses over time and the long-term effects as perceived by them.

The third section of the book reports on the women's sexuality in five different arenas. Chapter 4 discusses the study findings pertaining to body perception and reproduction. Chapter 5 discusses the study findings related to sexual preference and sexual "lifestyle." Chapter 6 discusses the study findings regarding sexual functioning.

The fourth section of the book, consisting of Chapters 7, 8, and 9, presents case narratives of the interviewed women. The women are clustered according to their level of distress over their adult sexuality. Discussions in each chapter relate to commonalities and differences within and across groups.

The fifth section of the book discusses treatment and self-help recommendations. Chapter 10 discusses cognitive and behavioral techniques and methods. Chapter 11 discusses physical and educational techniques and methods. An Epilogue provides a final summary.

I hope this book will serve the purpose it was intended to serve. As a woman who has struggled with healing her own sexuality as well as helping others heal theirs, I am pleased to be making the information available. My wish would be for survivors and professionals to benefit in all the ways which would enable them to do recovery work on sexuality together.

ACKNOWLEDGMENTS

OVER TIME MANY PEOPLE CONTRIBUTED to the development of this book. Eileen Nickerson, Hilary Bender, Carolyn Dillon, and Oliva Espin provided enthusiastic support as well as critical research review. My co-workers from Incest Resources, Inc., graciously tested the questionnaire used for the research and shared their reactions and observations. My colleagues, Patricia Hunt and Linda Nathan, amiably provided a reliability check on my analysis of the data from the interview portion of the research. Susan Snyder and Katie Logue skillfully typed, transcribed, and transformed. And Susan Barrows Munro provided the final touches to the work for W. W. Norton.

Throughout, Maggie Downes, Mercedes Cabral, and Linda Sargent encouraged me to persevere; Joseph Doherty lent his support to both the research and the writing; our beautiful son, Neil, reminded me daily that childhood can truly be a joyful time; and, as always, the memory of my maternal grandmother, Beatrice Peterson, sustained me.

As I complete this book, my thoughts are with my mother, Virginia Westerlund, who suffered and grew with me as I healed from the incest. This book speaks to her pain and her strength as well as mine, and to the love we have for one another as women today.

Women's
Sexuality
After
Childhood
Incest

annie died the other day

never was there such a lay—
whom,among her dollies,dad
first("don't tell your mother")had;
making annie slightly mad
but very wonderful in bed
—saints and satyrs,go your way

youths and maidens:let us pray

e.e. cummings

INTRODUCTION

IT IS CURIOUS that as late as the mid-1980s researchers had yet to ask women with incest histories to describe their sexuality. Incest is, after all, sexual by definition, whatever the offender motivations involved. One would reasonably expect childhood incest to have pronounced effects on adult sexuality in females. And one would reasonably expect researchers to have completely investigated the topic.

Yet, although an influence on future sexuality had been documented by then (Bess & Janssen, 1982; Courtois, 1979b, 1980; Courtois & Watts, 1982; Finkelhor, 1980; Fritz, Stoll, & Wagner, 1981; Herman, 1981; Hirschman, 1980; Meiselman, 1978, 1980; Russell, 1986; Tsai, Feldman-Summers, & Edgar, 1979; Tsai & Wagner, 1978; Westerlund, 1983), descriptive material was distinctly lacking (Meiselman, 1978; Tsai & Wagner, 1978; Westerlund, 1983). Little was actually known in regard to the nature of sexuality in women with incest histories. Studies conducted to specifically investigate aspects of sexuality were rare (Becker, Skinner, Abel, Axelrod, & Cichon, 1984; Becker, Skinner, Abel, & Treacy, 1982; Boekelheide, 1978; Lang-made, 1983; McGuire & Wagner, 1978; Tsai et al., 1979). Articles address-ing the treatment implications of study findings related to sexuality were even more rare (Faria & Belohlavek, 1984; McGuire & Wagner, 1978).

At the time this study was undertaken, it was generally assumed that incest victims would later be at risk for sexual exploitation, pornography, or prostitution. There were, however, other outcomes with respect to sexuali-ty that had been widely ignored. Outcomes troublesome to society seemed guaranteed to receive a certain amount of attention. No such guarantee seemed to exist for those outcomes that didn't affect society, however troublesome they may have been to the women themselves and however commonly they may have occurred.

As is true today, the number of women with incest histories in the United States was impossible to determine in the mid-1980s. Estimates had ranged from one in a million suggested as late as 1975 (Henderson) to one-third of all women (Belmonte & Boyer, 1983). The estimated figure of ten percent of U.S. women that had appeared in the literature for some time then was based upon several large-scale surveys of predominantly white, middle-class women (Finkelhor, 1979; Kinsey, Pomeroy, Martin, & Gebhand, 1953; Landis, 1956). Random sample surveys on the incidence and prevalence of sexual abuse histories among adult females in the United States (Russell, 1986; Wyatt, 1985) had indicated figures from these surveys were 16 percent and 21 percent respectively. These figures did not include cases involving exhibitionism or sexual advances and propositions not culminating in direct physical contact. They also did not include those women unwilling to report an incest history to a researcher with whom they had no ongoing relationship, and those women unable to report an incest history due to repression.

Among clinical populations, the percentage of women with incest histories appeared to be higher. Reports by Woodbury and Schwartz (1971) and Rosenfeld (1979) had indicated prevalence rates among general outpatient therapy populations of 30 percent and 33 percent, respectively. These figures were consistent with Bess and Janssen (1982) who reported that 31 percent of their subject group, which was selected at random from all persons presenting for outpatient psychiatric intake, disclosed an incest history. Clearly, the number of women with incest histories was sizable.

Of those women, it was again impossible to know how many perceived that their sexuality had been affected by the incest experience. In a study of 83 survivors of sexual assault including incest survivors (Becker et al., 1982), 41 percent of the women had reported sexual problems which they attributed to their experiences with rape and/or incest. In a later study of 371 sexual assault survivors including incest survivors (Becker et al., 1984), the figure was again 41 percent. While the authors had not provided separate figures for the incest survivors, they had noted that the incidence of sexual problems was higher among the incest survivors than it was among the rape survivors in these samples.

Certainly women with sexual abuse histories had often been encountered among women treated for problems of sexual functioning (McGuire & Wagner, 1978). In one study, 90 percent of the women being treated had been raped during childhood, 23 percent by fathers and stepfathers (Baisden, 1971).

Women with incest histories had also frequently reported sexual difficulties in therapy (Bess & Janssen, 1982; Courtois & Watts, 1982; Herman, 1981; Hirschman, 1980; Meiselman, 1978, 1980; Tsai & Wagner, 1978; Westerlund, 1983). The percentage of complaints regarding sexual impairment had ranged from 55 percent (Herman, 1981) to 87 percent (Courtois, 1980; Meiselman, 1978). These figures were substantially different from those reported by therapy patients without incest histories. In Meiselman's (1978) study, complaints of sexual problems for the incest group were 87 percent compared to 20 percent for the control group. Bess and Janssen (1982) reported similar findings of 70 percent compared to 18 percent in psychotherapy groups consisting of both males and females. Hirschman (1980) found that, even compared with clients whose fathers were seductive, incest clients experienced greater impairment in their sexual relations.

Yet, as a result of our limited knowledge, the treatment of problems related to sexuality in women with incest histories had been woefully neglected by therapists and sex therapists alike. Current sex therapy techniques at the time were in many instances inappropriate or ineffective with women with incest histories. The well-known sex therapy volumes (Kaplan, 1974; LoPiccolo & LoPiccolo, 1978; Masters & Johnson, 1970) did not expressly discuss the treatment of incest cases. Techniques specifically prescribed for women with incest histories were virtually nonexistent, whether one considered present sex therapy approaches or psychotherapy approaches.

By the mid-1980s sexuality had long been recognized as an aspect of women's lives that had profound implications for health and psychological well-being. Incest had been recognized as a trauma that had been experienced by a conservatively estimated 12 million women in the general population of the United States (Russell, 1983). Given those facts, the failure of researchers to have addressed the issue was, to say the least, regrettable. The inadequacies of our knowledge at the time regarding sexuality in women with incest histories will become more painfully obvious in the chapter that follows. So, too, will the stereotypes that, in the absence of knowledge, surrounded women with incest histories and their sexuality when this study was undertaken.

1

~~~~

Myth and Reality

THERE ARE SEVERAL QUESTIONS that people routinely ask, or would like to ask, about sexuality in women with incest histories. They are:

1. Is it true that incest inevitably leads to "promiscuity"?
2. Do many incest victims become prostitutes and pornography queens?
3. Is "frigidity" only "natural" in a woman with an incest history?
4. Do incest survivors often become lesbians?

Why these particular questions? Because all have been rumored to be true.

The myths and realities that pertain to the sexual lives of women with incest histories have been inextricably interwoven for decades now. Contributing to the confusion of the two are a variety of factors related to the research literature on incest, particularly in the earlier literature, including the highly select and nonrepresentative nature of incest samples. A closer look at those factors is included in this review of what had been written about sexuality in women with incest histories prior to this study.

It should be noted that much significant work has appeared on incest and sexuality over the past five years that is not reported on here. Some very important recent works are mentioned in the treatment chapters and are included in the treatment and self-help resources section at the end of the book. These should not be overlooked, but should be understood to have not yet had an impact when this study was undertaken. The literature reviewed here reflects the knowledge on the subject at the time and provides an accurate context in which to consider the study.

Overview of the Literature

Historically, studies of women with incest histories emphasized "promiscuity" and prostitution as outcomes (Gordon, 1955; Greenwald, 1958; Hersko, Halleck, Rosenberg, & Pacht, 1961; Howard, 1959; Kaufman, Peck, & Tagiuri, 1954; Kubo, 1959; Lukianowicz, 1972; Maisch, 1972; Medlicott, 1967; Rascovsky & Rascovsky, 1950; Sloane & Karpinski, 1942; Weinberg, 1955). There are several reasons for this:

1. In the past, incest samples were drawn primarily from clinic and court populations. Such samples were skewed toward psychological disturbance and toward sexual behaviors outside the norm.
2. Sexual "acting out" is considered a social problem in women and prostitution a threat to the community. Thus, such behaviors both attracted interest and were defined as worthy of study. In fact, in the literature of the past, "promiscuity" was presented (along with the failure to marry) as the only conclusive evidence of harm to women with incest histories (Herman & Hirschman, 1977). Such measures of damage reflect the value placed on feminine "virtue" and on the role of wife in our culture.
3. During those years in which our society was most sexually repressive and most mindful of the double standard, the labeling of women as "promiscuous" was a common practice. Indeed, such women may have merely engaged in premarital sex with more than one partner or been involved in some form of extramarital activity. Whatever was considered outside the norm for female sexual behavior at the time was viewed as deviant, however.
4. Additionally, it was often convenient to label the victim "promiscuous." To do so shifted the responsibility from the offender to the victim, providing an effective, if transparent, rationalization for the offender's behavior. As several later authors noted (Herman, 1981; Rush, 1980; Westerlund, 1986), incest victims were repeatedly blamed for what happened to them; "promiscuity" in the victim was but one defense offered in incest cases.

Sexual nonresponsiveness in women with incest histories was ignored historically for similar reasons. Since it is neither conspicuous nor antisocial, it received little attention. The community may, in fact, view nonresponsive women as well-adjusted if their sexuality is considered unimportant. Given that in the past there were no societal expectations with regard to sexual responsiveness and orgasm in women, nonresponsiveness was hardly conceived of as a problem, even by women themselves.

Remarkable as it may seem today, prior to the 1960s the very existence of a female orgasm was actually under question. This is reflected in the fact that difficulties related to sexual responsiveness including orgasmic dysfunction were not even mentioned in most of the earlier incest studies (Bender & Blau, 1937; Bender & Grugett, 1952; Sloane & Karpinski, 1942; Weinberg, 1955).

The early literature on women with incest histories limited discussion regarding their sexual functioning to mentions of "asceticism," "frigidity," or unspecified "sexual problems" (Berry, 1975; Greenland, 1958; Hersko et al., 1961; Howard, 1959; Kaufman et al., 1954; Landis, 1940; Lukianowicz, 1972; Magal & Winnick, 1968; Masters & Johnson, 1970; Molnar & Cameron, 1975; Rascovsky & Rascovsky, 1950). Moreover, "frigidity" was rarely cited in conjunction with any discussion of inadequate desire, arousal, and/or orgasm, but rather has referred to sexual aversion or to avoidance of sex with husband or male partner (Greenland, 1958; Hersko et al., 1961; Howard, 1959; Landis, 1940; Lukianowicz, 1972; Magal & Winnick, 1968; Rascovsky & Rascovsky, 1950). Thus, "frigidity" was viewed as a problem more in terms of female sexual compliance or noncompliance than in terms of the female's subjective experience.

For many years, a general lack of knowledge regarding female sexuality prevailed. This influenced what little description was offered of sexuality in women with incest histories. As late as 1972, in a discussion of the aftereffects of incest, Lukianowicz described "promiscuity" as an outcome category as if it existed separate from the outcome category he labeled "frigidity." "Promiscuity" is obviously often coincident with "frigidity." Such gross misunderstanding of the nature of female sexuality is fortunately not often encountered today.

Between the mid-1970s and mid-1980s, following on a wave of consciousness-raising regarding violence against women and children, incest was "rediscovered." Largely as a result of the influences of feminism, societal attitudes toward incest gradually changed over this period. This allowed women with incest histories to begin to more openly identify themselves and to more honestly discuss their experiences. The liberalization of sexual attitudes and the advancement of information related to female sexuality over this time period concurrently encouraged women with incest histories to more freely report on their sexuality. Thus, the literature from this time period differs from that which preceded it both in tone and in content, as the following discussions illustrate.

"Promiscuity"

"Promiscuity," both pre-incest and post-incest, was widely discussed in the literature prior to this study.

Pre-incest "promiscuity" was, in fact, in many instances suggested as a precipitant for incest. Given that incest routinely occurs well before adolescence, such suggestions might just as routinely have been dismissed. In actuality, even among populations of adolescent incest victims reported by "the authorities" or referred by the courts (Gligor, 1966; Maisch, 1972; Weinberg, 1955), "promiscuity" prior to the incest had been found in only a small minority of cases. Maisch (1972) found that 13 percent of the 76 daughters in his sample had had "undesirable sexual relations" before the incest occurred. It is unclear what sexual relationships were considered "undesirable" in West Germany at the time. Excluding long-term sexual relationships from her definition, Gligor (1966) found that only four percent of her U.S. sample of 57 daughters had been simultaneously involved sexually with two or more partners prior to the incest.

Reports of pre-incest "promiscuity" among samples drawn from other research settings were rare particularly when definitions of "promiscuity" were based upon realistic rather than idealistic standards. Meiselman (1978) asked the therapists of the daughters in her psychotherapy sample about pre-incest "promiscuity," using as criteria having had sex on a very casual basis or having changed sexual partners every few weeks or months. Only one case of "promiscuity" prior to the incest was reported among the 38 daughters in her sample of 47 females representing the major socioeconomic classes and ethnic groups.

"Promiscuity" subsequent to the incest was more frequently encountered. Although an impression had been created in the literature that "promiscuity" was a general and fixed characteristic of women with incest histories, a period of post-incest "promiscuity" for a minority of females had been the most common finding since the early incest studies (Kaufman et al., 1954; Kubo, 1959; Weinberg, 1955), including at least one U.S. study with a substantial and representative sample (Weinberg, 1955). The percentage of females labeled "promiscuous" had varied widely from study to study. At one extreme, Lukianowicz (1972) found that 42 percent of the 26 daughters in his sample were "promiscuous" following the incest. At the other extreme, Molnar and Cameron (1975) found no cases of "promiscuity" among the 10 daughters in their sample.

Several reasons exist for the wide discrepancy in reported percentages in the literature. Some studies assessed their subjects only shortly after the incest or followed them only through mid-adolescence (Gligor, 1966; Maisch, 1972; Weinberg, 1955). Such samples tended to reveal only compulsive sexual behavior as an outcome. Other studies provided follow-up reports, but generally on biased samples located through juvenile residences, public agencies, and the like (Howard, 1959; Kubo, 1959; Lukianowicz, 1972; Rascovsky & Rascovsky, 1950; Sloane & Karpinski, 1942). Such samples tended to include mostly "acting out" females who exhibited a variety of behaviors, including sexual behaviors outside the norm. Time was also an important factor. Studies conducted in similar research settings during different time frames may well be discrepant. For example, Medlicott found "promiscuity" in 35 percent of the 17 daughters in his psychotherapy sample interviewed in 1967; Molnar and Cameron found none among the ten daughters in their psychotherapy sample interviewed in 1975. One factor contributing to this difference might well have been the changes in general definitions of "promiscuity" resulting from the sexual revolution of the late 1960s and early 1970s. In the earlier studies, definitions were, for the most part, unstated. Additionally, the nature of the clients engaged in psychotherapy changed somewhat during those years as a result of increased public acceptance of mental health treatment. Cross-cultural differences in general definitions of "promiscuity" must also be considered, since many countries (Argentina, Canada, France, Great Britain, Israel, Japan, New Zealand, Northern Ireland, Norway, Sweden, United States, West Germany) were represented by the earlier incest studies.

While there was little agreement with respect to definitions or percentages in the literature prior to this study, post-incest "promiscuity" had nonetheless been a consistent finding. This had been true for the later U.S. studies as well. Herman (1981) reported that 35 percent of an all-white psychotherapy sample of 40 daughters had been "promiscuous" at one time by their own definition. This contrasted with the 15 percent figure reported by the comparison group of 20 women whose fathers were seductive but not incestuous. Meiselman (1978) found that 19 percent of the 23 incest daughters over 18 and 71 percent of the eight incest sisters over 18 in her psychotherapy sample had gone through a period of post-incest "promiscuity" (according to her definition as stated earlier in this chapter). Meiselman did not provide a "promiscuity" figure for the control group.

Both Herman (1981) and Meiselman (1978) emphasized the transitory nature of "promiscuity" in women with incest histories. Meiselman noted that "promiscuity" was generally outgrown in the twenties and that very few of the women in her sample had actually been labeled "promiscuous" as a result of a chronic pattern.

Finkelhor (1980) also concluded that the impact of incest on sexual activity is greatest in early adulthood. In a survey of predominantly white college students, Finkelhor discovered that the 75 females with sibling incest histories reported substantially higher levels of sexual activity than the 395 females without such histories. On closer examination he found that the difference between groups disappeared as adulthood progressed and the nonincest females caught up.

Boekelheide (1978) also reported on college females with incest histories, briefly describing three cases. It is interesting to note that two out of the three cases discussed were young women entering therapy with the wish to change a previous "promiscuous" pattern.

Langmade (1983) found in his study of women in psychotherapy that the 34 incest subjects of his study reported significantly less sexual activity than the 34 matched controls. In this instance the subject age range was 19 to 41 years, with a mean age of 29.7 years.

Women seen in later adulthood had been noted to sometimes exhibit different patterns than they had in early adulthood. Westerlund (1983) had commented on this, stating that compulsive sexual responses to incest could be but one side of an alternating pattern in which inhibited sexual responses would also be seen over time.

Most of the later reports on "promiscuity" in women with incest histories were specific to clinical samples. This was important to note, since women with incest histories in therapy were more likely to report "promiscuity" than women with incest histories not in therapy. Tsai, Feldman-Summers, and Edgar (1979) found that, among women molested as children, 43 percent of the clinical group of 30 reported having 15 or more sexual partners, whereas only 17 percent of the nonclinical group of 30 women reported the same. It was also important to take into account that "promiscuity" existed in the general population as well. This seemingly obvious fact had often been overlooked by those examining reported percentages in women with incest histories. Tsai et al. (1979) utilized a third group of 30 in the above-mentioned study, women not molested as children and not in therapy. Nine percent reported having 15 or more sexual partners.

In summary, the literature prior to this study presented some evidence of an association between incest and later "promiscuity." Pre-incest "promiscuity" was apparently rare. While the literature dispelled the notion that women with incest histories were generally "promiscuous," it suggested that a period of post-incest "promiscuity" was not uncommon for a substantial number, but still a minority, of women. A chronic pattern of "promiscuity" had been the exception among women with incest histories studied through that time, although conspicuously "promiscuous" females had been well attended to in the literature.

Prostitution

Like "promiscuity," prostitution was extensively discussed as an outcome of incest in the literature prior to this study.

Although the incidence of prostitution had generally been small, cases had been mentioned with regularity. In one of the early follow-up studies, Sloane and Karpinski (1942) reported that one of their five cases of incest had subsequently been involved in a period of prostitution. Lukianowicz (1972) found four cases of prostitution in his sample of 26 daughters. Most commonly, studies, including at least one large U.S. study with a representative sample (Weinberg, 1955), had indicated that a minority of women with incest histories who were "promiscuous" in adolescence later became involved in prostitution (Gagnon, 1965; Kubo, 1959; Lukianowicz, 1972; Sloane & Karpinski, 1942; Weinberg, 1955).

Later U.S. studies with substantial incest samples had revealed fewer cases of prostitution, although this may have been due in part to differences in sample characteristics. Meiselman (1978) found only one woman in her sample of 23 daughters over the age of 18 who had been involved in a period of prostitution. While Meiselman's sample included a "healthy representation of the major ethnic groups and socioeconomic classes" (p. 56), it was nonetheless select in that it was a psychotherapy sample. Herman (1981) reported two women in an all-white psychotherapy sample of 40 daughters.

Despite the rather small numbers, cases of prostitution had attracted a great deal of attention in the literature. This had apparently been due primarily to the dramatic nature of prostitution as a form of "acting out" in females.

Although there had been little evidence to support the notion that many women with incest histories became involved in prostitution, there had been substantial evidence to support the notion that many prostitutes had been involved in incest. Weinberg (1955) commented on the association between prostitution and early sexual exploitation, citing a Swiss study of prostitutes conducted in 1912 in which 30 percent were found to have been sexually abused as children. In a study of 20 "call girls," Greenwald (1958) regularly discovered early sexual exploitation by adult males as part of the females' histories. In several instances, the adult males involved were stepfathers and other relatives.

After the mid-1970s several U.S. studies provided overwhelming evidence linking prostitution to juvenile sexual abuse. James and Meyerding (1977a) found that 46 percent of a sample of 136 prostitutes had been sexually abused by an adult during childhood. Incestuous abuse was involved in over 36 percent of the cases. In a second study James and Meyerding (1977b) found that 65 percent of a sample of 20 adolescent prostitutes reported early sexual abuse. The offender was a relative in over 38 percent of these cases. Silbert and Pines (1981, 1983) similarly reported that 60 percent of their sample of 200 street prostitutes had been sexually abused as juveniles, two-thirds by fathers and surrogate fathers. Brothers and uncles were frequent offenders as well.

The association between prostitution and childhood sexual abuse appeared not only to be strong, but also to be specific to intrafamilial as opposed to extrafamilial sexual abuse. Vitaliano and James (1977) discovered that a significant difference between 126 prostitutes' and 129 nonprostitutes' reports of juvenile sexual abuse occurred only for related abuse; that is, prostitutes experienced significantly more incest than nonprostitutes.

While studies had repeatedly demonstrated that incest was commonly found in the background of prostitutes, it was important not to interpret as indicating that incest led to prostitution. It was likely in some instances that incest led to runaway behavior, which in turn led to vulnerability to prostitution. No causal connection between incest and prostitution had been established.

In summary, although prostitution had been emphasized in the literature prior to this study, a period of prostitution had not been a common finding among women with incest histories studied. It appeared that a small minority of women who had become "promiscuous" following the incest had later become involved in prostitution, but that even among "promiscuous" females, the majority would not move on to prostitution.

Sexual Preference

Most of the earlier incest studies (Gligor, 1966; Hersko et al., 1961; Lukianowicz, 1972; Magal & Winnick, 1968; Maisch, 1972; Molnar & Cameron, 1975; Weinberg, 1955) omitted mention of homosexuality; in fact, whether they even inquired about sexual preference is unclear. Kubo (1959) was one of the few to mention homosexuality specifically, stating that none was found among the 27 daughters and sisters in his sample. In several of the early follow-up studies (Bender & Grugett, 1952; Rasmussen, 1934; Sloane & Karpinski, 1942), there were also no findings of homosexuality.

A few of the early clinical studies reported findings of homosexuality, but did not specify numbers. Kaufman et al. (1954) and Heims and Kaufman (1963) reported that some of the incest daughters in their samples of 11 and 20, respectively, had been involved homosexually subsequent to the incest, but they did not report on the nature of the relationships. It is unclear whether they were sexually consummated relationships or were same-sex attachments typical of adolescent females. The only early clinical researcher to provide an actual figure was Medlicott (1967), who reported that 29 percent of his sample of 17 daughters manifested "serious homosexual problems."

Given the attitudes toward homosexuality that prevailed at the time of these early studies, one would not expect women to have disclosed a homosexual preference, particularly in those instances where no ongoing relationship existed with the researcher. The general absence of information regarding sexual preference in the early incest literature thus comes as no surprise.

Although the early incest literature generally failed to comment on female homosexuality, several early homosexuality studies did comment on a possible association between childhood incest and the development of a lesbian identity. Gundlach and Riess (1967), in a U.S. study of 217 middle-class lesbians and 231 middle-class non-lesbians, reported that 54 women had experienced rape or attempted rape at or before the age of 15. Of those 54 women, 39 were lesbians and 15 were non-lesbians. Gundlach (1977) reported in a follow-up study that a significant difference in the proportion of lesbians and heterosexual women occurred only for sexual abuse that was incestuous or nearly incestuous. Among those who were abused as children by an unknown assailant, the number of females who were homosexual as adults was not disproportionate. However, of 17 women who were sexually abused by a relative or close family friend as a child, 16 were lesbians as adults.

While these figures indicated an association between incest and female homosexuality, they did not demonstrate any causal connection. It was important to recognize that the vast majority of the lesbians in these study samples (83 percent and 79 percent, respectively) reported no heterosexual trauma in their histories, incestuous or otherwise.

Likewise, even though Simari and Baskin (1982) found that 38 percent of their demographically diverse lesbian sample of 29 reported incestuous experience, that nonetheless left 62 percent with no such experience. Furthermore, Simari and Baskin found that 29 percent of the females in their sample who had experienced heterosexual incest had identified themselves as homosexual prior to the incest.

In at least one instance, a claim of a causal connection between adult lesbianism and childhood incest had been made. Silbert and Pines (1983), in regard to their study of 200 San Francisco prostitutes, reported: "The present study also found that sexual abuse affected sexual preference. Only eight percent of the subjects in the present study were lesbians, but of those who reported being lesbian, 60 percent were sexually exploited as juveniles" (p. 288). Since the same figure (60 percent) was given for report- ed sexual abuse in the total subject population, their conclusion did not logically follow from their findings.

While there had generally been consistently frequent findings of incest histories among lesbian women studied, there had not been consistently frequent findings of lesbianism among women with incest histories studied.

Finkelhor (1980) examined levels of homosexual activity in 684 predomi- nantly white male and female college students, 99 of whom had sibling incest histories and 585 of whom did not. No significant differences in homosexual activity were found between the incest and nonincest groups, which included 75 females and 395 females, respectively. The figure for the incest group was 10 percent and the figure for the nonincest group was 8 percent. Langmade (1983) similarly found no significant difference in homosexual activity between 34 adult female incest subjects in psycho- therapy and 34 matched controls.

Meiselman (1978) reported that 30 percent of the 23 incest daughters over 18 in her psychotherapy sample "had become gay or had significant experiences or conflicts centered on homosexual feelings" (p. 245), while none of the eight incest sisters over 18 "had adopted a gay orientation" (p. 283). Meiselman concluded that incest may be "specifically associated with a later report of homosexuality in a significant minority of the cases" (pp. 245–246).

The tentativeness of Meiselman's conclusion seemed appropriate, par- ticularly given that the early sexual experiences of homosexual and hetero- sexual women could be quite similar. Gundlach (1977) reported the follow- ing regarding 225 homosexual adult females and 233 heterosexual adult females: "Many heterosexual women (42 percent) had had one or more homosexual experiences. Among the lesbians, 76 percent had had sexual intercourse with a man" (p. 369).

In contrast to Meiselman (1978), Herman (1981) reported that "a small minority" of the 40 incest daughters in the much narrower psychotherapy sample she examined had experimented with lesbian relationships, but that only two women out of 40 developed a confirmed lesbian identity. Herman further reported that three other women in this sample identified themselves as bisexual.

Clearly, there was considerable variation in the literature reports on sexual preference in women with incest histories. Studies had agreed on only one point, that the majority of women with incest histories were heterosexual as adults.

Researchers had additionally attempted to find a possible connection specifically between homosexual incest and later homosexuality. Finkelhor (1980) noted that, taking a subsample from his study of the 26 persons (gender unspecified) whose sibling experiences had been homosexual, he had found higher levels of adult homosexual activity in the incest group. These findings, again, did not necessarily imply a causal relationship between homosexual incest and later homosexual activity. It was possible that the females involved in homosexual sibling incest were homosexually oriented in the first place and sought homosexual contacts, sexual and/or otherwise. Simari and Baskin (1982) found that 75 percent of the lesbians in their study who had experienced homosexual incest had identified themselves as actively homosexual before the incestuous activity. Furthermore, none of the females reported the homosexual incest experience as negative.

In summary, no causal relationship had been established between incest and homosexuality, despite researchers' attempts to correlate both heterosexual and homosexual incest with later lesbian identity. Although incest and lesbianism had been associated with one another in the literature, the nature of this association was unknown. What was known was that the majority of women with incest histories had remained, as Herman (1981) described it, "steadfastly, even doggedly heterosexual" (p. 104).

The fact that researchers had not attempted to correlate incest and heterosexuality spoke to the relative valuation of heterosexuality as compared with other choices in our culture. For it could have been argued that incest survivors' need for "normalcy," their need to prove that they could function sexually with men, their need to avoid sexual "secrets," and their need to avoid disclosures and confrontations might motivate them to choose heterosexuality. Devaluations of heterosexuality based upon such assumptions of negative rather than positive motivation had not appeared in the literature. Not to suggest that they should have, but this illustrated the way in which our society's traditional view of celibacy, bisexuality, and lesbianism as failures of heterosexuality had influenced the research on sexual preference in women with incest histories.

Sexual Functioning

The "Overview of the Literature" earlier in this chapter included discussion of the nature of the incest literature pertaining to sexual functioning prior to the mid-1970s. The later literature from the mid-1970s to the mid-1980s pertaining to sexual functioning will be reviewed now as it relates to the following areas: reports of no sexual problems, sexual aversion, sexual desire, sexual arousal, orgasm, and other related findings.

Reports of No Sexual Problems

While satisfactory sexual relationships had been reported by women with incest histories (Fritz, Stoll, & Wagner, 1981; Meiselman, 1978; Tsai & Wagner, 1978; Westerlund, 1983), such reports were apparently in the minority.

Although Fritz et al. (1981) found that 77 percent of college females sexually molested as children reported no difficulties with sexual adjustment, their sample of 42 included both females molested outside and those molested within the family. Since many studies had reported that extrafamilial abuse of females was more common than intrafamilial abuse (Finkelhor, 1979; Gagnon, 1965; Kinsey et al., 1953; Landis, 1940; Landis, 1956; Russell, 1983, 1986; Wyatt, 1985), it was likely that Fritz et al.'s sample consisted primarily of females who experienced extrafamilial abuse. Given that extrafamilial abuse was, in general, considered less traumatic than intrafamilial abuse (McFarlane & Waterman, 1986; Russell, 1986), it seemed that fewer reports of sexual problems might be expected in adulthood by females molested outside, as compared to within, the family. Had Fritz et al. reported separately on the unspecified number of females in their sample who had experienced incest, there might have been fewer reports of no sexual problems.

Other studies of demographically diverse sexual assault survivors (Becker, Skinner, Abel, Axelrod, & Cichon, 1984; Becker, Skinner, Abel, & Treacy, 1982) had found that 41 to 43 percent of females reported no sexual problems. The samples in these instances of 371 women and 83 women, respectively, included adult survivors of rape as well as adult survivors of childhood incest. It is unclear what portion of the 41 to 43 percent were women with incest histories, but the authors did note that incest survivors were found to have a higher incidence of sexual problems than rape survivors.

Investigations specific to women with incest histories that had provided percentages (Courtois, 1980; Herman, 1981; Meiselman, 1978) had indicated that reports of no sexual problems were in the minority (13 percent of a sample of 30, 45 percent of a sample of 40, and 13 percent of a sample of

23, respectively). It was important to note that all of these studies had been based upon clinical samples, however dissimilar otherwise, and that like information was not available for nonclinical samples of women with incest histories.

Thus, while it could not be assumed that all women with incest histories experienced sexual problems, adult sexual impairment had been associated with childhood incest. Among women with incest histories seen clinically, it was more likely that sexual problems would be reported than not (Bess & Janssen, 1982; Courtois, 1980; Courtois & Watts, 1982; Herman, 1981; Hirschman, 1980; Meiselman, 1978, 1980; Tsai & Wagner, 1978; Westerlund, 1983).

Measures of sexual satisfaction (Current Sexual Behaviors and Satisfaction Questionnaire; Sexual Experiences Questionnaire) had confirmed that clinical samples of women with incest histories experience less sexual satisfaction than both clinical controls without incest histories (Langmade, 1983) and nonclinical controls with incest histories (Tsai et al., 1979). It had also been documented that women with incest histories experienced greater sex anxiety (The Sex Anxiety Inventory) and greater sex guilt (Mosher Forced Choice Sex Guilt Subscale) than controls (Langmade, 1983). Both could interfere with sexual functioning during one or more of the sexual phases of desire, arousal, and orgasm. Additionally, avoidance of sex could be motivated by either or both.

Sexual Aversion

While the incidence of avoidance of sex among women with incest histories had not in itself been investigated, reports of aversion to sex had certainly appeared in the literature (Herman, 1981; Meiselman, 1978; Tsai & Wagner, 1978; Westerlund, 1983). Partly due to the fact that definitions of aversion had generally gone unstated in the incest literature, it was impossible to say how common sexual aversion might be. It was apparent, however, that many women with incest histories who reported sexual dysfunctions experience fear of sex which might or might not have been associated with aversion and which might or might not have been translated into avoidance of sex. Becker et al. (1982) reported fear of sex in 9 out of a sample of 12 women with incest histories. In a larger sample of 28 incest survivors, Becker et al. (1984) found that 64 percent reported fear of sex.

Sexual Desire

An absence of sexual desire in women with incest histories had been commented on by several authors (McGuire & Wagner, 1978; Silbert & Pines, 1983; Westerlund, 1983). Becker et al. (1982) found that 4 out of a sample of

12 incest survivors reported a desire dysfunction. Similar results were obtained among a sample of 28 women with incest histories by Becker et al. (1984) who reported a figure of 35 percent. It had been noted that desire dysfunctions were significantly correlated with arousal dysfunctions in women with incest histories (Becker et al., 1982).

Sexual Arousal

The figures for arousal dysfunctions in women with incest histories reported by Becker et al. (1982) and Becker et al. (1984) were 42 percent and 50 percent respectively. Sexual nonresponsiveness of varying severity had frequently been reported in the literature (Herman, 1981; McGuire & Wagner, 1978; Meiselman, 1978; Tsai & Wagner, 1978; Westerlund, 1983). A pattern of arousal contingent upon control had been noted by several authors (Meiselman, 1978; Tsai & Wagner, 1978; Westerlund, 1983).

Orgasm

Meiselman (1978) had stated:

> It seems that an incest association is a relatively rare source of orgasmic dysfunction in women, since Masters and Johnson mentioned only one case of orgasmic dysfunction out of their sample of 342 in which incestuous experience with a father was a crucial factor in the failure of sexual function. (pp. 242–243)

This conclusion was based upon three very faulty assumptions: (1) that incest survivors with orgasmic dysfunction would have sought treatment with Masters and Johnson, (2) that Masters and Johnson would have routinely inquired about incest prior to 1970, and (3) that incest survivors would necessarily have disclosed their history to Masters and Johnson.

It was unknown, in fact, how many women with orgasmic dysfunction happen to also be women with incest histories. What was known was simply that orgasmic dysfunction existed as a problem among incest survivors. In Meiselman's own study, 74 percent of a subsample of 23 incest daughters reported having had "one or more heterosexual relationships in which orgasmic dysfunction was a major problem" (p. 234). Many other authors had found orgasmic dysfunction in women with incest histories who reported sexual problems (Becker et al., 1982; Becker et al., 1984; Herman, 1981; Silbert & Pines, 1983; Tsai et al., 1979; Westerlund, 1983). Among such samples of women, 8 to 10 percent had reported primary orgasmic dysfunction and 14 to 33 percent had reported secondary orgasmic dysfunction (Becker et al., 1982; Becker et al., 1984).

It was important to keep in mind that U.S. women in general included an estimated 10–33 percent with incest histories (Belmonte & Boyer, 1983; Finkelhor, 1979; Kinsey et al., 1953; Landis, 1940; Landis, 1956; Russell, 1983, 1986; Wyatt, 1985). Of the estimated 10–12 percent of women in the U.S. population who never experienced orgasm (Hite, 1976; Masters & Johnson, 1970), we had no way of knowing how many had incest histories and how many did not. Orgasmic dysfunction as a problem in women with incest histories could neither be minimized nor assumed to be a greater problem than it might have been in women without incest histories.

Two phenomena related to orgasm that appeared to be highly specific to women with incest histories had been noted in the literature. The first was the ability to be orgasmic only when the sexual partner was new, i.e., "unrelated" (McGuire & Wagner, 1978; Meiselman, 1978; Westerlund, 1983). The second was the ability to be orgasmic in the absence of sexual desire, arousal, and/or pleasure (McGuire & Wagner, 1978; Tsai & Wagner, 1978; Westerlund, 1983).

Other Related Findings

Several other findings related to sexual functioning had been mentioned in the incest literature prior to the study. These included negative or distorted body perception (Faria & Belohlavek, 1984; Westerlund, 1983); flashbacks during sexual activity, which had been reported with regularity by women with incest histories (Becker et al., 1984; Herman, 1981; Meiselman, 1978; Tsai & Wagner, 1978; Westerlund, 1983); discomfort with sadomasochistic fantasies and/or behaviors, which had been occasionally reported by incest survivors (Meiselman, 1978; Westerlund, 1983); and complaints of vaginismus and dyspareunia, which had appeared to be quite rare (Becker et al., 1982; Becker et al., 1984).

Summary on Sexual Functioning

While there were women with incest histories who experienced no difficulties with sexual functioning, such women were evidently in the minority. Various sexual dysfunctions had been reported by women with incest histories, including fear of sex, desire dysfunctions, arousal dysfunctions, primary orgasmic dysfunction, secondary orgasmic dysfunction, vaginismus, and dyspareunia. Multiple dysfunctions were more commonly reported than single dysfunctions (Becker et al., 1982; Becker et al., 1984). Response-inhibiting dysfunctions such as fear of sex, desire dysfunction, and arousal dysfunction had been found to be approximately four times more common than orgasmic problems in women with incest histories and over twenty times more common that intromission problems such as vaginismus and dyspareunia (Becker et al., 1982; Becker et al., 1984). Several authors had emphasized the chronicity of sexual dysfunctions in incest survivors (Becker et al., 1982; Becker et al., 1984; Becker, Skinner, Abel, & Cichon, 1986; McGuire & Wagner, 1978; Meiselman, 1978; Westerlund, 1983).

Sexual Adjustment Outcome Factors

Several studies had attempted to identify the factors that contributed to the presence or absence of sexual problems in women with incest histories. Unfortunately, findings had been contradictory more often than not.

Among the variables investigated, the findings had been as follows: frequency had been found significant (Tsai et al., 1979) and not significant (Courtois, 1979a, 1979b); duration had been found significant (Tsai et al., 1979) and not significant (Courtois, 1979a, 1979b; Finkelhor, 1980; Langmade, 1983); age at first experience had been found significant (Courtois, 1979a, 1979b; Finkelhor, 1980) and not significant (Becker et al., 1984; Langmade, 1983; Tsai et al., 1979); age at last experience has been found significant (Tsai et al., 1979) and not significant (Finkelhor, 1980); the degree of coercion had been found significant (Becker et al., 1982; Finkelhor, 1980; Fritz et al., 1981) and not significant (Becker et al., 1984; Courtois, 1979a, 1979b); and attempted or achieved penetration had been found significant (Becker et al., 1982; Tsai et al., 1979) and not significant (Becker et al., 1984; Finkelhor, 1980).

The single factor on which there had been agreement with regard to effect on sexual adjustment had been that of self-blame. Levels of self-blame had consistently been found to be higher in incest survivors with sexual problems than in incest survivors with no sexual problems. Becker et al. (1984) found that 82.8 percent of the sexually dysfunctional incest survivors in their sample held themselves partially responsible for their assaults. The figure for the sexually functional group was 31.6 percent. Other authors (Becker et al., 1982; Fritz et al., 1981; Tsai et al., 1979) had not provided figures, but had indicated that significantly lower levels of self-blame had been found in sexually adjusted women with incest histories.

It had tentatively been concluded (Becker et al., 1982; Fritz et al., 1981) that self-blame was related to having sexually complied when no "force" was used. While such an explanation was certainly plausible, it seemed decidedly simplistic and likely only to yield yet another study attempting to correlate degree of coercion and level of self-blame. Many additional factors might be involved in self-blame which researchers had failed to identify due to unfamiliarity with the totality and the uniqueness of the incest experience. Several that immediately came to mind were maintaining secrecy, experiencing physiological arousal, accepting rewards for sexual behavior, and being blamed by others in response to disclosure.

It had repeatedly been demonstrated that sexual adjustment could not be readily predicted on the basis of knowledge pertaining to specific variables related to the incestuous abuse. The incest experience was clearly a highly subjective and complex experience. Even without regard for post-incest factors, it seemed that response to the incest experience could be expected to prove idiosyncratic.

Conclusions

The literature written prior to this study made several things clear. One was that the development and expression of sexuality in women could be substantially altered by sexual trauma. The second was that incest, as a form of sexual trauma involving coercive seduction, betrayal of trust, and an injunction to remain silent, could predispose women to problems with intimacy and sexuality. The third was that a variety of adult difficulties with sexual adjustment and with sexual functioning had been associated with childhood incest.

Also apparent in reviewing the literature prior to the mid-1980s were the limitations of that body of research. Most glaring was the sense that while the sexual problems experienced by women with incest histories had been categorized and catalogued, the subjective experience underlying the difficulties and dysfunctions had been largely ignored. Little effort had been made to study sexuality as perceived by the incest survivors themselves. Thus, although information and statistics had been obtained, insight into the personal implications of an incest history had been forfeited. Under such circumstances, help could be offered to women with incest histories only on the basis of knowledge that was, at its best, superficial and, at its worst, contradictory and unenlightened.

The research pertaining to women with incest histories was clearly troubled by a number of methodological problems and by bias. Although the literature from the mid-1970s to the mid-1980s addressed some of the problems and biases, others remained.

Among the later studies described here pertaining to sexuality, some combined reporting on both intrafamilial and extrafamilial childhood experiences (Fritz et al., 1981; McGuire & Wagner, 1978; Silbert & Pines, 1983; Tsai et al., 1979; Tsai & Wagner, 1978); some combined reporting on adult and child sexual assault (Becker et al., 1982; Becker et al., 1984; Becker et al., 1986); some combined reporting on women and men (Bess & Janssen, 1982; Finkelhor, 1980; Fritz et al., 1981; Simari & Baskin, 1982); and some combined reporting on exploitive and nonexploitive experiences (Finkelhor, 1980; Fritz et al., 1981; Simari & Baskin, 1982). While such studies were useful for comparative purposes, extracting information specific to women with incest histories in such instances proved difficult. Moreover, conclusions about women with incest histories have sometimes drawn from such studies without regard for the differences between subsamples included.

Conclusions were also sometimes drawn from studies of college populations (Boekelheide, 1978; Finkelhor, 1980; Fritz et al., 1981) without regard for the characteristics of such groups. Periods of sexual adjustment and degree of sexual experience are of considerable importance in studies on sexuality.

An additional difficulty was the inconsistency of reporting regarding sexual preference. Studies that had included only heterosexual participants had not stated so, with the exception of Tsai et al. (1979). Some researchers had mentioned that they inquired about homosexuality (if not bisexuality and celibacy), but then failed to report on it (Fritz et al., 1981; Hirschman, 1980). Others had neither indicated whether they inquired about sexual preference nor provided information on it (Becker et al., 1982; Becker et al., 1984; Courtois, 1979a, 1979b, 1980; Herman & Hirschman, 1977; Tsai & Wagner, 1978). In the few instances where some information had been provided, sexual preference had nonetheless been omitted in the demographics (Bess & Janssen, 1982; Herman, 1981; Langmade, 1983; Meiselman, 1978).

The problems and biases of the later studies reported here limited their usefulness as other problems and biases outlined in this chapter limited the usefulness of the earlier research. It was the intent of this study, to whatever degree was possible, to address these problems and biases.

2

The Study and the Participants

THE PURPOSE OF THE STUDY on which this book is based was to investigate and describe body perception, reproduction, sexual preference, sexual "lifestyle," and sexual functioning as experienced by women with incest histories and as perceived by them as having been influenced by the incest. Given the intent of the study, qualitative research methods were most applicable. Those methods will be discussed in general fashion here, but readers unfamiliar with qualitative research and readers given to analyzing studies from a quantitative knowledge base should turn first to Appendix A: Methodology.

The Study Sample

The participants for this study were recruited from the self-help support groups facilitated by Incest Resources in Cambridge, Massachusetts, during 1985. This nonprofit counseling and educational organization was co-founded by the author in 1980. Several organizational characteristics influenced the nature of the sample.

1. As a counseling and self-help organization, Incest Resources attracts women who are actively seeking resolution and recovery from the incest experience. While the majority of the women who attend-

ed the self-help support groups from which the sample was drawn were in psychotherapy, the population was not a therapy population per se. Women who attended the meetings were incest survivors primarily residing in the Boston area who were able to contact the organization on their own initiative and who were able to function well in relatively unstructured discussion groups of 25–35 women. They were also women who were able to challenge themselves emotionally with additional work outside of psychotherapy and women who valued and were able to utilize the support of other incest survivors.

2. As a predominantly white organization, Incest Resources attracts a predominantly white population. Very few women of color attended the self-help support groups facilitated by Incest Resources in 1985 and few volunteered to participate in the study.

3. As a feminist organization affiliated with the Cambridge Women's Center, Incest Resources attracts women of all sexual preferences. The high percentage in the sample of women representing sexual preferences other than heterosexuality is reflective of the population that attended the self-help support groups in 1985 and is reflective of other populations of women that meet at the Cambridge Women's Center.

The sample was thus drawn from a nonrepresentative population of women who considered themselves to have been affected by the incest, but who were functioning at a sufficiently healthy level to utilize self-help, and who differed perhaps from the larger population of women with incest histories in terms of their style of dealing with the incest experience outside of traditional psychotherapy. Study participants were additionally volunteers and thus, by definition, self-selected. There is no way of knowing whether women selected themselves as participants due to their relative dissatisfaction with their sexuality and awareness of the impact of the incest in that area or their relative comfort and ease with discussing their incest history and their sexuality.

Also, while the return rate was surprisingly high given the nature of the study, there is no way of knowing whether those who did not return the questionnaire (40 percent) all found it "too painful" or "too revealing," as suggested by those who did convey their reasons for nonparticipation (approximately one-third). In any event, those who selected themselves as participants may well have differed from those who did not return the questionnaire (as well as from the larger population of women with incest histories) in terms of their sexuality. (The limitations of the study and researcher bias are discussed both at the end of this chapter and in Appendix A.)

Definitions

Three criteria were used to determine a participant's inclusion in the study. First, a participant had to have been involved as a child and/or adolescent in sexual activity with a family member. However, that family member did not have to have been related by blood, since it is the author's belief (and that of others) that definitions of incest which exclude other than blood relatives are legalistic and unnecessarily restrictive. Since the issues for the victim are not appreciably altered by such measures of relatedness, such distinctions are arbitrary. On the other hand, women sexually victimized as children and/or adolescents by individuals outside the family do differ sufficiently from women victimized within the family (Russell, 1986) to have been excluded from this study.

Second, a participant had to be at least 25 years of age to ensure that an adequate period of adult sexual adjustment had been attempted.

Third, a participant had to be female. The decision to limit the study to women was based upon the fact that sexual victimization results in somewhat different issues for males than it does for females (Finkelhor, 1979, 1980; Fritz et al., 1981; Simari & Baskin, 1982). One would expect this to be particularly true with respect to sexuality, given differences in the sexual socialization of males and females in our society. Also, the use of male as well as female participants would have necessitated comparisons and it was beyond the intent and scope of this study to address such areas.

Additional criteria involving relationship of the offender to the participant, gender of the offender, nature of the sexual activity, and so forth were avoided.

For the purpose of this study, incest referred to sexual activity between the subject and a family member during childhood and/or adolescence. Sexual activity included kissing and/or fondling, manipulation of the male and/or female genitalia, oral-genital contact, simulated intercourse, vaginal intercourse, and anal intercourse. Also included were activities which did not result in direct physical contact, such as genital exhibition or masturbation by the offender in the presence of the subject and "peeping." Subjects were self-identified as having an incest history. Sexuality, as defined in this study, encompassed body perception, reproduction, sexual preference, sexual "lifestyle," and sexual functioning. Included as aspects of sexual functioning were sexual fantasy, desire, arousal, orgasm, and satisfaction.

The Subjects

Seventy-two questionnaires were distributed, with a return rate of 60 percent, resulting in a sample of 43 women. Of those 43 women, 38 (88 percent) volunteered to be interviewed as well. A subsample of ten women representing various sexual preferences (i.e., heterosexual, lesbian, celibate, undecided, and bisexual) and sexual "lifestyles" (i.e., "lifestyles" characterized by aversion, inhibition, compulsion, celibacy, "promiscuity," prostitution, and sadomasochism) was drawn based upon the questionnaire responses. Subjects with a capacity for self-examination and with an ability to effectively articulate their thoughts and feelings in a self-generated manner were sought. Additional factors considered in the selection of the interview subjects were (1) the identity of the offender (in order that survivors of father-daughter, brother-sister, grandfather-granddaughter, uncle-niece, and mother-daughter incest all be represented); (2) the age of the woman (in order that women in their twenties, thirties, and forties all be represented); (3) the race of the woman (in order that women of color be as fully represented as possible); (4) the socioeconomic status and the religion of the woman in the present as well as in the family of origin (in order to represent different classes and religious groups); and (5) whether the woman had children or not (in order to represent women both with and without children).

The Questionnaire

The Westerlund Incest Survivors Questionnaire (Appendix B) covers the following three areas:

1. Demographic information related to both family background and present status of the respondent.
2. Historical information related to the respondent's incest experience and its perceived effects. Included are both factual information and information pertaining to the respondent's cognitive, affective, behavioral, and integrative responses.
3. Information related to the respondent's present adult sexuality. Included are questions concerning body perception, reproduction, sexual preference, sexual "lifestyle," and sexual functioning, as well as questions pertaining to the perceived effects of the incest experience on the respondent's sexuality.

The questionnaire was designed to elicit responses and minimize omission by providing "cues" to prompt the participants' thinking without forcing a misrepresentational answer. The construction of the questionnaire, including the selection of "cues," was based upon input from several hundred women with incest histories whom the author had spoken with throughout the five-year period prior to its final design. In addition to "cues" that were considered potentially applicable, a category labeled "other" was always provided to invite accuracy and elaboration by the respondents. Special care was given to avoiding language that was value-laden, judgmental, blaming, heterosexist, or otherwise oppressive that might have negatively influenced disclosure.

The questionnaire was tested for suitability, adequacy, and clarity prior to its use by the staff members of Incest Resources, a group comprised of six women of various sexual preferences with incest histories. These six women formally completed the questionnaire and provided their feedback on each individual item as well as on the questionnaire as a whole. Refinements and revisions were made accordingly.

The questionnaire provided an effective way to reach a substantial number of women with incest histories from whom to establish a range of variation with respect to sexuality. The greater safety and anonymity of the questionnaire encouraged the participation of women who might have refused to participate in the more threatening and more exposing face-to-face interviews.

(For a detailed account of the procedures used for recruiting the subjects and administering the questionnaire, the interested reader is referred to Appendix A.)

Demographic data from the returned questionnaires were summarized using sample percentages and means, and the open-ended data from the questionnaires underwent analysis based upon an adaption of the method of qualitative analysis described by Lofland (1971). (For a fuller discussion of the actual procedures used in the data analysis, the interested reader is referred to Appendix A.)

The Interviews

Focused interviews were conducted (and audiotaped) with a subsample of questionnaire respondents who represented various sexual preferences and sexual "lifestyles" within the range established by the questionnaire. The "focused interview" developed by Merton, Fiske, and Kendall (Sjoberg & Nett, 1968) is used with individuals known to have been involved in a particular experience when the researcher has already provisionally analyzed that experience. The interviews allowed the author to explore the data generated by the questionnaire in greater depth. The interviews were focused on the subjective experiences of the individuals, with the objective being to understand the personal meaning given to the experience by each individual.

In keeping with this objective, the interview was unstructured and open-ended, initiated by a single question (Appendix C) designed to avoid influencing the subject's direction or prioritizing of areas under investigation. An interview guide rather than a structured protocol was prepared for the interviews (Appendix D), based upon analysis of the questionnaires. The interview guide was consulted to ensure that key topics were covered in the interviews. These topics were inquired after if they were not addressed in the whole of the interviewee's spontaneous response.

The open-ended style of the interview permitted the interviewee to disclose in her own manner and time, interviews lasting one and one-half to three hours. Rapport was enhanced by the fact that the interviewees had previously met the author at the self-help support groups when the study was announced, were aware of the author's similar history, and had already participated in the questionnaire portion of the study. The latter enhanced rapport by providing the interviewees in advance with a sense of the author's thinking regarding incest and sexuality and by acquainting the researcher in advance with the interviewees via their questionnaires. (For a detailed account of the procedures used for conducting the interviews, the interested reader is referred to Appendix A.)

Analysis of the data from the transcribed interviews was based upon an adaption of the method of thematic analysis described by Taylor and Bogdan (1984). (For a fuller discussion of the actual procedures used in the data analysis, the interested reader is referred to Appendix A.)

General Research Questions

The author approached the study with the following assumptions:

1. Incest is a major psychological trauma in the lives of women.
2. Incest affects the development and expression of sexuality in women.
3. A variety of sexual "lifestyles" are adopted by women with incest histories.
4. A variety of difficulties related to sexuality are experienced by women with incest histories.

5. Women with incest histories are not likely to seek formal sex thera-py if dissatisfied with their sexuality.

With the above assumptions serving as a starting point, the author approached the study with the following general research questions:

1. What are the perceptions of these women of the incest experi-ence?
2. What are the perceptions of these women of their sexuality?
3. What effects do these women perceive that the incest experience has had on their sexuality?
4. How do these women experience those effects?
5. What has been helpful and what would be helpful to these women in terms of increasing comfort, pleasure, and satisfaction with their sexuality?

The Questionnaire Participants

The women who participated in the questionnaire were self-identified incest survivors involved in a self-help community of women with incest histories. They chose to participate for several reasons, including a desire to support research in the area of sexuality, a desire to contribute to the eradication of myths and stereotypes about incest, and a desire to be involved in a project from which they might derive a sense of empower-ment. Most of the women found their participation evocative and discom-forting, yet positive in some way. The following response illustrates a num-ber of the common reactions:

This questionnaire has been one of the most difficult tasks I've ever completed. It became almost an obsession with me. It became every-thing I've thought of in the past week. . . . There were so many things this survey made me remember, things that might have taken much longer for me to remember. It also helped me to make some connections between my behavior as a child and as an adult. It gave me a basis to go back and look at my childhood and adolescence in a structured way. . . . I don't feel so isolated from, so different from the child I was. There were times when I was completing this survey that I just wanted to trash the entire project. The feelings were so intense, so much hurt, so much anguish, wanting so much for it not to have happened, so much guilt, so much pain. . . . Now that I've finished this I feel scared. It feels very strange to take all of the skeletons out of the closet, set them down on paper, and then mail them to someone I don't really know. Of course, if I wanted to make up an excuse to not mail this I could just refuse to participate, but I don't really want to do that because I also feel pride in participating in the survey. It means something to me. It's important that people understand more about incest. It's important that it stop.

For apparently similar reasons, 60 percent of the women provided with questionnaires were motivated to complete and return them. The demographic data provided in the following sections are based upon analysis of the 43 questionnaires returned.

Questionnaire Participant Demographics

Age

The age of the questionnaire participants at the time of the study ranged from 25 to 50 years, with a mean age of 34.3 years.

Race and Ethnicity

Forty-one of the 43 questionnaire participants (95 percent) were white Americans, 40 of European descent (English, Scotch, Irish, Dutch, German, French, Italian, Portuguese, Greek, Swedish, Russian, Czechoslovakian, Yugoslavian, Polish, Armenian) and one of European and West Indian background. The remaining two participants (5 percent) were Hispanic women, one from Puerto Rico and one from the Dominican Republic.

Religious Affiliation

Almost one-third of the questionnaire participants (30 percent) had no religious affiliation at the time of the study. Twenty-six percent (26 percent) of the respondents were Protestant (82 percent of whom were practicing), 16 percent were Jewish (100 percent of whom were practicing), and 12 percent were Catholic (20 percent of whom were practicing). Of the remaining women, three were Wiccan, two Buddhist, one a Secular Humanist, and one a Native American Spiritualist, all of whom were practicing their religion.

Education

The level of education of the questionnaire participants ranged from having completed high school to having completed a doctoral degree. Seven percent (7 percent) of the questionnaire respondents had completed high school, 23 percent had completed some college, 35 percent had completed a bachelor's degree, 28 percent had completed a master's degree, and 7 percent had completed a doctoral degree.

Occupation

A wide variety of occupations was reported by the questionnaire respondents. Twenty-one percent (21 percent) of the participants were professionally involved in the arts and the media, 19 percent were involved in counseling and education, 16 percent were employed in a secretarial capacity, 14 percent were occupied as doctoral students, 9 percent were psychotherapists, 7 percent were nurses, 5 percent were in sales, and 5 percent were in business and industry. Of the remaining women, one was a postdoctoral fellow and one was disabled and not employed at the time of the study.

Socioeconomic Status

The socioeconomic status (self-determined) of the majority of the questionnaire participants (65 percent) was middle class. Thirty-three percent (33 percent) of the participants were working class and 2 percent upper class.

Sexual Preference

The largest number of questionnaire respondents reported themselves to be heterosexual (42 percent) followed by lesbian (35 percent). Of the remaining participants, 9 percent stated that they were celibate, 9 percent were undecided, and 5 percent were bisexual.

Relationship Status

The largest number of questionnaire participants were living with a life partner (42 percent) or partner (5 percent) at the time of the study. Of the remaining respondents, 16 percent were involved in a significant (self-defined) relationship, 12 percent were involved in a relationship but not (by self-definition) a significant one, and 25 percent were not involved in any relationship.

Children

The majority (60 percent) of the questionnaire participants did not have children at the time of the study. Of the 40 percent who did, the number of children ranged from one to three, with a mean of 1.9 children per respondent. The mean age of all the children was 12.9 years.

Therapy

The vast majority (98 percent) of the questionnaire respondents reported having had experience with psychotherapy. Length of time in psychotherapy ranged from eight months to 15 years, with a mean of 6.4 years. Ninety-five percent (95 percent) of the participants had been in individual psychotherapy, 65 percent had been in group psychotherapy, and 63 percent had been in both. Eighty-four percent (84 percent) of the participants were in psychotherapy at the time the study was conducted. Only 5 percent of the respondents had been in sex therapy and none was at the time of the study.

Summary of Questionnaire Participant Demographics

The demographic data on the questionnaire respondents presented here are summarized in Table 1 (Appendix E).

The Interview Participants

The ten women who participated in the interviews were selected from among the 38 questionnaire respondents (88 percent) who volunteered to be interviewed. Women were chosen on the basis of the questionnaire responses to provide a group of participants representing various sexual preferences (i.e., heterosexual, lesbian, celibate, undecided, and bisexual) and sexual "lifestyles" (i.e., "lifestyles" characterized by aversion, inhibition, compulsion, celibacy, "promiscuity," prostitution, and sadomasochism). In addition, the identity of a woman's incest offender(s) was considered along with demographic diversity. Age, race, socioeconomic status and religion (in the present as well as in the family of origin), and children/no children were other factors taken into account in the selection of the interview participants. Hispanic women were, by intent, more represented in the interview group than in the questionnaire group. Otherwise, the demographic trends of the two groups were similar.

Interview Participant Demographics

Age

The age of the interview participants at the time of the study ranged from 27 to 49 years, with a mean age of 34.9 years.

Race and Ethnicity

Eight of the ten interview participants were white Americans, seven of European descent, and one of European and West Indian background. The remaining two participants were Hispanic women, one from Puerto Rico and one from the Dominican Republic.

Religious Affiliation

Four of the interview participants had no religious affiliation, two were Catholic, two were Jewish, one was Protestant, and one was Buddhist. Of the six with an affiliation, four reported themselves to be practicing their religion.

Education

The level of education of the interview participants ranged from having completed high school to having completed doctoral coursework. One woman had completed high school, one woman had completed some college, four women had completed bachelor's degrees, two women had completed master's degrees, and two women were completing doctoral degrees at the time of the study.

Occupation

A variety of occupations was engaged in by the interview participants. Three women were involved in the arts and the media, three women were involved in counseling and education, two women were doctoral students, one woman was employed in a secretarial capacity, and one woman was employed in business and industry.

Socioeconomic Status

The socioeconomic status (self-determined) of seven of the interview participants was middle class. Three participants were working class.

Sexual Preference

Four of the interview participants were lesbian, three were heterosexual, one was celibate, one was undecided, and one was bisexual. Six of the ten participants were sexually experienced as adults with both genders.

Relationship Status

Five of the interview participants were living with a life partner at the time of the study. Of the additional participants, two women were involved in significant (self-defined) relationships, two women were involved in relationships but not (by self-definition) significant ones, and one woman was not involved in any relationship.

Children

Six of the ten interview participants did not have children at the time of the study. Of the four who did, the number of children ranged from one to three, with a mean of two children.

Therapy

All of the interview participants had experience with psychotherapy. Length of time in psychotherapy ranged from one to 15 years, with a mean time of seven years. All of the interview participants had been in individual therapy, and six of the participants had been in group therapy. Eight of the ten participants were in therapy at the time of the study. None of the interview participants had been in sex therapy.

Summary of Interview Participant Demographics

The demographic data on the interview participants presented here are summarized in Table 2 (Appendix E).

The Study Limitations

Although incest has been described as "relentlessly democratic" (Butler, 1978, p.24), the study participants did not display an even distribution of demographic variables. As with other incest studies, the sample was neither random nor representative. In fact, many of the participants might be described by others, if not by themselves, as well-educated, psychologically sophisticated, East Coast feminists. Findings from such a select group of women clearly may not apply to other groups of women with incest histories. Unsound extrapolation may occur if the reader does not remain aware throughout of the nature of the sample.

Unsound interpretation may likewise occur. For example, in this study women of color are very much underrepresented and women of sexual preferences other than heterosexuality are very much overrepresented. Both are functions of sampling method; that is, the sample was drawn from a skewed population of women. The reader should obviously not conclude from this study that women with incest histories are in almost every instance white. Neither should the reader conclude that women with incest histories are often lesbian. Since the sample is neither random not representative, the study must be understood to provide limited information with limited generalizability. (For a discussion of the lesser limitations related to the research design, the interested reader is referred to Appendix A.)

Researcher Bias

Another factor to mention briefly before moving on to the findings is bias. The reader should remain aware throughout that the author is a woman with an incest history who is a founding member of the self-help community of women with incest histories from which the study sample was drawn. The very same attributes that assisted the research design, collection, and analysis were also potential sources of bias, as was the author's feminist perspective. The study findings should be considered accordingly with some measure of reserve. (For a description of the reliability check carried out as a safeguard against bias, the interested reader is referred to Appendix A.)

3

The Incest and Its Impact

THE HISTORIES OF THE WOMEN who participated in this study are all unique. Each woman survived a childhood like no other and each woman has lived an adulthood like no other. In subsequent chapters the voices of the participants will be heard as they describe their individual experiences. In this chapter the incest histories of the women will first be looked at collectively, and the impact of the incest on their lives will be examined in a general fashion to provide context for what follows.

The participant data provided in the following sections relate to family background, incest background, and incest experience. Data on the questionnaire participants are presented first, followed by data on the interview participants. (For a complete summary, the reader is referred to Tables 3, 4, 5, 6, 7 and 8, which appear in Appendix E.)

Histories of the Questionnaire Participants

Socioeconomic Status of Childhood Family

The majority of the questionnaire participants (54 percent) were from middle-class backgrounds, 37 percent were from working-class backgrounds, and 9 percent were from upper-class backgrounds (as self-determined).

Occupation of Childhood Family Breadwinner

A wide variety of occupations was reported for the major breadwinner of the questionnaire participants' childhood families. In the largest number of childhood families, the major breadwinner worked in a white-collar position (43 percent). In 30 percent of the childhood families, the major breadwinner worked in a blue-collar capacity. There were a number of childhood families headed by lawyers and physicians (20 percent), and a few childhood families were military families (7 percent).

Religious Affiliation of Childhood Family

Only 7 percent of the questionnaire respondents reported no religious affiliation for their childhood family. Thirty-seven percent (37 percent) of the childhood families were Protestant, 35 percent were Catholic, and 21 percent were Jewish. Seventy-eight percent (78 percent) of the families with a religious affiliation practiced regularly.

Number of Children in Childhood Family

Most commonly, the questionnaire respondents reported four children in their childhood family. The number of children ranged from 1 to 9, with a mean of 3.8 children per family.

Birth Position in Childhood Family

Middle children were most common among the questionnaire participants (40 percent), followed by youngest (30 percent), eldest (23 percent), and only children (7 percent). The majority of the respondents (60 percent) were eldest or only daughters, however.

Siblings Incestuously Abused

Sixty-three percent (63 percent) of the questionnaire respondents with siblings reported that at least one other sibling had been abused. In 56 percent of these instances, one or more younger siblings were involved; in 28 percent of the cases, one or more older siblings were involved; and in 16 percent of the cases, both older and younger siblings were involved. In 5 percent of the cases, siblings were impregnated. The majority of the siblings abused were female (85 percent). Only 7 percent of the respondents with siblings reported that no siblings had been abused. Thirty percent (30 percent) of the respondents did not know whether their siblings had been abused or not.

Age of Respondent During Incest

Age of onset ranged from 1 to 14 years, and age of cessation ranged from 5 to 20 years. The mean age of onset was 5.2 years, and the mean age of cessation was 13.4 years. The incest was reported to have taken place over a period of from 1 to 14 years, with the mean number of years the incest lasted 8.4.

Identity of the Incest Offender

The majority of the offenders were fathers (59 percent) including two stepfathers and one surrogate father. Brothers were next often encountered as offenders (13 percent), including one stepbrother. All of the brothers were older than the respondents, with a mean age difference of 4.5 years. Grandfathers, including two stepgrandfathers, accounted for 11.5 percent of the offenders, and 10 percent of the offenders were uncles, including one greatuncle. Of the female offenders (6.5 percent), all were mothers.

Number of Incest Offenders

The majority of the questionnaire participants (68 percent) reported one incest offender. Twenty-one percent (21 percent) of the participants reported two incest offenders, 9 percent of the participants reported three incest offenders, and 2 percent reported four incest offenders. A total of 63 offenders was reported by the 43 respondents.

Forms of Coercion Used by the Offender

A majority of the questionnaire respondents had experienced force at some time during the sexual abuse (58 percent). Pressure was as often experienced (58 percent) as force, and threat of force was more often experienced (63 percent). Threat of loss of love (49 percent), bribery (42 percent), and threat of consequences to others (33 percent) were other forms of coercion commonly encountered. Less often experienced by the respondents was the administration of drugs and/or alcohol to ensure compliance (9 percent).

Nature of the Sexual Activity

A variety of sexual activities was reported by the questionnaire respondents, with most women having experienced kissing and/or fondling (95 percent), manipulation of male and/or female genitalia (84 percent), and oral-genital contact (70 percent). Almost half the respondents (49 percent) reported vaginal intercourse, and almost one-eighth of the respondents (12 percent) reported anal intercourse. Less common activities included simulated intercourse (37 percent), vaginal and anal penetration with objects (7 percent), "inspections" of sexual areas of the respondent's body for the gratification of the offender (7 percent), and the administration of douches and/or enemas for the gratification of the offender (2 percent). Many respondents (56 percent) additionally reported sexual activity not involving direct physical contact, including "peeping" by the offender, genital exhibition or masturbation by the offender in the presence of the respondent, "sharing" of pornographic materials with the respondent, and rape of a sister or mother in the presence of the respondent. Over one-fifth of the respondents (21 percent) noted that the offender engaged in sexual activities with them involving domination and pain for purposes of heightened gratification. Seven percent (7 percent) of the respondents reported being involved in group sex, and 5 percent reported being involved in sexual activity with animals. Five percent (5 percent) of the respondents were impregnated by the offender.

Frequency of the Sexual Activity

Frequency of the sexual activity varied considerably depending upon the type of sexual activity, the time available to the offender, the likelihood of being discovered, and the accessibility of the respondent to the offender. Most commonly, participants reported that sexual activity took place on a daily to monthly basis. Less than one-quarter of the respondents (23 percent) reported abuse that occurred several times a year. In all instances of abuse that occurred once or twice (16 percent), the offender was a relative from outside the home who did not have regular access to the respondent.

Reason Incest Ended

In the majority of cases (75 percent), the incest was not disclosed during childhood. In those instances in which disclosure did take place, responses by adults (mothers, grandmothers, a father, a neighbor, a teacher, hospital personnel, and a psychiatrist) included shock, disbelief, anger directed at the respondent, avoidance, and inaction. In only two instances, one in which the respondent told her mother and one in which the respondent told her grandmother, did disclosure result in cessation of the sexual abuse.

In all but these two instances, the incest ended for reasons other than disclosure. Either decreased access to the respondent or increased risk of discovery was generally involved.

For many of the questionnaire respondents (38 percent), the abuse ended as puberty was reached, when the onset of menstruation was imminent or had occurred, when the respondent had attained a greater degree of freedom of movement outside the home, and when the respondent had achieved a greater understanding of the implications and exploitive nature of the sexual activity. Almost two-thirds (63 percent) of the questionnaire respondents with siblings indicated that the offender had moved down a line of children in their families. This movement was apparently related to the fact that younger children were not yet fertile, were more accessible, more compliant, and less potentially (or actually) threatening than older children in the family. Upon entrance into adolescence, in fact, several of the respondents (15 percent) became sufficiently threatening and/or oppositional to succeed in ending the sexual abuse themselves.

In instances where the sexual abuse ended other than at puberty, the separation of the offender from the respondent was often involved (30 percent). This occurred when the offender left the home or geographic area or when the respondent went away to boarding school or left home for college, work, or early marriage. In some instances (12 percent), it was unclear why the abusive acts ceased.

Histories of the Interview Participants

Socioeconomic Status of Childhood Family

Five of the interview participants were from working-class backgrounds, three were from middle-class backgrounds, and two were from upper-class backgrounds (as self-determined).

Occupation of Childhood Family Breadwinner

Four of the interview participants were from families in which the major breadwinner worked in a blue-collar capacity, and three participants were from families in which the major breadwinner worked in a white-collar capacity. Two participants were from families headed by physicians, and one participant was from a military family.

Religious Affiliation of Childhood Family

Only one interview participant was from a childhood family with no religious affiliation. Of the other participants' childhood families, three were Protestant, three were Catholic, and three were Jewish.

Number of Children in Childhood Family

The number of children in the interview participants' childhood families ranged from 2 to 7, with a mean of 3.7 children per family.

Birth Position in Childhood Family

Five of the interview participants were middle children, four were youngest children, and only one was an eldest child. Five of the interview participants were eldest or only daughters, however.

Siblings Incestuously Abused

Seven of the interview participants were from families in which at least one sibling had been incestuously abused. In one instance, a sibling had been impregnated. Over four-fifths of the siblings abused in the interview participants' families were female. Younger siblings were abused with the same frequency as older siblings.

Age of Participant During Incest

The age of the interview participants at the onset of the incest ranged from 1 to 11 years. The age of the interview participants at the cessation of the incest ranged from 6 to 19 years. The mean age of onset was 5.6 years, and the mean age of cessation was 13.8 years. The incest took place over a period of from 1 to 15 years, with the mean number of years the incest lasted 8.2.

Identity of the Incest Offender

The greatest number of offenders named by the interview participants were fathers (44 percent) followed by brothers (17 percent), grandfathers (11 percent), uncles (11 percent), mothers (11 percent) and one grandmother (6 percent).

Number of Incest Offenders

Four of the interview participants had been incestuously abused by one offender. Five participants had been incestuously abused by two offenders, and one participant had been incestuously abused by four offenders.

Coercion Used by the Offender

Force was experienced by two of the interview participants and threat of force by five of the interview participants at some time during the incestuous abuse. Three of the participants experienced pressure, three experienced the threat of loss of love, and three experienced bribery. One participant experienced the threat of consequences to others, and one participant was given drugs and/or alcohol to ensure compliance.

Nature of the Sexual Activity

A variety of sexual activities was experienced by the interview participants. Sexual activity not involving direct physical contact, such as sexualized comments, "check-outs," "peeping," and/or genital exhibition by the offender, was experienced (in addition to direct physical contact) by seven of the participants. Eight of the participants experienced kissing and/or fondling, eight participants experienced manipulation of male and/or female genitalia, seven participants experienced oral-genital contact, and six participants experienced simulated intercourse. Five of the interview participants experienced vaginal intercourse, and one participant experienced anal intercourse. Three participants were subjected to "inspections" of sexual areas of their body, and one participant was subjected to enemas for the sexual gratification of the offender. Two participants were exposed to sexual sadism on the part of an offender. One participant was impregnated by an offender.

Frequency of the Sexual Activity

Frequency of the sexual activity varied from once to daily, depending upon the type of sexual activity, the time available to the offender, the likelihood of being discovered, and the accessibility of the participant to the offender. Five of the interview participants most commonly experienced sexual activity on a weekly basis, and three of the participants most commonly experienced sexual activity on a daily basis. One participant generally experienced sexual activity on a monthly basis, and one participant generally experienced sexual activity several times a year. Three participants with multiple offenders experienced sexual activity once or twice with a secondary offender. In these instances the offenders were relatives from outside the home who had only limited access to the participants.

Reason Incest Ended

For five of the interview participants, the incest ended as a result of separation from the offender. For two participants the incest ended as a result of circumstances related to puberty, and for one participant the incest ended due to increased threat of disclosure. Two participants were uncertain why the incest had ended.

Comparison of Interview and Questionnaire Participants

An examination of Tables 6, 7, and 8 (Appendix E) in conjunction with Tables 3, 4, and 5 (Appendix E) reveals that the interview participants were comparable to the larger pool of study participants, the questionnaire respondents. Women from working-class and upper-class backgrounds were, by intent, more represented in the interview group than in the questionnaire group. Otherwise, the trends in family background were similar. Women who were abused by more than one offender were more represented in the interview group than in the questionnaire group (two women, in fact, did not identify a second offender until the time of the interview). Otherwise, trends in incest background were similar. The women interviewed experienced force less often as a form of coercion but experienced sexual activity on a more frequent basis than the questionnaire group. Otherwise, the trends in incest experience were similar. Thus, for the most part, the interview group was representative of the larger pool of study participants.

Participant Profile

The participant profile offered in this section and the profiles of the offender and the perceived protector offered in the next section were constructed from the questionnaire data. While such profiles are, of necessity, overly general and imprecise, they provide a means of summarizing what was most salient about each group.

The "typical" respondents in this study were white, middle-class, college-educated women in their thirties, working regularly and attending psychotherapy weekly while involved in a committed heterosexual or lesbian relationship.

The "typical" study respondents came from middle-class or working-class families in which they were one of four children, most likely a middle or youngest child. Their homes were characterized by traditional values; an acceptance of patriarchy; a lenient or resigned attitude toward alcohol abuse, unpredictable behavior, and/or physical violence; and a tendency to minimize or deny problems.

From the ages of 5 to 13, the "typical" respondents were sexually abused by a father or older brother who threatened force and used force more often than not and who engaged in vaginal and/or anal intercourse more often than not in addition to other sexual activities.

During childhood the "typical" respondents told no one about the incest, but as adults they disclosed the abuse to family members as well as friends. As often as not, they also confronted the offender about his actions, with generally unsatisfactory outcomes.

Family Portrait

A total of 63 offenders was reported by the 43 questionnaire respondents. Fifty-one of the 63 offenders (81 percent) were described.

The profile of the offender that emerged from the questionnaire was of a man who presented as "your generic man" and "ordinary citizen." He was generally respected in the community as a man who adequately provided for his family, embraced traditional values and conventional attitudes about sex, practiced religion as often as not, and seemingly functioned appropriately for the most part on a social basis. Within the home, this same man was authoritarian, unpredictable, and as often given to physical violence as not. He was frequently known to have been abused emotionally or physically and infrequently known to have been abused sexually as a child. He was very likely to be abusing alcohol as an adult, much less likely to be abusing other substances, including drugs and food. On an intimate level, he functioned interpersonally with little skill as a partner, parent, and friend. If and when he was confronted regarding his abuse, he relied on denial, minimization, and/or rationalization, thus either refusing to admit the abuse or refusing to accept responsibility for it.

Female offenders, all of whom were mothers, were too few in number (four) to even attempt to construct a profile. However, some findings should be mentioned. In all four instances of sexual abuse by mothers, the father or father figure in the home was also an offender. Two mothers were known to have been sexually abused as children, one mother was known to have been emotionally and physically abused as a child, and the childhood history of the fourth mother, who was psychotic much of the time, was not known. Three of the four mothers were substance abusers (food, food and alcohol, and alcohol and drugs). Unlike the male offenders who were described as superficially competent, the female offenders were described as visibly disturbed. They were characterized as inept, fearful, immature, socially isolated, and lonely.

Almost 60 percent of the respondents emphasized that at the time of the sexual abuse there was no one whom they perceived as a protector, that such an idea was alien to them. Twenty-one percent (21 percent) of the respondents did not describe a perceived protector. Of the respondents (79 percent) who did, all but two described mothers. One respondent described a father, and one respondent described a sister.

The profile of the perceived protector that emerged from the questionnaire was of a woman with low self-esteem who was often known to have been emotionally, physically, and/or sexually abused as a child and who was dependent emotionally and/or financially on her role within the family. She was often, but not always, described as distant and emotionally undemonstrative and as uncomfortable or fearful with regard to sexual matters. Most striking was the consistency of reports regarding her avoidance of conflict and confrontation, her lack of assertiveness or opposition in response to domination, oppression, and/or violence in the home, and her minimization or denial of problems related to the family.

Participant Responses to the Incest

During the sexual activity, the most common responses were dissociative reactions. Psychic "numbing" was reported by 77 percent of the respondents. Participants often described feeling "nothing" physically or being "dead" or "detached" emotionally while the abuse was occurring. Such feelings were generally reported as associated with a sensation of self-estrangement and/or unreality. Fifty-one percent (51 percent) of the respondents reported leaving their bodies, and 40 percent of the respondents reported observing themselves from nearby.

Many respondents relied on a combination of such mechanisms to "get through." For example:

Physically I had to go numb. . . . I think I would have died otherwise. Once I had numbed myself physically, I had to do the same thing emotionally. I accomplished this by disassociating the event from myself. . . . It was almost like dissecting yourself. . . . I guess, in a way, I left my body. It wasn't my body anymore, it was someone else's. It was a very weird feeling. Sometimes I actually felt like there were two separate bodies—two different people. . . . I usually watched what was taking place from across the room or from above. The "person" watching experienced all of the feelings in a detached manner while the person it was happening to was "dead." Or, sometimes the person it was happening to would be screaming and crying, while the person watching only observed and felt nothing.

Sexual arousal was experienced at some time by over half of the respondents, and orgasm was experienced at some time by over a quarter of the respondents. Physiological pleasure was accompanied by intense negative affects, including disgust, fear, shame, guilt, confusion, and anger.

Following the sexual activity, mood and behavioral changes were commonly experienced. Sleep habits, eating habits, and health were also commonly affected.

The most frequently reported defense mechanism in response to the incest was repression, followed by denial and minimization. Repression was reported as a primary defense by over 85 percent of the respondents. Only six respondents reported always remembering their abuse. Incest memories most commonly surfaced when respondents were in their late twenties and early thirties.

Adult coping responses often included the development of a preoccupation with activity or achievement. Such a preoccupation was reported in the domestic, social, and/or academic realm(s) by 72 percent of the respondents. The development of social and/or sexual avoidances was reported as a response to the incest by 67 percent of the respondents.

Other responses during adulthood included a continued reliance on psychic "numbing" and/or dissociative states reported by 53 percent of the respondents and self-medication (i.e., treatment of one's own symptoms) with alcohol, drugs, and/or food. Fifty percent (50 percent) of the respondents reported having self-medicated with alcohol, 40 percent reported having self-medicated with food, and 35 percent reported having self-medicated with drugs. Thirty-seven percent (37 percent) of the respondents engaged in acts of self-mutilation, and 35 percent of the respondents attempted suicide subsequent to the incest.

Perceived Effects of the Incest

The impressionistic material offered in this section was generated from the participants' answers to the open-ended items on the questionnaire and the respondents' spontaneous reporting throughout. The material thus offers the reader an overall sense of what the participants themselves perceived as significant and gave priority to in the absence of suggestion. While general in nature, as with the participant profile and family portrait offered earlier, the material provides an overview of the meaning the incest has had in the lives of the participants. Perceived effects are discussed as they pertain to personality, health, work, parenting, spirituality, intimacy, and sexuality.

Personality

All of the respondents reported that their personality had been altered in some way by the incest experience. "Emotional numbness" and "a lack of spontaneity" were often described. Many respondents reported a chronic vulnerability to depression, and some respondents reported recurrent suicidal ideation. A variety of personality features, from "passive" to "compulsive" to "paranoid," were perceived as related to the incest. Universally experienced difficulties with trust extended from "guardedness" to "suspiciousness of everyone's motives" to "hypervigilance as a way of life" to "a lack of trust in life itself."

Many of the respondents reported that a sense of stigmatization, isolation, and alienation from humanity had resulted from the incest and had influenced their adult personality. A number of respondents described themselves in connection with this as in some respect developmentally delayed. A unanimous complaint was of persistent problems with negative self-image and low self-esteem.

Health

Over one-third of the respondents reported health problems as one of the long-term effects of the incest. Stress-related conditions, including digestive disorders and permanent sleep disorders, were most commonly reported in relation to the incest. Chronic postural problems associated with depression and/or body shame were also attributed to the incest. Several respondents who were still recovering their incest memories reported severe anxiety attacks, multiple symptoms of post-traumatic stress disorder (including high levels of flashback activity and physical sensations related to reexperiencing the trauma), and/or continuous gynecological dysfunctions. Several other respondents reported similar symptomatology during memory retrieval in the past.

Additionally, a transitory or permanent pattern of substance abuse specifically related to the incest was reported by 40 percent of the respondents. Alcohol was most commonly abused, followed by drugs and food. Multiple abuses were reported by a number of respondents. Newly sober respondents were particularly vulnerable to flashback activity.

Work

Over half of the respondents reported that the incest had negatively affected their work. Many problems associated with work were described as related to the incest. Among those most commonly reported were difficulties with authority figures or co-workers related to power, control, and trust issues; difficulties with new tasks, with decision-making, and with achieving recognition related to low self-esteem and fear of attack; and difficulties with memory, concentration, and completion related to general anxiety and/or depression.

Over one-third of the respondents stated that they had not reached their potential as a result of the incest. Several such women wondered where they might be today had the incest never happened. In contrast, over one-quarter of the respondents stated that they had become "over-achievers" as a result of the incest. Many of these women reported that they were "driven" to achieve in the interest of their self-esteem and that they were often unable to take pleasure in their accomplishments because they were "never enough."

Parenting

All of the respondents with children (40 percent) reported that the incest experience had affected their parenting in some way. Over one-third of the respondents with children reported that they were more sensitive and responsive to their children's needs as a result of the incest experience. However, almost half of the respondents with children described themselves as too troubled, anxious, or depressed due to the incest to be as energetic and giving with their children as they would have liked.

Overprotectiveness was a tendency that almost all of the respondents with children reported having to fight against in order not to pass their "terror," "pessimism," or "mistrust" along to their children. Respondents often reported having difficulty leaving their children in the care of others. Worries over the nature and adequacy of their children's sexual abuse prevention training, general sex education, and gender socialization were rather commonly reported. One-fourth of the respondents with children reported that a child of theirs had been sexually abused. A few of the respondents with children reported a constant concern that their children would perceive them as helpless or ineffective in the way that they perceived their own mothers; such women blamed themselves whenever anything painful occurred in their children's lives.

Discomfort with handling the genitals of children during diapering and/ or bathing and discomfort with being physically demonstrative with children were reported by almost one-third of the respondents with children. This was generally experienced in association with a sense of confusion regarding the boundaries between nonerotic and erotic touch and nonexploitive and exploitive touch. Out of a fear of being "intrusive," "inappropriate," "seductive," or "stimulating," some respondents felt unable to express affection spontaneously with their children.

Finally, parenting issues related to children's contact with or estrangement from the respondent's childhood family, including the offender, were not uncommonly mentioned as problematic.

Spirituality

Over half of the respondents reported having rejected or embraced religion as a result of the incest experience. For some, the notion of a God became absurd in the context of the abuse that was occurring. For some, religious practice was associated with family hypocrisy and thus became meaningless or abhorrent. Some respondents decided that God couldn't possibly love them because they were such "sinners"; others decided that, although no one else loved them, maybe God did. Whether faith provided comfort or brought additional pain, the majority of the respondents believed that the incest had influenced their spiritual development.

Intimacy

Problems with intimacy were universally reported, most commonly difficulties related to trust, self-esteem, power, and control. A preoccupation with safety in relationships, a tendency to conceal feelings, a fear of betrayal and abandonment, a sense of confusion regarding limits and boundaries, a pattern of self-reliance as well as responsibility for others, a longing for dependency, and a difficulty with self-protection were all frequently described. Some respondents reported avoiding intimacy, and several mentioned using alcohol, drugs, or food as "a safe companion" to "fill the emptiness" and "provide comfort."

Over half of the respondents reported having been attracted to unavailable or rejecting partners. A pattern of such involvements was frequently perceived as related to the incest. A number of respondents described reenacting the incest experience by maintaining sexual involvements with a series of partners who couldn't be "won" emotionally. Such partners, like the incest offender, provided an initial "illusion" of giving emotionally while receiving sexually and thus often "became obsessions" as unresolved issues surfaced for the respondent. Particularly as issues related to power and control were replayed, disillusionment and loss similar to that experienced with the incest followed.

Many respondents reported having been involved in physically or sexually abusive relationships. Physically abusive relationships were not reported with great frequency. Sexually abusive relationships were quite commonly reported. Almost half the respondents had been raped one or more times as adolescents or adults by acquaintances, dates, and/or husbands. Two respondents additionally reported having been sexually exploited by male therapists (only half the respondents had been in treatment with a male therapist). Four respondents reported that it was in the context of an abusive relationship that their incest memories had surfaced.

An additional problem in relationships reported by over one-quarter of the respondents was an inability to integrate emotional intimacy and sexual intimacy. Thus, the development of erotic interest was accompanied by emotional detachment, and the development of emotional attachment was accompanied by erotic disinterest. This "split" was perceived as directly attributable to the incest experience.

Sexuality

The respondents unanimously agreed that the incest experience had negatively influenced their adult sexuality. Many respondents expressed anger over the influence the incest continued to exert over sexual comfort, pleasure, and satisfaction. Comments included:

> I'm tired of pretending to feel sexual and I'm angry at feeling like I've failed as a woman.

> I'm angry that I'll never be "normal" sexually, that there will always be something wrong with me.

> I'm angry that I can't be as sexual as I'd like when I know I have the right to experience good sex.

> I'm angry that I have to work so hard to feel safe.

> I'm angry at having to be scared.

> I'm angry at my father for generating fear that gets displaced onto my sexual partner.

One respondent summed up her discontent with the comment, "My sexuality doesn't belong to me, it belongs to the incest."

A variety of problems related to sexuality were reported as attributable to or associated with the incest. Several aspects of sexuality were felt by the respondents to have been influenced. These are discussed at length in the chapters that follow.

4

Body Perception and Reproduction

FIVE ASPECTS OF SEXUALITY in women with incest histories were investigated in the study reported on here. They were: body perception, reproduction, sexual preference, sexual "lifestyle," and sexual functioning.

The first of these five aspects, body perception, had received but brief mention in the literature prior to this study (Faria & Belohlavek, 1984; Westerlund, 1983). The second, reproduction, had not been discussed at all in the literature. The significance of these omissions will soon be apparent, as the findings relevant to body perception and reproduction are presented. Not only are the potential effects of incest on these two areas of sexuality numerous, but their impact on a woman's overall sense of self and identification as a woman may clearly be profound.

Body Perception

Negative and/or distorted body perception was reported by 74 percent of the respondents. Many respondents reported that their childhood perception of their body as "dirty," "nasty," "bad," "evil," "out of control," or "untrustworthy" was difficult to overcome. Several respondents reported perceiving their body as "the cause of the abuse." The following sections on body hatred, "ownership," control, estrangement, fitness, illness, body and gender, and physical appearance expand upon the issues and feelings reported in relation to body perception.

Body Hatred

A number of respondents (30 percent) reported "hating" their body. This was generally described as related to the body's association with physical and/or emotional pain. For some respondents, this hatred was expressed by an attitude that it was "OK to abuse," "endanger," or "damage" their body with food, drugs, alcohol, "promiscuity," self-mutilation, and even suicide. Anger and guilt were both apparently related to body hatred. Respondents commonly spoke of abusing themselves as a form of "self-punishment." One respondent stated, "Substance abuse is a way to hurt yourself, a way to make yourself as disgusting and ugly as you feel inside." Another respondent reported, "Promiscuity was a way to 'beat up on' my body which I hated and thought deserved to be denigrated." A third respondent wrote, "I punish myself for my 'sins' by eating and being overweight. It's a form of self-punishment since my body makes me feel shame."

For a number of respondents (35 percent), body hatred or body devaluation was expressed via neglect of exercise, nutrition, and/or hygiene. One respondent reported, "My body never meant anything to me. It was used as a waste receptacle and I saw no reason to take care of it—except when I was pregnant and responsible for another human being." A second respondent wrote, "My body isn't part of me, it's not mine, so I don't pay attention to it."

Body "Ownership"

A sense of not "owning" the body was reported by several respondents (16 percent). Comments included:

> My body doesn't belong to me—it's as if because he possessed it, he owns it. It feels like a house I can be thrown out of at any time.

> My body isn't mine. I have no rights over it. I have no boundaries.

> I don't feel as if my body is my own and I can make it act, make it respond, make it do what I want.

> My body isn't really mine. I just happen to be in it. But it's not as if it's my own. It doesn't do what I want it to do.

Body Control

Complaints of not feeling in charge of the body were rather common (28 percent). This feeling was, in many instances, related to arousal and/or orgasm during the incestuous acts. Physiological arousal during the incest was described by a number of the respondents as a "betrayal" by the body. One respondent explained, "Because I experienced physical pleasure in spite of all the negative emotions, I feel like I can't trust my body not to betray me. I can never know what it might go and do on me." Another respondent reported, "I have a terror of my body and the things it might do. My body isn't a comfortable place to be in."

Body Estrangement

Some respondents (19 percent) reported that they dealt with the "betraying" body by consciously disowning it. One respondent wrote, "It's not sex that's shameful, but my body wanting to have sex. I don't want anything to do with my body." A second respondent stated, "I can't be in my body fully because I'm afraid to physically feel." A third respondent reported, "I feel I have no power over my body, so I pretend I don't have one."

Other respondents (9 percent) reported chronic detachment from the body, without any conscious effort to disown it. Comments included:

I don't know how to be in my body, to feel as if I'm really in it.

My body is somehow separate from me, unknown in some ways and mysterious.

My body is like a stranger to me, somehow disconnected from the real me.

Sometimes such feelings were linked to a pattern of reliance on dissociative states. For example: "I was out of my body most of the time for many years. Later I didn't know how not to be."

Fitness

For many respondents (42 percent), feelings of detachment, lack of control, and powerlessness related to the body were ameliorated by exercise and athletic programs. A number of respondents reported a "need" for such activity as a means of feeling "in myself," "physically whole," "in charge of my body," "less vulnerable," "less fearful of violation," "more powerful," and "purged of the incest." One respondent reported that the only pleasure associated with her body was that derived from athletics. Several respondents reported that exercise or athletic programs had helped them to feel "less ashamed" of their bodies. All of the respondents who reported a highly positive body perception (16 percent) regularly engaged in physical activity, exercise, and/or athletics.

Illness

Illness was described by several respondents (16 percent) as a "betrayal" by the body and/or a confirmation of their lack of control over the body. An intolerance for illness was confounded for some women by fears regarding their physical normality. Several respondents described feeling anxious that they were "not put together right," were somehow "abnormal inside," were "internally deformed" or "damaged" or had "contracted some horrible disease and didn't know it." One respondent wrote that her body wasn't experienced as real but as a "facade" that made her "appear to be human." Such feelings were linked by several respondents to the sense of stigma, isolation, and alienation from humanity associated with the incest.

Body and Gender

A few respondents (7 percent) experienced doubts as to whether they were actually female. One respondent wrote, "I sometimes feel afraid that I'm not really female, that I've just been tricked and have tricked everyone else in turn." Another respondent stated, "I sometimes wonder if I'm really a man accidentally in a female body." This confusion in some instances was linked to an attempt to deny the "female" aspects of the self associated with vulnerability and fear. One respondent described "pretending to be a male persona so much as a child" that she later "felt like a male and not a female." Additionally, two respondents reported feeling that they were "imposters" as adult females.

Several respondents (12 percent) reported difficulty embracing a female identity. One respondent wrote, "I don't want to have breasts, I don't want to have a uterus, I want not to be female." Another respondent stated, "If I were a male, I would not be disgusting to others and to myself."

For a majority of the respondents (63 percent), the equation of "femaleness" with rape and abuse remained strong. Many respondents reported fear associated with revealing the "feminine" aspects of their body. Several respondents reported associating being noticed with being violated in some way and expressed a wish to be "invisible." One respondent explained that she didn't want to work out because "people notice you and I want to be physically invisible." Another respondent reported that she always dressed down in loose clothing so as not to "be flashy and attract attention" to herself. Several other respondents also mentioned deliberately choosing "ill-fitting" or "colorless" clothing in order "to look less attractive" and "to avoid notice." One respondent reported that she couldn't allow herself to gain weight because "to be bigger means to be more visible and to be visible means attack." Respondents were often very conscious of their weight in relation to how it revealed the sexual aspects of their bodies.

Several respondents purposefully gained weight "to be less curvaceous," "to bury myself in my body," "to be undesirable," "to make myself untouchable" or "to hide." Another means of "hiding" reported by the respondents was poor posture. Several women reported that they didn't carry themselves well due to "fear" or "self-consciousness."

Physical Appearance

Whether attractive or not, many respondents (44 percent) reported feeling unattractive or "ugly" due to the incest. An intolerance for outward flaws and a sense that such flaws were evidence of a negative internal quality were often expressed. Respondents frequently reported having difficulty accepting compliments regarding their appearance. Several respondents stated that they were unable to realistically assess their own appearance and had difficulty believing that others found them attractive.

Reproduction

The development of reproductive capacity was reported as an unwelcome event by many of the respondents (56 percent). Discomfort with the physical changes that occurred at puberty and denial or rejection of "womanhood" during adolescence were often described.

As adults, respondents frequently experienced feelings in relation to reproduction that were reminiscent of the incest experience, most commonly fear, shame, and confusion. For example, menstruation was sometimes accompanied by fear because it was associated with feeling a loss of control over the body and its activities. Or, symptoms of reproductive dysfunction were accompanied by shame because such symptoms were experienced as a "betrayal" by the body and a confirmation of the respondents' suspected "abnormality" and/or female "inadequacy." Or, an unwanted pregnancy was accompanied by confusion because it was associated with "having given over all power and control" to a sexual partner without awareness. The following sections on reproductive decision-making, pregnancy, birth, and nursing expand upon the commonly reported feelings and issues related to reproduction.

Reproductive Decision-Making

Reproductive decision-making often involved deliberation that was painful due to fear and confusion. Many respondents (56 percent) reported having concerns that they might not be good parents. For example: "I wonder do I have it in me to give to a child when I wasn't given to and emotionally nourished as a child—will I be drained of what little I do have emotionally? Reproduction doesn't feel like a free choice to me." Respondents reported fearing that they would be "overprotective," that they would "abandon" or "fail to protect" their children, that they would be "inappropriate," "seductive," "harmful," or "abusive" (emotionally, physically, and/or sexually).

Two respondents reported deciding not to have children because of their fears of being abusive, and one respondent reported choosing to have fewer children so she wouldn't be "tested too much as far as my potential to become abusive." Three additional respondents reported choosing to have no children, and three others reported choosing to have fewer children "because of the incest." Thus, a total of nine respondents (21 percent) reported deciding to have fewer or no children for reasons related to the incest experience.

A few respondents (7 percent) felt that they "couldn't possibly bear a normal child." This conviction was grounded in negative and/or distorted self-perceptions related to the incest. Such respondents continued to perceive themselves as "evil," "inhuman," or "alien" as adults. One respondent expressed a fear of an "outside force" being involved with pregnancy, as in the film *Rosemary's Baby*. Another respondent reported that she feared she would have a "monster" somehow reflective of her own "secret evilness."

Several respondents (9 percent) reported wanting to be single or adoptive parents because they did not want to have a child with a man, did not want to have a man be significant to their child, or did not feel they could ever trust the father not to abuse the child. One respondent expressed a desire to have only sons, thinking that they might be less vulnerable to abuse.

Pregnancy

Twenty-five of the questionnaire respondents (58 percent) had been pregnant one or more times. Only 35 percent of the respondents had biological children. Two respondents reported having miscarried welcomed pregnancies. Twelve respondents (including four respondents with children) reported having aborted or miscarried one or more unwanted pregnancies.

Many of the respondents who became pregnant (80 percent) reported that pregnancy brought up a mixture of feelings related to the incest experience. A sense of having the body being "taken over by another" and "doing things all on its own" seemed reminiscent of the incest to a number of respondents who became pregnant (28 percent). A feeling of shame associated with pregnancy was reported by a few respondents who became pregnant (12 percent) who perceived the pregnancy as evidence to the outside world of their previously unrevealed "badness." One respondent reported feeling more fearful and vulnerable during pregnancy because the pregnancy "called attention to" her. In contrast, another respondent reported feeling "safer" during pregnancy because she was "no longer sexual and the maternity clothes covered all."

Changes in sexual activity during pregnancy were reported by most of the respondents who became pregnant (60 percent). Some respondents who became pregnant (28 percent) reported feeling repulsed by their sexual partner during pregnancy or repulsed by the idea of intercourse. A few respondents who became pregnant (12 percent) reported a fear that the baby might be damaged by sexual activities that were "incest-like." For example, "During the first couple of months I had irrational fears about harming the baby by intercourse because it seemed 'incestuous' to have my husband's penis so close to the baby." Some of the respondents who became pregnant (16 percent) welcomed pregnancy as a "relief from the sexual demands" of their partners. One respondent wrote, "When I was pregnant I could get the holding and caretaking I wanted without sex. I felt a sense of dread when the pregnancy was over in regard to this."

Birth

Of the respondents with children, one was an adoptive parent, one was a stepparent, and the remainder were biological parents. Fifteen of the questionnaire respondents (35 percent) had experienced childbirth one or more times.

As with pregnancy, birth was reported by many of the respondents with biological children (80 percent) to have brought up a mixture of feelings related to the incest experience. One respondent reported associating childbirth to forced intercourse. Another respondent reported "hating" her body during birth "because it was the first time since the incest" that she "had no control over what it was doing and what was happening" to her. Most of the respondents who gave birth (60 percent) mentioned difficulties associated with having their bodies "out of control again" and with having to be "dependent again" upon others during birth. One respondent reported feeling "betrayed again" by her body when a caesarian section was required. Two respondents reported experiencing such intense shame upon being exposed at delivery that they were unable to watch their children's births.

Nursing

Most of the respondents with biological children (80 percent) had nursed one or more of their children. One respondent reported that she hadn't nursed because she was "repulsed" by the idea of having something "attached to" her breast. Two other respondents reported that they hadn't nursed, but did not comment further.

The experience of nursing was reported by many of the respondents who nursed (75 percent) to have been influenced by the incest. Two respondents stated that they had discontinued nursing because larger breasts made them feel self-conscious. Two other respondents reported difficulty with nursing due to feeling unable to call their bodies their "own." A number of the respondents who nursed (42 percent) experienced fears about not being able to nurse associated with feeling like an "inadequate" or "abnormal" human being or a female "imposter." Such women reported being "surprised" that they were capable of nursing.

Several respondents who nursed (33 percent) experienced fears during nursing that their body would "betray" them by becoming aroused. For example: "I was always apprehensive that I might get aroused sexually by the nursing baby." And, "If I had gotten aroused, I'm sure I would have felt like an incest offender." One respondent reported feeling "uncomfortable about the vaginal contractions" experienced during nursing.

Two respondents who nursed were unable during the nursing period to have both their child and their partner touch their breasts because it was "too confusing." Many of the respondents who nursed (58 percent) reported that nursing gratified their need for physical closeness and "connectedness" more satisfactorily than sexual activity with their partner.

Only three respondents with biological children described the experience of pregnancy, birth, and nursing in a highly positive way. In these few instances, the respondents reported that an "affirmation of normalcy" and "a sense of power" as a woman were associated.

Discussion

The findings presented here related to body perception and reproduction extended beyond the literature of the time and thus could not be comparatively reviewed. Both of these aspects of sexuality in women with incest histories had been altogether neglected by researchers. In part, this might have been due to the characteristics of the prior research. Since few efforts have been made to study sexuality as perceived by women with incest histories themselves, perhaps it should not have been surprising that researchers have failed to identify some of the major areas in need of investigation.

Given that incest is taken in as an experience through the body and that it occurs during childhood when body concept is developing, there would be every reason to suppose that women with incest histories might demonstrate disturbances in body perception. With this vulnerability to negative and/or distorted body perception, there would also be every reason to suppose that women with incest histories might be vulnerable to disturbances in their perception of reproductive function/ dysfunction, pregnancy, birth, and nursing, since all of these are experienced through the body.

The findings of the study clearly indicate that women with incest histories may experience a variety of difficulties related to both body perception and reproduction, and that these difficulties may be attributable to or associated with the incest experience. The unavailability of information in the past incest literature pertaining to these two aspects of sexuality became rather tragic in light of the numerous findings reported here.

Since body perception has the capacity to affect exercise, nutrition, hygiene, substance use/abuse, weight, physical fitness, and the experience of illness in women with incest histories, professionals involved in the medical and health fields need to begin to routinely ask women whether they have such histories. Likewise, gynecologists, childbirth educators, obstetricians, and obstetrical nurses need to know if the women they serve have known or suspected histories of incest. Only then can effective interventions be made to address the potential complications of providing education and care to this group of women.

Research investigation regarding body perception and reproduction from the viewpoint of medical and health professionals is sorely needed in addition to study by mental health professionals. This would provide a more integrated conceptualization of the problems that women with incest histories may experience in these two areas, and would inform interdisciplinary provision of services to such women.

5

Sexual Preference and Sexual "Lifestyle"

WOMEN WITH INCEST HISTORIES had often been stereotyped or further stigmatized by the literature when this study was undertaken, particularly in relation to sexual preference and sexual "lifestyle." In Chapter 1 some of the factors underlying the history of stereotyping were revealed. The reader will be better able to appreciate some of the problems outlined in that discussion as the findings relevant to sexual preference and sexual "lifestyle" are presented here. The reader should remain aware, as emphasized in Chapter 2, that the sampling method used for this study predisposed for an overrepresentation of women of sexual preferences other than heterosexuality. Conclusions should not be drawn from this study about the relative frequencies of the various sexual preferences among women with incest histories in the general population. As will be seen from the section that follows, the sample was unusual in terms of the relative percentages of the various sexual preferences and in terms of the percentage of women sexually experienced as adults with both men and women.

Sexual Preference

The questionnaire respondents reported their sexual preference as follows: 42 percent heterosexual, 35 percent lesbian, 9 percent celibate, 9 percent undecided, and 5 percent bisexual. Many respondents (56 percent) reported both certainty and satisfaction with regard to sexual preference. Seventeen percent (17 percent) of the heterosexual women, 100 percent of the lesbian women, and 50 percent of the undecided women were sexually experienced as adults with both genders. All of the celibate women were sexually experienced as adults with men only. Thus, a total of 51 percent of the respondents were sexually experienced with both genders, and a total of 49 percent of the respondents were sexually experienced with men only. The issues and feelings commonly reported in relation to sexual preference are discussed in the following sections on incest associations, dissatisfaction and preference, confusion and preference, and assumptions and preference.

Incest Associations

Several respondents (16 percent) associated their sexual preference with the incest experience. Within this group, respondents whose preference was celibacy predominated (71 percent). Comments included:

Celibacy was chosen because I didn't want anyone touching my body, even myself.

Celibacy was chosen to avoid feeling sexual at all, to avoid the guilt and shame, to avoid being touched. I hated touch, I was disgusted by it.

Celibacy gives *you* control over your sexuality.

Celibacy is safer than sex with a partner.

Respondents who had not yet established a strong sexual identity also spoke of an association with their incest history. For example:

I want to be in a relationship with a man, but fear being used, being hurt, having him turn out to be a monster.

I don't want to be celibate, but I don't want to be hurt or to hurt anybody.

I *can't* be heterosexual. I can't relate to men sexually.

A few respondents (7 percent) reported that a sexual relationship would be difficult for them with either gender as a result of the incest. For example: "It seems unimportant who I'm sexual with — it's arbitrary when I don't know if I can ever be sexually happy with anyone."

Dissatisfaction and Preference

Of the respondents who had established a strong sexual identity, there were several who expressed dissatisfaction, all of them heterosexual. One respondent expressed a wish to be celibate but stated that she couldn't because she was "with a life partner." A few other respondents expressed a wish to be lesbian, one reporting, "Then I wouldn't have to deal with this," another reporting, "Men are too much work," and a third reporting, "It *must* be easier!" A fourth respondent who was heterosexual wrote, "Although I sometimes wonder if I'd be better off lesbian, I know lesbians who have the same problems relating to their lovers that I do."

Approximately one-third of the heterosexual respondents reported being attracted to women but dissuaded from lesbianism or bisexuality by the "social censure," "societal attitudes," or "oppression" associated with these choices. Some of these respondents reported dissatisfaction with their preference and others reported confusion.

Confusion and Preference

A third of the respondents reported confusion related to sexual preference and uncertainty over their choice. Comments included:

> I don't know what my identity is, but I'm dissatisfied with the [heterosexual] label I've given to myself.

> How is it I fantasize about women but have never considered myself a lesbian?

> My sexual feelings for men confuse me. Going from a lesbian to a bisexual identity is very difficult.

> I'm celibate, but . . . I can't make up my mind whether to try a lesbian relationship or forget it.

One respondent summed up her confusion with the question, "What do I do—try out heterosexuality, celibacy, lesbianism, and bisexuality, until I find something that fits?"

For a number of the respondents, the confusion over their choice was related to confusion over what was sex and what was affection. A few respondents (7 percent) specifically mentioned being sexual with both genders when, in fact, they only wanted the friendship and affection of one of those genders. An additional respondent reported reacting to her "affection" for same-sex friends with "homophobia" because of her difficulty distinguishing between sex and affection.

Sometimes the confusion related to sexual preference included confusion over "the why of it." One respondent questioned her celibacy, stating, "Is this what I really want or am I just denying part of myself?" A lesbian respondent reported experiencing "uncertainty over whether incest made heterosexuality impossible as a life choice." A respondent who was undecided wondered, "If I was never attracted to women until I started to work on the incest, then aren't I just choosing because of my terror of men?" And a heterosexual respondent reported, "Maybe I just want to say to the world, 'I'm not maimed for life, you know.'" Whatever sexual preference was chosen, some respondents (14 percent) wondered about their sexual identity free of the incest trauma.

Assumptions and Preference

A number of respondents expressed concern that others might automatically attribute their sexual preference to the incest. Several respondents expressed resentment that others had, in fact, done so in the past.

Assumptions of traumatic causation were reported to have contributed to difficulties experienced by 40 percent of the lesbian respondents when they were coming out as lesbians. Almost half of the lesbian respondents (47 percent) reported that they felt they had had a more difficult time coming out as lesbians because of the "double stigmatization" of incest and lesbianism. A "flight into compulsive sex with men" to avoid feeling "marked" again was described by one-third of the lesbian respondents.

While lesbian respondents more frequently encountered devaluation of their preference on the basis of the incest experience, respondents of all preferences, including respondents who reported certainty and satisfaction, felt vulnerable to negative judgments and assumptions regarding their sexual preference. Celibates as well as lesbians expressed concerns that their choice would be viewed as a "cop-out." Heterosexual respondents expressed concerns that their choice would be viewed as "an attempt to prove something." And bisexual respondents expressed concerns that their choice would be viewed as indicative of "confusion," "ambivalence," or "lack of commitment." Such concerns were unfortunately sometimes confounded by the respondents' exposure to feminist prescriptivism based upon notions of "politically correct" sexuality.

Sexual "Lifestyle"

A variety of sexual "lifestyles" was reported by the questionnaire respondents. Many respondents reported changes in "lifestyle" over time or a pattern of alternation between "lifestyles" during adulthood. Sexual "lifestyle" was often felt to reflect the incest experience. The following sections on aversion, inhibition, compulsion, celibacy, "promiscuity," prostitution, "the split," and sexual orientation expand upon the issues and feelings related to sexual "lifestyle."

Aversion

A "lifestyle" in which aversion predominated was reported by 14 percent of the respondents. Descriptions of sexual repulsion accompanied by sexual avoidance were categorized as aversion. "Fear of sex" and/or "fear of men" were not in and of themselves indicative of aversion. Both were commonly reported but in many instances were not associated with repulsion and were not accompanied by avoidance.

Feelings of fear were reported by all of the respondents whose "lifestyle" was predominantly characterized by aversion. Some respondents (5 percent) reported fear that was "disguised" as disgust. Other respondents (9 percent) described experiencing a "terror" of the physical and/or emotional "pain" associated with sex.

Anger was related to aversion in that half of the respondents whose "lifestyle" was predominantly characterized by aversion "hated" sex because it was viewed as something they were forced to do. The resentment felt over having to comply during childhood was sometimes expressed via avoidance or refusal in adulthood. As one respondent commented, "I learned to consider 'normal' sex deviant or perverse, something that had to be done. I hated sex throughout my marriage and looked for ways to get out of it." Another respondent stated, "I sometimes feel like my reaction to my husband is just a matter of 'you can't make me.'"

Inhibition

A "lifestyle" in which inhibition predominated was reported by 63 percent of the respondents. Sexual thought, feeling, behavior, and/or activity were described as having a constrained quality that was felt as unnatural.

A number of respondents (14 percent) felt that "pleasure seeking" was shameful and an indication of their "evilness." They thus avoided sexual pleasure so as "to avoid feelings of self-blame and guilt" related to the incest. Several respondents (9 percent) reported that inhibition was related to feeling "undeserving" of sexual pleasure. Inhibition was sometimes mentioned as a way to "resolve" confusion regarding sex and affection (7 percent). It was also mentioned by one respondent as a way to deal with confusion regarding desire and fear. As this respondent explained, "By choosing sexlessness I avoid being pulled in two different directions."

Fear was often reported in relation to inhibition. For some respondents (9 percent) the only way to eliminate the fear was to control sexual feeling. Other respondents (30 percent) reported a sense of, "I can't control my feelings, so I must control my actions." One respondent explained, "Even if I feel desire, I don't act on it. I control my sexual behavior because that's how you get hurt in relationships."

An "obsessive" need for trust and control encouraged some women to be more active sexually with themselves than with partners. A number of respondents (23 percent) reported frequent sexual fantasies and frequent masturbation, but infrequent or limited sexual activity with partners due to the associated vulnerability. One respondent stated, "My reliance on masturbation and nonvaginal sex to reach orgasm is a way to stay in control and to keep men out of my body, a way of protecting myself."

Anger was also reported by a number of respondents (21 percent) in relation to inhibition. One respondent explained, "My way to be 'in power' sometimes is to say 'No!' but it's an automatic no, it isn't really a choice." Another respondent wrote, "If sex renders you weak and defenseless, then a way to be powerful is to refuse sex." In addition to being associated with power and control issues, anger was in some instances associated with trust and self-esteem issues. For example: "I can't believe that I'm wanted for more than sex sometimes, so I *have* to refuse."

Compulsion

A "lifestyle" in which compulsion predominated was reported by 23 percent of the respondents. Sexual thought, feeling, behavior, and/or activity were described as having a driven quality that was felt as unnatural.

Issues of self-esteem were sometimes related to compulsion. For example: "Compulsive sexual behavior serves as a validation of my badness" and "Compulsive sex gives me a reason for the guilt and shame I feel anyway."

A few respondents (7 percent) reported an identity dependent upon the sexual self. Comments included:

Sex is all I'm good for.

Sex is the only reason I'm alive.

If I'm not sexual, I don't exist, so I'm compulsive about sex, I'm obsessed.

Compulsive sex was felt by several respondents (9 percent) to provide a way to express anger at oneself. One respondent described compulsive sex as "a self-abuse tool." Another respondent commented, "The 'sexual' impulses are really impulses to be self-abusive. Anger's the real drive, not sex."

For some respondents (7 percent), compulsive sex provided a way to express anger at others. For example: "I test men repeatedly just to prove they're all the same. Even the ones you think are your friends can be had. In the end they'll all betray you for sex." One respondent described using sex "as a tool to manipulate others to get what you want, to make them 'pay' with gifts."

Some respondents (9 percent) reported issues of power and control related to compulsion in sexual behavior. One respondent stated, "Pursuing attractions compulsively is related to a feeling of power it gives me." Another respondent described repeatedly sexualizing friendships as "an exercise routine in power and control." In some instances the power or control was described as "an illusion thereof."

A few respondents (7 percent) reported that compulsiveness brought relief from unpleasant emotions. One respondent described her "compulsive sexual behavior" as "an attempt to undo the fear and powerlessness." Another respondent described using sex as a way to avoid feelings. She wrote, "Compulsion is a means of avoiding emotional feelings by focusing on physical feelings — lusting serves as a cover — instead of feeling emotional pain you feel sexual pleasure."

Two respondents (5 percent) reported that compulsive sex during young adulthood was related to confusion. One respondent commented, "My sexual behavior was a reflection of the state of my mind — I was all over the place." Another respondent reported, "I was totally hypersexual. I didn't have any notion of what sex was really about and I was completely confused about sex and affection."

For a few respondents (7 percent), compulsive sexual behavior was related to a fear/pleasure bond that was felt to be the result of the incest. One respondent explained, "The mix of pleasure and fear means I have to change partners a lot. The excitement fades when someone becomes familiar and the 'danger' is gone." A second respondent elaborated, "My excitement is greater when fear is blended so I sometimes feel driven in my pursuit of sexual pleasure." A third respondent reported, "I feel helpless sometimes because pleasure is associated with fear. I'm 'obsessed' with sex as a result of it."

Celibacy

A period of celibacy was reported by 49 percent of the respondents. The term celibacy was generally used by the respondents to indicate abstention from all sexual activity with a partner(s). In very few instances was the term used to indicate abstention from masturbation as well.

Celibacy was reported by many respondents (33 percent) as associated with the avoidance of feelings of guilt, shame, and fear. Some respondents reported that "asexuality" meant "freedom" from the shame and self-blame that accompanied sexual pleasure. Other respondents reported that celibacy provided a way to be "in control" and to "not have to live with fear all the time." As one respondent explained, "Safety is my first priority and the only time I *know* I'm safe and in charge is when I'm with me."

"Promiscuity"

A period of self-defined "promiscuity" was reported by 47 percent of the respondents. In the majority of instances (70 percent), the "promiscuity" took place in adolescence (ages 13 through 17) and/or in young adulthood (ages 18 through 22).

"Promiscuity" was viewed by many of the respondents (35 percent) as both a means to express anger at oneself and a means to express anger at others. Several respondents spoke of "promiscuity" as a way of "abusing" or "punishing" themselves. Underlying this self-directed anger was a sense of guilt and shame, of "deserving no better." For some respondents (9 percent), negative and/or distorted body perception was involved. For example: "I was reckless with my body as if it weren't my own. It was disassociated from me as a person. I endangered my body because it had no value to me except insofar as it could 'control' others."

"Promiscuity" was perceived by a number of respondents (14 percent) as providing "a sense of control," since the sexual activity was "self-initiated" and involved "acting on another rather than being acted upon." One respondent reported, "By sleeping with *everyone*, I made sure I had no sexual feelings for anyone that were outside of my control."

An "illusion of power" or "a reversal of the power dynamic" through "promiscuity" was described by a number of respondents (16 percent). Several of these respondents spoke of enjoying the power associated with the role of sexual "aggressor."

For a few respondents, being the "aggressor" meant "demeaning and disempowering men by having them sexually." One respondent stated, "I'd pick them up, use them, hurt them, and reject them. I used to kick them out before breakfast."

As some respondents described expressing anger at men via "promiscuity," other respondents (7 percent) described expressing anger at their childhood family. For example:

I couldn't stand the hypocrisy! As kids we were expected to go to church twice on Sundays, to service in the morning and to youth group at night. In between my father would be screwing all of us. I became promiscu-

ous in adolescence and stayed that way all through college. It was my "revenge," my way of humiliating my family, my way of telling on them without telling.

Whatever satisfaction was derived from the expression of anger through "promiscuity," respondents who had been "promiscuous" tended to report (70 percent) that "promiscuity" was "emotionally self-destructive" for them. As one respondent commented, "In the end, of course, the person I was hurting most was me. It took me a long time to realize that, to see how destructive it all was."

A few respondents (9 percent) reported "promiscuity" with one gender or the other related to a period of confusion regarding sexual preference. In all but one instance, this was heterosexual "promiscuity" associated with an attempt to deny lesbianism.

Two respondents (5 percent) reported "promiscuity" that was motivated in part by fear. One respondent stated, "I was sexually provocative in early adolescence and promiscuous in college. I was trying to get another man to claim me so my father wouldn't be able to." The other respondent reported, "I wanted to escape from my father. I had to belong to another male so I wouldn't belong to my father anymore."

A few respondents (9 percent) reported that in an ironic way "promiscuity" had helped them "become more sexual" since it involved "repeated confrontations with the guilt and shame," "seizing power instead of giving it up," and "challenging the fear instead of running from it." One respondent described the "limitations" of addressing the incest issues via "promiscuity." She stated, "It doesn't help integrate sex and love. It doesn't involve any real emotional vulnerability, so the trust and intimacy issues get completely ignored."

Alternation

Alternation between "promiscuity" and celibacy was reported by 21 percent of the respondents. Thus, the percentage of respondents reporting a period of celibacy without a period of "promiscuity" was 28 percent and the percentage of respondents reporting a period of "promiscuity" without a period of celibacy was 26 percent.

Prostitution

A period of prostitution was reported by 12 percent of the respondents. Of these five respondents, two were also involved in pornography during the period of prostitution. Two of the five respondents reported having prostituted for drugs. One respondent was involved in prostitution during adulthood from the ages of 22 to 26. In all other instances, the period of prostitution occurred during adolescence (ages 13 through 17) or young adulthood (ages 18 through 22).

Prostitution was reported as related to self-esteem and/or power issues. Distorted body perception was associated in that the body was not one's own but "belonged" to the pimp and was there to be "possessed" by others. Negative identity was associated in that the respondents felt that they were "only good for sex" or "deserved to be treated like a whore." A sense of "having power over men sexually" was reported in conjunction with "using them via sexuality, having disdain for them and for their sexual desires." At the same time a sense of "turning over all power to men" was reported in conjunction with "giving them whatever they wanted" and "letting the pimp run your life no matter what."

"The Split"

In association with sexual "lifestyle," "the split," the nonintegration of emotional intimacy and sexual intimacy, was reported by a number of respondents (28 percent). One respondent described "the split" as follows: "I can't allow myself to get close because I'm afraid of losing my sexual desire and feelings. The only way I can continue to want sex is to maintain emotional distance." Other descriptions of respondents' experience of "the split" included: "I can't have my sexual life and my home life in the same place. Everything's in separate compartments." And, "So much for monogamy, it isn't an option."

Some respondents (5 percent) reported that "the split" encouraged "promiscuity," since they experienced difficulty being sexual with a familiar partner. A familiar partner was sometimes perceived as more "dangerous," since to be known involved having one's "badness" discovered. Other respondents (5 percent) reported that "the split" was more "a consequence" of their "promiscuity." For example: "I punish men with my sexuality. Therefore, I can't be sexual with anyone I love or even like."

Some respondents (12 percent) reported "the split" in association with inhibition. In one instance a respondent described longing for and seeking a loving, asexual relationship. She reported:

I don't want sex, I want holding and warmth and love without sex. I guess what I want is what I was supposed to have as a child and never got. I can't desire men I care about and I don't want men I care about desiring me. It's as if some part of me is always saying, "If you really loved me, you wouldn't want sex."

In other instances where "the split" was reported in association with inhibition, commitment rendered the partner more "related" or "more like family," with a resultant loss of sexual desire. In some instances, sex became more emotionally conflictual with the "relatedness," and in other instances sex became associated with duty as in the incest.

Some respondents (7 percent) reported "the split" in association with compulsion. In these instances, committed relationships were avoided due to associations with manipulation, loss of power, and betrayal. Two respondents (5 percent) reported a pattern of precipitously ending relationships and "jumping into" new ones when commitment threatened. One respondent reported a pattern of "betraying the partner first on the assumption that, of course, they will betray you once they become meaningful."

Sexual Orientation

A masochistic orientation was reported by three of the respondents (7 percent). For two of these three women, orgasm was contingent upon humiliation or pain. An additional four respondents (9 percent) had experimented with sadomasochism but had found their experiences unsatisfying. Masochistic orientation in fantasy was reported by 12 additional respondents (28 percent) who had had no experience with sadomasochism. For half of these women, orgasm was contingent upon masochistic fantasy.

None of the respondents reported an orientation toward children. Three respondents (7 percent) reported sexual fantasies of children which they had never enacted and occasional sexual impulses toward children which they controlled. Three other respondents (7 percent) reported having engaged in sexual acts with children during early adolescence. None of the respondents reported sexual activity with children as adults.

None of the respondents reported an orientation toward animals. Three respondents (7 percent) reported having sexual fantasies involving animals. Of these three women, two had had oral-genital contact with animals during their adulthood. None of the women reported involvement in sexual activity with animals at the time of the study.

Discussion

The findings presented here related to sexual preference supported a previous finding of confusion in women with incest histories (Meiselman, 1978). Two explanations for this phenomenon emerged from the study.

Both confusion between affection and sex arising from the incest experience and confusion over the role of the incest in choice-making may contribute to self-doubts over sexual preference in women with incest histories. Neither of these factors had been explored previously in relation to confusion over sexual preference in incest survivors.

The findings neither supported nor challenged Meiselman's (1978) suggestion of an association between incest and female homosexuality. While a large percentage of the study sample was lesbian, the sampling method predisposed for this finding, as emphasized in Chapter 2. The substantial number of lesbian participants in this study should not be interpreted as confirmation of a high incidence of lesbianism among women in general with incest histories.

Since the author does not assume that lesbianism (or celibacy or bisexuality) is a failure of heterosexuality, it was not an intent of this study to investigate the role of the incest trauma in the establishment of a lesbian (or celibate or bisexual) identity. Nonetheless, some relevant information emerged from the study. The findings suggest that some women (in this instance, predominantly celibate or undecided women) may themselves attribute their sexual preference to the incest experience. This finding could not be compared with the findings of previous studies relevant to incest and sexual preference (Finkelhor, 1980; Langmade, 1983; Meiselman, 1978), since participants' own perceptions were not reported. In only one instance was the perspective of the study participants on this issue mentioned. Herman (1981) reported that two lesbian women (out of a sample of 40 incest survivors) had themselves attributed their preference to the incest.

The need for researchers (and others) to allow women with incest histories to express their own thoughts regarding sexual preference is underscored by the study's finding that women with incest histories may commonly expect to have their choice devalued by others on the basis of their history. The literature on sexual preference prior to this study clearly gave women with incest histories, particularly lesbians, little reason to anticipate otherwise.

The findings presented here related to sexual "lifestyle" supported previous findings of an association between incest and later "promiscuity" (Boekelheide, 1978; Finkelhor, 1980; Herman, 1981; Meiselman, 1978; Tsai et al., 1979). In agreement with other reports (Boekelheide, 1978; Finkelhor, 1980; Herman, 1981; Meiselman, 1978), a transitory period of "promiscuity" (in this instance, self-defined) was found to be rather common, particularly during adolescence and/or young adulthood. A period of celibacy, however, was even more common among the participants of this study. This finding could not be compared with previous study findings, since past researchers did not inquire about celibacy.

In agreement with previous studies (Herman, 1981; Meiselman, 1978), a period of prostitution was not a frequent finding among the study's participants. The percentage revealed was rather small, although higher than the figures from the Herman (1981) and Meiselman (1978) studies. The discrepancy may be due to sampling differences or to a greater degree of disclosure having been achieved in this study. As with "promiscuity," prostitution was most likely to have occurred in adolescence or young adulthood.

Finally, the findings suggest that in later adulthood sexual "lifestyles" dominated by inhibition may be more common than "lifestyles" dominated by compulsion or aversion. These results could not be compared with previous study results since such patterns had not been examined in women with incest histories. The findings were, however, in apparent agreement with Finkelhor (1980), who concluded that the impact of incest on sexual activity is greatest in early adulthood, and with Langmade (1983), who found significantly less sexual activity in incest subjects than in matched controls among women with a mean age similar to that of this study group.

6

Sexual Functioning

WHILE SOME OF THE RESEARCH prior to this study pertaining to sexuality in women with incest histories had specifically addressed sexual functioning, a sense of the subjective experience of such women had not been conveyed. As the findings on sexual functioning are presented here, the complexity of the underlying issues for these women will be revealed.

All of the questionnaire respondents reported that the incest experience had influenced their adult sexual functioning. A range of comfort and discomfort was described, with all of the respondents reporting that several aspects of adult sexual functioning were affected rather than one discrete area. These aspects are discussed in the following sections on sexual fantasy, desire, arousal, orgasm, "the split," and satisfaction.

Sexual Fantasy

An absence of sexual fantasy was reported by 16 percent of the respondents. Three respondents reported that they didn't fantasize at all. Two respondents reported that they weren't able to allow fantasy due to associated negative affects. Two respondents reported that they were unable to hold an image due to the intrusion of incest-related images.

Almost a third of the respondents (30 percent) reported the occasional presence of the offender in their fantasies. Most of the respondents experienced this as outside of their control and described the fantasies as "intrusive" and "unwelcome." As one respondent explained, "These 'fantasies' aren't created, they just happen. I feel as if my mind is attacked by these thoughts." Several of the respondents experienced occasional fantasies of the offender as voluntarily engaged in, but conflictual. One respondent stated, "I try not to engage in fantasies about him anymore because I don't think they're good for my healing or recovery."

Whatever the nature of the respondents' fantasies, difficulty accepting them was generally described (70 percent). A few respondents (12 percent) reported that they were "able to enjoy" their fantasies because they were "able to separate thought from action" and knew they "wouldn't act on them."

Sexual fantasy as an activity was seen as "bad" by a number of the respondents (37 percent). Descriptions ranged from "unwholesome" to "impure" to "dirty" to "raunchy" to "a sign of being promiscuous." One respondent explained, "Fantasizing is evidence of your sexual nature, therefore your blame and your badness." Several respondents (16 percent) spoke of having their fantasies somehow "found out" by others and of having their "desire" or their "sexual side" thus revealed. Magical thinking of this nature was accompanied by expectations of being "taken advantage of," "humiliated," or "robbed of self-esteem" by those who were able to read their minds. Such fears were linked by some respondents to an earlier fear of having their demeanor somehow reveal the incest.

Over half of the respondents (51 percent) reported guilt and/or shame in association with the content of their sexual fantasies. In a number of instances respondents reported that their fantasy partners were "inappropriate" (30 percent). A few respondents reported discomfort over experiencing desire (as evidenced by fantasies) for anyone but their marital partner. Other respondents reported shame or guilt over fantasies of the offender, children, or persons of the nonpreferred gender. Several respondents described conflict over fantasizing about people whom they knew personally, conflict that was apparently related to their own sensitivity to exploitation. For example: "You shouldn't 'use' unsuspecting others in this way." And, "I feel like I'm 'violating' them or 'betraying' them even if I never act on it."

Fantasy activities as well as fantasy partners were sometimes judged "inappropriate" by the respondents (28 percent). Fantasies that involved humiliation, force, violence, or pain were often accompanied by "intense" guilt. One respondent commented, "Incest survivors shouldn't have violent fantasies and shouldn't be aroused by 'forceful' sex even if no one is really hurt." Another respondent stated, "I feel like I'm perverted because of my fantasies of physical abuse and punishment." A third respondent reported, "I keep wishing I didn't have sadomasochistic fantasies and that I weren't aroused by thoughts that are self-abusive." One respondent summed up her dissatisfaction with the content of her fantasies with the comment, "I don't approve of most of my fantasies."

Confusion in association with sexual fantasies was reported by a number of the respondents (21 percent). Questions asked included:

How can an incest survivor have fantasies about children? Am I sick?

Why do I have fantasies about men when my preference is for women?

How come sadomasochistic fantasies that are abusive arouse me?

How come only sadomasochistic fantasies bring me to orgasm and nothing else works?

A few respondents (7 percent) experienced confusion over their role in the incest as a result of their sexual fantasies. One respondent wrote, "It's not 'normal' to have fantasies that are violent or humiliating. Maybe I'm sick or damaged. I must have liked those things that happened." Another respondent wrote, "If I have these fantasies of being raped I guess that's what I wanted. I must be perverted even though they frighten me."

Control issues were a concern for several respondents (16 percent) in relation to sexual fantasy. Some women felt uncertain whether their fantasies "owned" them rather than vice versa and whether the fantasies had "power over" them. Respondents spoke of feeling "helpless" to "control" their fantasies, to "change" their fantasies, or to "not respond to" their fantasies. For example:

It makes me angry that my mind isn't free of degrading and humiliating fantasies. They're an intrusion and I feel helpless against them. I feel attacked by my own fantasies and yet the only way to orgasm is to give in.

Several respondents (14 percent) reported a need to "shut out" their fantasies because they felt "out of control." Other respondents continued to engage in their fantasies despite such feelings. For example: "I feel out of control if I'm in the aggressor role, but I like the feeling of power." A few respondents (7 percent) reported magical thinking in association with thought and action. For example: "If I don't control my fantasies, that's what I'll go out and do."

Sexual Desire

An absence of sexual desire was reported at the time of the questionnaire by 14 percent of the respondents. Such women described having no sexual desire for a period of time from "several years" to "most of my life." An additional 16 percent of the respondents spontaneously reported an absence of sexual desire for a period of time in the past. Respondents with no sexual desire reported feeling "abnormal," "not human," "like an imposter as a woman," and "guilty" in relation to their partners. Several respondents (12 percent) reported that a sense of "relief" accompanied sexual desire. One respondent explained, "I fear slipping back into being shut down sexually even though I'm currently active." Another respondent reported, "I fear that I may never feel sexual again. I think, don't get too busy or too sick for sex, or you might never regain interest."

Interference with the sexual desire phase of sexual functioning was reported by 53 percent of the respondents. Such interference took many forms.

Guilt and/or shame in association with sexual desire were reported by a majority of the respondents (53 percent). For some respondents (21 percent) shame interfered with initiating sexual activity since to do so involved the acknowledgment of sexual desire. One respondent stated, "When I feel sexual desire, I feel ashamed, I feel that I'm dirty and bad." Another respondent commented, "I control my sexual desire because I don't like the feeling of guilt that comes with it."

In some instances (9 percent), the presence of sexual feeling was perceived as evidence that the incest was the respondent's fault. One respondent wrote, "Feeling sexual is equivalent to being responsible for the incest." Another respondent reported, "If I weren't a sexual person, i.e., 'bad,' he never would have done what he did. If I'm sexual, it's my fault." Such conclusions in some instances resulted in feelings of sexual desire being accompanied by "self-loathing" or "self-hatred."

Some respondents (23 percent) reported perceiving sex as "dirty" or "disgusting" due to the "secrecy" that surrounded the incest, the "sneaky" behavior of the offender, the "animalistic" behavior of the offender, or the "body odors" of the offender. Such women felt unable at times to act on their sexual desire without viewing themselves as "dirty" or "disgusting" by association. One respondent explained, "If I feel sexual then I'm just as bad as them [the offenders]."

Some respondents (23 percent) reported that they denied or attempted to deny their sexual desire using the same coping mechanisms used during childhood. For example: "I turn away from my sexual feelings and split them off like I did as a child to protect myself from shame." And, "I go sexually 'dead,' into 'nothingness' so I have no sexuality to feel bad about. It's what my body and emotions were like during the time of the abuse."

Confusion was felt by a number of respondents (37 percent) to inhibit both sexual desire and the expression of sexual desire. For a few women (7 percent), confusion between desire for affection and desire for sex led to total inaction. In such instances women felt unable to deal with their concerns about expressing affection and "having things turn sexual." One respondent asked, "Can I have love, nurturance, and closeness without having to pay for it with sex?" Another respondent wondered, "Can I have physical touch without sex being assumed?"

A few respondents (7 percent) reported confusion over what was fear and what was desire. In these instances, sexual excitement seemed indistinguishable to the respondents from fear. Related to this confusion was sometimes a secondary confusion for respondents over whether they were attracted or repulsed. In some instances the attraction was to someone who resembled the offender in appearance or behavior, and this created confusion.

Of the many respondents who reported "confusion" over their choice of "inappropriate" partners, some (7 percent) were immediately aware of this whenever sexual desire was felt. One respondent commented, "I always wonder, will my sexual desire just lead me into another nonnurturing relationship?" Another respondent stated:

> I continually choose inappropriate love objects — men who aren't interested in me, men who aren't available, men who are gay — I don't trust my sexual desire so I don't like to feel it. It confuses me that it always leads to a dead end. It's as if my sexual desire has been "corrupted" by my "obsession" with safety.

For a number of respondents (16 percent), confusion was related to the mixture of feelings experienced with sexual desire. One respondent reported, "I feel torn in two directions, wanting to satisfy strong sexual needs and yet being unable to due to fear. I end up with feelings of being trapped and desperate. I feel tormented and just want to be sexless." Another respondent reported, "Sexual desire is something you have to fight with to control, something I'd rather not have because it feels too strong and powerful. Yet it also feels good, it makes you feel normal, and that's confusing."

Power and control issues were frequently referred to (44 percent) in the respondents' comments about sexual desire. Women sometimes felt uncertainty with regard to their wants and limits in sexual interaction and therefore inhibited desire or the expression of desire. A number of respondents (28 percent) reported that they were "unable to say no" to partners' wishes or tended to "relinquish all power" to the partner. Some such women reported that sexual desire was accompanied by a "sense of helplessness," of being "at the mercy of my desires," of having "lost control of things," a "powerlessness" that they "would rather avoid" since they didn't think they would "be able to protect" themselves.

Concerns about losing all power and control in a sexual relationship were reflected in respondent questions such as:

What is consent and what is coercion?

What is consensual and what is exploitive?

Can I be coerced to be sexual?

If I desire someone, what can they do to me and what can't they do?

If I don't surrender all control and do anything they want, am I enough as is?

If I don't please a partner, what can happen to me?

If I have sex with someone, do I "belong" to them?

Is my body my own or does possession mean ownership?

Can I lose my boundaries?

Can I lose my identity?

Can I be taken over, made soul-less, a puppet without a will of my own?

Such concerns for some respondents (12 percent) were so strong that sexual desire was immediately lost unless they were in the "aggressor" role. A few respondents (7 percent) reported being "unable to maintain desire" if a partner they were interested in approached them. As one respondent explained, "Desire depends upon having total control in the sexual encounter. If you can't make the moves yourself, all is lost."

Some respondents (16 percent) feared their own power and control in sexual interactions. For some respondents (7 percent), taking the initiative in expressing sexual desire was felt as "an identification with the offender." Uncertainty over whether a partner "would feel able to say no if not interested" or "would be overpowered" was reported.

Concerns over the nature of the respondents' own sexual power were reflected in respondent questions such as:

Can I take others over?

Do I sexually use people?

Can I make people sexual slaves?

Do I take advantage of others sexually?

Do I use sex to exploit people?

Do I hurt and reject people through sex?

If I have the power will I "bully" others?

Such concerns influenced desire or the expression of desire in a number of instances.

Sexual Arousal

An absence of sexual arousal was reported at the time of the questionnaire by 26 percent of the respondents. Such women described experiencing little or no erotic pleasure during sexual activity. An additional 9 percent of the respondents spontaneously reported an absence of sexual arousal for a period of time in the past.

Interference with the sexual arousal phase of sexual functioning was reported by 84 percent of the respondents. Arousal interference included flashbacks reported by 63 percent of the respondents, vaginal pain specific to penetration/intercourse reported by 23 percent of the respondents, vaginal pain not specific to penetration/intercourse reported by an additional 16 percent of the respondents, vaginal closure specific to penetration/intercourse reported by 28 percent of the respondents, inadequate lubrication reported by 9 percent of the respondents, and a number of other forms of interference.

Guilt and/or shame in association with sexual arousal were reported by a majority of the respondents (56 percent). Some respondents (19 percent) reported that if they felt sexual pleasure they immediately felt "bad." One respondent explained, "Arousal is even more shameful than desire because you're acting on the desire instead of ignoring it." In a few instances (9 percent), respondents reported that they didn't feel entitled to sexual pleasure. For example: "I don't feel I deserve sexual pleasure because I'm such a bad person. I need to be denied to be punished."

A number of respondents (28 percent) consciously inhibited their arousal. One respondent explained, "If I get really aroused, I feel evil so I have to control it." Another respondent stated, "I shut off the sexual arousal so I won't have to feel guilty." A third respondent reported, "If you can be aroused you must be sexual, therefore to blame—you must have really wanted the abuse." Some respondents (12 percent) reported allowing themselves sexual pleasure and "paying for it later" with guilt and shame.

A third of the respondents reported that they experienced arousal, but found that shame inhibited their expression of arousal. These respondents reported a number of concerns in relation to partners' reactions to them. One respondent stated, "If I start enjoying things too much, I feel like I'm exposing myself and I can feel shame." Several respondents reported feeling that their arousal would "put people off" or "disgust and scare" others. For example: "I sometimes think my sexual feelings in arousal are perverted and will turn off my partner."

Many respondents (37 percent) spoke of an association between a fear of judgment and the incest. One respondent commented, "I expect to be judged by a partner as I judged myself during the incest." Another respondent stated, "If I'm being very sexual I'm afraid my partner will be thinking, 'So this is how she acted with her father.'" A third respondent explained, "Just as I considered my father's arousal disgusting and dirty, I assume my own arousal will seem that way to others."

Sometimes shame prevented the respondents from engaging in specific sexual activities. Several women (12 percent) reported that they were unable to be actively involved in stimulating a partner because if they were "into it" they would feel "bad" about themselves. As one respondent commented, "I want to sexually excite my partner, but I don't know how to be comfortable with that." A few respondents (7 percent) reported being "too embarrassed" to stimulate themselves in any way in front of a partner as well.

Sometimes the fear of opening up in front of a partner was due to fears of being "violated" which were frequently experienced (37 percent). One respondent explained, "If I become too aroused, if my partner sees that, I won't be able to protect myself." Another respondent stated, "If I don't monitor the arousal, I'll be vulnerable to attack." A third respondent reported, "If I let go with a partner, I'll lose myself, I'll be left unprotected."

Respondents (14 percent) also reported feeling that they could be "humiliated" by arousal. For example: "I'm afraid of being laughed at for revealing my sexual self to a partner, for a partner being able to arouse me." One respondent wrote of an aspect of her incest experience shared by a few respondents, "My father would stimulate me until I came and then he would laugh at me in scorn." In addition to being "violated" or "humiliated," respondents feared being "used" or "exploited" if their state of arousal became evident. Control was thus an important issue to many respondents (49 percent) in relation to arousal. As one respondent commented, "Being in control is the only way I can manage the anxiety."

For a number of respondents (35 percent), "numbing out," "disconnecting," or "disassociating" provided a sense of control that was comforting. One respondent reported, "When I'm aroused and feeling out of control, I go numb and then I feel back in control." Another respondent wrote, "Even though I can't control my body, at least I can control the feelings."

Some respondents (14 percent) found it confusing, however, to feel physical pleasure in the absence of emotional pleasure. One respondent stated, "I think to myself, if I get aroused I must be a sexual person, but I don't feel like a sexual person. There's no emotional enjoyment in it." Another respondent reported, "Following my childhood pattern I find myself responding sexually while withdrawing emotionally and feeling confused."

Confusion also sometimes accompanied situational "panic." Several respondents (14 percent) described an "eerie" feeling of déjà vu accompanied by "intense" fear in association with specific sexual situations. In the absence of incest memories relevant to the same sexual activity, such women reported a sense of puzzlement about their "panic." Similar puzzlement and confusion were reported by two respondents in relation to vaginal, clitoral, and/or anal pain experienced during sexual activity. Flashback images sometimes resolved such confusion later on.

Many respondents (58 percent) experienced confusion between their partner and the offender when reliving the incest during flashbacks. It was not uncommon for women to scream in rage at partners during flashbacks. Some women "attacked" their partners at such moments and remained concerned thereafter that they would "overpower" or "abuse" them again.

Power was an important issue for many respondents (47 percent) in relation to arousal. One respondent stated, "Arousal is contingent upon a sense of equality in the relationship." Several respondents reported that when a partner was "aggressive" or "took the initiative," it felt as if the partner was "taking away" their "power." This "loss of power" was associated with difficulty maintaining arousal.

A number of respondents (44 percent) reported that arousal was "impossible" when it was felt that a partner couldn't be refused or had to be pleased. One woman stated, "To be sexually aroused, I have to feel that what I'm doing is a complete choice." Conditions that felt "coercive" were associated with the incest experience and were likely to result in "fears about being forced" and "fears about being used." One respondent reported, "When it feels like a demand or like I'm being 'instructed,' I'm unable to be receptive or flexible. I associate to the offender and automatically shut down."

Situations that felt "coercive" were also frequently reported to result in anger (35 percent). One respondent wrote, "If it seems like I have no power, like I have no choice, I get angry. I become unresponsive and sexually passive. The more it seems like I have to satisfy the other person, the less I bother trying to please." Another respondent reported, "I don't like complying with sexual demands—I don't do much to satisfy if I feel it's expected—I just won't go out of my way."

Orgasm

Primary orgasmic dysfunction, the inability to orgasm under any circumstances, was reported at the time of the questionnaire by 5 percent of the respondents. Inability to orgasm other than by masturbation was reported by 7 percent of the respondents. Inability to orgasm during vaginal penetration/intercourse while receiving additional clitoral stimulation was reported by 12 percent of the respondents.

Several respondents (12 percent) reported experiencing orgasm in the absence of felt desire, arousal, and/or pleasure. Two women (5 percent) reported that they were orgasmic but did not find orgasm gratifying.

Interference with the orgasmic phase of sexual functioning was reported by 26 percent of the respondents. Orgasmic interference included vaginal or pelvic pain during orgasm reported by three respondents (7 percent) and a number of other forms of interference.

A few respondents (7 percent) reported that shame prevented them from stimulating themselves in front of a partner even if masturbation or additional clitoral stimulation was the only way to achieve orgasm. A few respondents (9 percent) similarly reported difficulty due to "embarrassment" or "awkwardness" with acting in a manner that would hasten or enhance their orgasm. Fear of judgment for "being a sexual person" was generally related to such inhibition.

Most respondents (79 percent) reported that orgasmic capacity was related to the development of trust with a partner. Respondents often stated that it was only over time that they had learned to overcome the fear associated with being "so exposed" or "so vulnerable" during orgasm. For example: "It took me a long time to realize that 'surrender' wasn't synonymous with violation."

Closely related to the issue of trust was the issue of control. Orgasm was often associated with "being out of control" or "letting a partner take control of things." Several respondents (14 percent) reported difficulty "giving over control to a partner." As one respondent reported, "I sometimes think, 'Do I want an orgasm or not? Can it happen outside my control?'" For some women, such concerns were related to the fact that arousal and/or orgasm had occurred during the incest and were unwelcome. One respondent commented, "I learned that my body could respond to someone even when I tried to be in control. Letting go and allowing someone to bring me to orgasm now is incredibly difficult."

"The Split"

In association with sexual functioning, "the split," the nonintegration of emotional intimacy and sexual intimacy, was reported by over a quarter of the respondents.

"The split" was reported in relation to sexual desire by 16 percent of the respondents. In these instances, sexual desire decreased as the sexual partner became more familiar and/or more intimate. With the development of emotional attachment, respondents found their desire "waning" or "dwindling away." Some respondents (7 percent) reported that in more emotionally intimate relationships, desire was lost because sex became associated with duty as in the incest. Other respondents (9 percent) reported that sexual desire was lost because sex "brought up more feelings" or "created more conflicts" in the context of an emotionally intimate or committed relationship that "felt like family."

A few respondents (7 percent) reported that loss of desire was related to the issue of dependency and its association with exploitation as in the incest. One respondent explained, "I knew the offender well when he turned on me. A sexual partner can do the same and in a domestic arrangement there you are dependent again, trapped again." Another respondent reported, "Whenever the topic of commitment comes up in a relationship, fear strikes and my desire goes down the tubes." A third respondent wrote:

> If there's one sure way to kill my sexual desire, it's to bring up the subject of living together. If I can't convince myself that I'm unattached and don't need the other person (i.e., convince myself that I'm safe), I can't feel sexual toward the person.

"The split" was reported by 9 percent of the respondents in relation to sexual arousal. In these instances, greater difficulty becoming and remaining aroused during sexual activity was experienced with familiar and/or intimate partners.

For two respondents, fear of judgment and resultant inhibition were involved. One respondent explained:

> If I don't care what the person thinks or feels about me, I'm totally uninhibited. But give me a partner I care about emotionally and want to

have care about me the same way, and I'm suddenly unable to relax and enjoy myself. I keep worrying that I might be too sexual, like maybe they'll know I've "been at it" since I was four or five, maybe I'll seem too "experienced."

Another respondent reported:

When a partner becomes "family," so to speak, it starts to feel strange. How can I possibly show how sexually excited I am without being disgusting to them? It's easier with a partner whose opinion I don't care about, whose approval I'm not looking for.

In two instances, flashbacks or fears that were only active in the context of a meaningful relationship were related. One respondent reported:

In more casual relationships I did OK, but once I got emotionally involved the associations to the incest got much stronger. I started having flashbacks during sex and I'd totally shut down. It still happens although it's not like when the incest first came up.

Another respondent wrote:

I never had flashbacks or panic attacks until recently when one particular partner became more meaningful to me. Suddenly the incest stuff was all over the place. Between the flashbacks and the crazy thoughts— that he was using me, that he was going to hurt me, that he was going to betray me—I couldn't function. It was enough to convince me that casual sex had its advantages.

In one instance (2 percent), "the split" was reported in association with orgasm. In this instance, the respondent was orgasmic only with a new partner.

Sexual Satisfaction

Approximately 60 percent of the respondents who were sexually active reported being "more satisfied than dissatisfied" during sex, with 25 percent of the respondents reporting total satisfaction at times. Satisfaction was related to experiencing a sense of "power," of "being alive," of "being normal" with sexual desire, arousal, and orgasm.

Approximately 40 percent of the respondents who were sexually active reported being "more dissatisfied than satisfied" during sex, with 13 percent of the respondents reporting total dissatisfaction at times.

Respondents were equally split on reports of dissatisfaction and satisfaction following sex. The primary factor contributing to dissatisfaction after sex was "a sense of having been used," which was very commonly experienced. Feelings of guilt, shame, fear, and sadness after sex also contributed to dissatisfaction.

Discussion

The findings presented here related to sexual functioning supported the findings of previous studies (Courtois, 1980; Herman, 1981; Meiselman, 1978) suggesting that the majority of women in therapy with incest histories might experience difficulties with sexual functioning. In this instance, the percentage of women reporting problems with sexual functioning was higher than in previous studies. This was very likely due to the fact that the study was specific to sexuality and necessitated reflection on a variety of questions directly related to sexual functioning. There is also the possibility that women experiencing greater sexual dysfunction self-selected to participate in the study.

The findings related to the "absence of" or "interference with" sexual desire, arousal, and orgasm were difficult to compare with the "dysfunctions" of desire, arousal, and orgasm referred to in previous studies (Becker et al., 1984; Becker et al., 1982). However, for the most part the patterns appeared similar. Difficulties with arousal appeared to be most common, followed by difficulties with desire and with orgasm. Also in concurrence with Becker et al. (1984) and Becker et al. (1982), the study suggested that several aspects of sexual functioning were likely to be affected, rather than one discrete area.

An unexpected finding of this study was the seemingly high incidence of complaints of vaginismus and dyspareunia. Previous studies (Becker et al., 1984; Becker at al., 1982) had suggested that such complaints were quite rare, although chronic nonsituational pelvic pain had been associated with a history of incest (Caldirola, Gemperle, Guzinski, Gross & Doerr, 1983). While the definitions of vaginismus and dyspareunia might have differed somewhat between studies, this would not appear to fully account for the discrepancy. It may be that the qualitative nature of the instruments used in this study contributed to a higher response rate.

Several phenomena that had been mentioned in the literature that appeared to be highly specific to women with incest histories were noted in this study. As in previous reports (Meiselman, 1978; Tsai & Wagner, 1978;

Westerlund, 1983), a pattern of arousal contingent upon control was a finding. Orgasm in the absence of desire and/or arousal, and orgasm contingent upon the unfamiliarity of a partner were also noted, as in previous reports (McGuire & Wagner, 1978; Tsai & Wagner, 1978; Westerlund, 1983).

Additional findings from the study relevant to interference with sexual functioning and sexual satisfaction went beyond the existing literature at the time. Disturbingly, more than a quarter of the respondents reported an inability to integrate emotional intimacy and sexual intimacy. The effects of "the split" on sexual functioning (as well as on sexual "lifestyle" as reported in Chapter 5) had not been examined in the past. Neither had the power and complexity of the incest feelings as they pertained to sexual functioning. The findings clearly demonstrated how fear, shame, guilt, anger and confusion related to the incest could compromise sexual fantasy, desire, arousal, orgasm, and satisfaction.

7

"Lucky" Women

ALL TEN WOMEN INTERVIEWED responded to the incest experience in very unique ways. Three women, whose chosen pseudonyms are Esther, Nancy, and Meg, will be presented in this chapter. Their narratives reveal the highly individualized nature of the personal connections made between the incest and their adult sexuality; yet some common themes will be seen. (For a summary of the themes from the interviews, the reader is referred to Table 9 in Appendix E.)

Esther

Esther is a 35-year-old woman who is occupationally involved in the media and the arts. She is a lesbian and has been involved for several years in a significant relationship which does not include children.

Esther is from a first-generation, working-class family of Eastern European Jews and is the second of two children. From the age of 7 to the age of 14, she was sexually abused by her older brother.

Esther perceives her sexuality as something she generally feels "pretty good about." She feels "amazingly lucky" not to have had her sexuality more negatively affected by the incest. Esther believes that the incest influence was minimized by her emphasis on her brother's activities as abusive rather than sexual.

I never connected the incest to sex. I made a split in my head about it thinking, "This isn't sex!" The incest seemed to be just an extension of the physical violence in my home, another manifestation of violence in a different form. It wasn't a subtle seduction or anything and in some ways I feel like that's what saved me from having my sexuality affected even more.

Having learned to appreciate and enjoy her body through physical labor, exercise, and dance, Esther derives a great deal of pleasure and comfort from her body. Movement provides a sense of freedom and control over her body that contradicts the feelings of being trapped and overpowered that she experienced during the incest.

I see movement and exercise as healthy, not just in the normal sense of healthy, but healthy in connection to the sexual abuse, that my body is doing what I want it to be doing and I have control over it. That makes me feel good in a very subtle kind of way.

When Esther is unable to exercise or to be physically active regularly she begins to feel "an energy block." She misses the physical and emotional "release" of exercise and becomes less positive in her perception of how her body looks and feels. "If I'm exercising I feel fine about my body, and when I begin to stop exercising for a while, that's when I feel shitty about my body. There's always that connection there."

Esther "can find a lot of fault" with her body appearance and particularly "hates" her thighs. This, she has come to understand, is related to having repeatedly had her brother's semen "all over them" and having generalized the associated negative feelings to her thighs. She explained, "That part of my body felt dirty and damaged. It's the incest connection, not the thighs themselves, that I hate."

Self-hatred associated with the body is sometimes experienced by Esther with illness. This seems very incest-related to her, the link being "I'm not like everybody else, I'm different from others." Additionally, Esther experiences a sense of having "lost control over" her body when it is not functioning well. This is accompanied by a strong sense of fear.

As an adolescent Esther had many fears about her bodily functioning, particularly her reproductive capacity. When menstruation was somewhat delayed Esther assumed she had been "ruined inside" by her brother's rape and was "permanently damaged."

As an adult Esther became pregnant twice, terminating both pregnancies. She was "intimidated and bullied" into the decision to abort the second pregnancy and in that process relived many feelings associated with the incest. Following the termination of that pregnancy Esther "shut down sexually" for a period of one year. This was in response to feelings of "violation and betrayal" reminiscent of the incest.

Esther remains ambivalent about having children, primarily due to fears of being an inadequate or abusive parent. These fears are related both to her own abuse history and to the absence of adequate role models during her childhood. If Esther does have a child, she would like to share parenting with several lesbian women, including her partner.

Esther's identity as a lesbian is a source of comfort, satisfaction, and pride. She has sometimes wondered whether she remained heterosexual for so long partly in response to the incest. Her "need to feel strong and in control before coming out as a lesbian," she explained, was related to "a fear of attack" associated with the Jewish holocaust (both parents are holocaust survivors) which, she suspects, was heightened by her incest history.

As with sexual preference, Esther has experienced changes in sexual "lifestyle" over time. Celibacy was adopted as a "lifestyle" by Esther in her late twenties for approximately two years. Inhibition has sometimes been predominant in Esther's sexual "lifestyle," most noticeably during the one-year period of lost sexual desire mentioned previously. Aversion and/or compulsion have not been predominant during any period.

At present, inhibition is predominant in Esther's sexual "lifestyle," in that she is in a relationship that has become sexually inactive. While Esther's sexual functioning is generally healthy in terms of adequate desire, arousal, and orgasmic capacity, she is often unable to act on her sexual desire. Her difficulty initiating sex with a partner is in large measure related to the incest. Having been coerced herself, she is extremely cautious about being "aggressive" and "pressuring or forcing anyone into sex." She explained:

I'm overly careful because the last thing I want to do is to be oppressive to others sexually. I think it's just an overidentification of my own, but that's definitely a place where the incest plays itself out—in power issues.

Esther also experiences some inhibition in fantasy and in masturbation due to shame associated with the incest.

That's definitely another place where the shame and the incest are— because it's so tied up. It was everything that he represented, and I think that's where I've jumbled up him entering my body versus me entering my own body.

In sexual activity with a partner Esther generally does not experience interference with sexual functioning. When she does, however, it is felt by her to be related to the incest.

Both arousal and orgasm are very connected to trust for me. When I'm not feeling trust, I can't have an orgasm. I generally can't even enjoy having sex if I'm not feeling safe. I find myself closing off and withdrawing, becoming less present like I did during the incest.

As Esther spoke about her sexuality, she became more aware of the ways in which the incest continues to affect her in the present. She found the interview "painful at times" as a result, but also found it "exciting to discover areas to work on in the future."

Nancy

Nancy is a 42-year-old woman who is occupationally involved in counseling and education. She is heterosexual and has been married since her early twenties. She and her partner have three children.

Nancy is from a Protestant middle-class family of English and Swedish descent and is the middle child of three. From the ages of 11 to 12 she was sexually abused by her older brother. She was also sexually abused once during that time period by her grandmother.

Nancy perceives her sexuality as something she's "not happy with too much right now" and sees the incest as related to her dissatisfaction.

For a short time after I became aware of the incest I felt freer, but that didn't last very long. I think I thought at first when I became aware of the incest, "Well, now I'm aware of it and I've talked about it so that's all over now." I didn't realize that it would be something that would be with me forever, be a part of me.

One of the ways in which Nancy has been able to make the incest less a "part of" her is by changing her body perception.

I was not considered a healthy child when I was young. I never was into athletics at all and I thought I wasn't athletic. I decided I wanted to have now what I didn't have then and I became a really strong swimmer even though I didn't learn to swim until I was an adult. I really take pleasure in my body when I'm swimming, and being physically fit gives me a real sense of pride.

Nancy's choice to take up swimming as her primary athletic activity was significant.

> *The incest took place in the water, in a pond, and I think my fears about the incest got attached to the water. I was always afraid of the water, always wondering, "Are there things down there that are going to get me?" Learning to swim was like I conquered it, even though I still have fear at times. I've done something about it.*

Other fears Nancy has experienced about her body have also been difficult to overcome.

> *It took me about six months to get pregnant the first time and I was convinced that I was not going to be able to have children. I was ready to apply for adoption right then and there. I just had this feeling that we wouldn't be able to have children and it would be my fault. That it would be because my internal organs weren't normal, because things somehow weren't right in there.*

Nancy was "glad in one sense" later on to have had caesarian births because "someone actually had looked inside and seen that everything really was all right and that I wasn't different in some way." She nonetheless continues periodically to experience concerns that "there is something wrong" with her.

Nancy also sometimes wonders if she is "less normal" than other women because she is "not sure what it means to be a sexual person."

> *I often feel like I'm really not a sexual person, that I'm sort of asexual. I've been consciously aware for quite a few years that I don't entice men, that I don't give men the come-on. I'm just a human being. I'm not a woman. I think of me more as a human being rather than as a woman.*

While Nancy is sometimes "confused" by her lack of a strong sexual identity, she does not experience doubts about her sexual preference. She has been exclusively heterosexual since adolescence and has always experienced satisfaction with her preference.

As with sexual preference, Nancy's sexual "lifestyle" has remained consistent over time. Nancy has never adopted celibacy as a sexual "lifestyle" and has "never considered celibacy a choice" in the context of marriage. While she has always found it "scary to think" that she is "really a sexual person," her "lifestyle" has never been characterized by aversion. Rather, inhibition has predominated.

> *I was never one who was out to be sexual with men and I've always thought of myself as not as sexual as other people. I guess I'd rather not think about that I'm a sexual person because I might just let loose and really feel I was a wild and crazy woman. The problem is I think I'd get out of control sexually, like my image of a prostitute. That would be out of control. It would be giving in all the way if I really allowed myself to feel sexual completely. It's as if I have almost like evil sexual powers that could take over.*

Nancy's feeling that she has "evil sexual powers" she traces more to the incestuous abuse by her grandmother than to that by her brother.

> *When I think of evil sexual powers I picture myself dressed up like a witch, all in black. And I think of my grandmother, and just the look on her face when she abused me, this bizarre look of ecstacy that was so scary and so confusing. So I have a fear that maybe I might be like that and I don't want to be like that.*

In keeping with her past pattern, Nancy's present sexual "lifestyle" is predominated by inhibition. The inhibition seems, however, more exaggerated to Nancy than in the past.

> *I remember having the flu, and first I had it and then my husband did. And we didn't have sex for about three weeks or something. And he started complaining, but I sort of felt like it didn't make much difference to me one way or the other. I really wouldn't care if I never had sex again sometimes. I guess that's really how I'm feeling at this point, which is kind of new. I'm not certain how much that's related to the incest and how much that's related to the relationship. But he complained to me that now I've brought this [the incest] all up with him again [by participating in the interview].*

When Nancy's partner is unsupportive of her efforts "to learn and to grow" or is disinterested in communication, she begins to feel "he is out for what he can get" in the relationship and she is likely to feel that she's "just a body or an object to be used." This feeling is intensified in sexual situations in which Nancy feels that "he's doing what he wants to do and there's no mutuality in it." "It feels like letting other people do things to me and I don't want anyone to do anything to me. I want to feel I'm part of it."

When Nancy's partner is feeling emotionally "needy" and possessive of her, "wanting" her "to be there continually," she begins to feel "trapped" and "invaded." These feelings occur in the sexual realm as well.

> I feel like there's this body up against me, and I can't get away. If I try to say no, he'll feel rejected. He's just around me and I don't have the freedom to move. And the fear of being invaded by foreign bodies, I think of the penis as a foreign body and I think of it as a weapon. With the incest I felt very closed in, very trapped.

One of the ways in which Nancy tends to respond to feelings of entrapment and intrusion is by "holding" herself "back" sexually.

> I don't give myself over completely. I have to save a piece of myself just for myself. I don't want him to be in control of me being aroused. I want to feel in charge of that myself. It feels like one area I can determine. I'll let him do what he wants to with me and I'll go along and I'll try to make him feel good, I'll be cooperative from an objective standpoint. But I can make the decision that I'm really not going to be totally involved.

When Nancy doesn't want "to be totally involved" she relies on the coping mechanism she utilized at the time of the incest.

> If I've decided I'm not in the mood, I'm just numb and nothing happens. I got really used to numbing out and I didn't have to think about what I was doing. And I think maybe I need to have a certain numbing out so that it keeps me in control because if I let myself feel completely then it would be like giving in to another person.

When Nancy is "in the mood," that is, when she is feeling that her husband "really loves" her, she then wants to be aroused and wants to have an orgasm although she still wants to be "in charge."

> I've always been able to have an orgasm when I want one. It's never been a problem. If I want one, I have one. But if I don't want one, I don't have one. And it sort of fascinates me that I seem to have control over that. He can do almost anything to me and if I've decided I'm not going to have an orgasm, I don't. But I don't think he wants me to have an orgasm because he wants me to feel good. He wants me to have one so

he'll feel that he's been a good masculine sexual partner. So it's really for him. I don't want him to make me feel good. I really want to be in charge of that myself.

Nancy's feeling that sex and even her orgasm are serving to caretake her partner and that her pleasure is irrelevant is reminiscent of the incest. "What my brother told me was, 'You need to do this to make me feel good.'" Nancy has "never felt that" she "really enjoyed orgasm" the way she thought she "was supposed to" or the way "other people maybe do."

It's a physical tension release, certainly. But I often haven't felt loved, and so I guess I would want to feel loved during sex to make that feel gratifying. It's physically gratifying, but not really emotionally gratifying. I've wondered, "Is this what it's like for other people?"

Nancy is aware that she has "always felt undeserving of sexual pleasure" and sees this as "probably connected with the incest and with feeling undeserving in general."

My brother was deserving and I really didn't matter. My mother taught me that women were there to do what men want, to make men feel good. That's what she told me and that's what my brother taught me, too.

Nancy's childhood lessons in the devaluation of women influenced her perception of adult sexual relationships between men and women.

That's a general belief that all society has, and that's just what life is about. That's what it means to be a woman, to do what the man wants you to do when he wants you to give him pleasure, and it doesn't matter if you want pleasure for yourself. You're really undeserving of pleasure. You're not supposed to have any pleasure. Sex is for the man, it's not for you.

Although Nancy finds it "difficult" to deal with the concept of sexual obligation to her husband given the coercion in her past, she still feels like "that's the way it is." "That's the way the world is. And that's just the expectation. I'm a woman and I'm married and that's what you do." As Nancy discussed her sexuality and the ways in which the incest has influenced her sexuality, she became more aware of the connections between the two. "There were things that never came up until today, things that never occurred to me. The interview made me look at some hard questions and made me stop and think about things I've never thought of before."

Meg

Meg is a 27-year-old woman who is occupationally involved in business and industry. She is bisexual and is not significantly involved in a relationship with a partner. She has no children.

Meg was raised in a middle-class Jewish home and is half Jewish, half West Indian. From the age of 10 to the age of 16 she was sexually abused by her father.

Meg perceives her sexuality as "problematic." "I'm afraid my body's not going to work. I'm afraid I'm going to be broken. I'm afraid after all this work I've done that I'm still not fixed for sex."

Meg emphasized that her sexuality was additionally influenced by two date rapes during young adulthood. She sees her incest experiences as having been "more subtle," although she sees "the two—the rape and the incest—as very related." She is convinced that, had it not been for the incest, she would never have been raped.

> I really feel like I was set up for the rapes. There was always this feeling that I had to be obedient. That was something I learned from my father as a child. Not questioning, not speaking up for myself, not knowing I had any rights, not being able to say no, not knowing that I had a choice. Had I learned different things, had I been taught self-esteem, self-respect or anything like that, I wouldn't have been raped at all.

Meg also "learned" from her father to devalue her body and to neglect her appearance.

> His attention scared me to death, it repulsed and disgusted me. I thought at the time that I felt ugly for other reasons. But his touching me and admiring my body made me so uncomfortable. It just had such a negative effect on me that it made me not want to be attractive. I didn't want to be noticed by anybody because there was this unwanted attention from him. I saw, and I still do see, real negative things about being attractive.

Over time and "with a lot of work" Meg has overcome her feelings of ugliness and has learned to appreciate and take pride in her body. Much of this came out of the three-year period of time when Meg was a lesbian separatist.

When I was a lesbian it was a good time for me, taking care of my body. I was a runner, I was physically active. Being removed from men was really good for my psyche, really healing. I was a lot more relaxed feeling like I didn't have to deal with men, I was just feeling a whole lot better as a human being, feeling a lot more comfortable about being a woman.

Meg has also developed her own self-concept of attractiveness over time and no longer needs to rely on the taste and perception of others.

When I came out as a lesbian I started dressing down again because that was the accepted mode of dress in that year. I was looking like every other dyke. When I started sleeping with men again I became more interested in being attractive in a mainstream sort of way. So it took me a long time to grow into feeling comfortable with myself and to feel okay about not making so many compromises about my appearance. Now whoever I'm with has to accept what I look like, how I dress, so I can be me for myself.

One of the aspects of bisexuality that is appealing to Meg is "the attitude that anything goes in terms of appearance, that whatever you want to look like is fine." Meg did not feel that same acceptance or absence of pressure to conform in either the heterosexual world or the lesbian community.

Meg's shifts between heterosexuality, lesbianism, and bisexuality have been difficult, although Meg is now very comfortable with her sexual preference.

When I came out as a lesbian I thought it was the answer to all my problems about sexuality. I was feeling like there was no way I could ever be sexual with a man again. I hated men so much, I was so afraid of them. And I thought that if I was with a woman then I would be safe and would live happily ever after.

Meg discovered that she "was unable to be sexual without problems" with women as well.

It was very frustrating for me. It ended up a whole lot easier to just not have sex. I was so disappointed to find out that being with women was not going to answer all my problems about sexuality, that I was really broken forever. I didn't know what it would take to make me feel like a sexual person again. I didn't think it would ever happen.

Meg remained "very much involved in the lesbian community, politically and socially identifying as a lesbian, but no longer sleeping with women." She was very open with her lesbian friends about having resumed sexual relationships with men and "that wasn't too well accepted." For the next year and a half, however, Meg was again exclusively heterosexual.

Part of my being sexual with men again was a real effort on my part to work on my sexual relations with men and trust, trusting somebody else with my body. There was no way I could continue to be alive and not do that, not deal with it. It was just too depressing.

While Meg succeeded in overcoming some of her problems with sexual functioning with men, she found her interactions with men, for the most part, emotionally unsatisfying.

Some guys don't even know what feelings are, they don't know how to be emotionally close to the other person. They want an ongoing sexual relationship but they don't want to make the emotional, not even commitment, but take a little baby step to open up a little bit. And that's a time when I can feel really used.

Meg no longer has any "expectation" with regard to having "a real relationship" with a man.

I'm not really interested in a long-term relationship with a man. It's not worth putting my energy into. I tried, but after a while I gave up trying to make that happen or trying to find a man who knew how to have feelings, who knew how to be intimate.

Meg has nonetheless remained interested in having sexual relationships with men.

I can be attracted to a man and I can sleep with him. I'm attracted to men and I'm attracted to women both. I would much sooner get involved with a woman because it feels easier to connect on more levels with a woman, easier to be close. If I wanted to just have sex for the sake of sex and fun, I'd sooner do that with a man.

Coming out as bisexual "made it okay" for Meg to be attracted to men as well as women. It also allowed her to work on sexual relationships with both men and women. "I really felt like I needed to get better, I needed to be able to be sexual with other people, whether my partner was a man or a woman."

"Getting better" has involved changes in Meg's sexual "lifestyle" as well as her sexual preference.

I've been single for a long time now. I've spent the past two years being single so I could work through an awful lot of things about what relationships were, what they were about, stuff like that. And also, during that time being casually sexual with people who I trusted so I could work out some of the issues about being sexual, being a sexual person.

What Meg has come to understand in that process is that "casual sex is easier" for her than intimate sex.

There's a split. I've been aware of that, that it feels really a lot easier for me to handle having sex without intimacy. To think of it as a one-time thing can make it very safe and very comfortable. Intimacy is just a really scary thing to think about. Trust is a real issue for me.

Underlying the issue of trust is an apparent association between intimacy and coercion via obligation.

There's something about not having to be responsible for the other person. It's a lot easier just to be with someone sexually when the sex isn't part of an expectation in a relationship. I guess I feel less pressure or no pressure. I feel a lot more able to let go if I don't have to do this ever again.

Meg is now aware that she has not been able to integrate emotional intimacy and sexual intimacy and that this has perhaps played a role in encouraging a nonmonogamous, casual sexual "lifestyle" during recent years.

Throughout the past, Meg's sexual "lifestyle," has alternately been predominated by inhibition and compulsion. Aversion has never been predominant in Meg's sexual "lifestyle," although it has been in evidence at times in the past.

During the time that Meg was "intensively" working on the incest she was sexually inactive. Her period of celibacy lasted approximately six months.

It was a time when I couldn't do a thing sexually. I was really turned off when I was dealing with the incest, thinking about it that way, feeling the emotions. I was completely shut down sexually, definitely disinterested. That's one period of time when I really questioned why I would ever want to be sexual.

In contrast, Meg was very sexually active as a young adult when the incest had more recently ceased and had not been dealt with.

In my late teens I was having sex with people who weren't interested at all in me. Being desired by somebody was important at the time. Having a sexual partner meant that I was attractive to somebody. The first year of college when I was 18 I was promiscuous.

Meg views her "promiscuity" in retrospect as related to the incest, although at the time she did not see the association.

A lot of my earliest sexual experiences with men had everything to do with feeling ugly and wanting to feel wanted. The caring I got from my father was next to nothing except for the unwanted sexual attention. I didn't see the promiscuity as connected with my self-esteem or self-perception. But I'm sure it was. I'm sure I was looking for affection more than sex or for something emotional rather than sexual. It didn't make sense. I slept with total strangers for no good reason.

Meg's current sexual "lifestyle" is characterized by a much higher frequency of sexual activity with herself than with a partner. This she sees as related to trust and control issues.

It's a lot more comfortable for me to be in control. I'm real clear about that. So that's where trust really feels like an issue. In my sexual fantasies I give up control and it's very exciting. But in real life, I won't at all. It's very frightening to give myself over to somebody else. It's incredibly scary. There's this terror that I'm going to be abused again.

Some of Meg's difficulties with sexual functioning, such as her fear of penetration, relate directly to the rapes rather than to the incest. Being able to have intercourse with a man was "a hurdle" for Meg to overcome that was "absolutely 100 percent associated with the rapes." Other aspects of sexual functioning that are problematic are more difficult to attribute solely to the rapes.

I block advances from other people, not just from men. I keep myself from feeling sexual sensations. It's like I'm not open to being touched by somebody else although I'm very open to touching somebody else. Being sexual feels real out of control, sort of like losing consciousness. And I have a really hard time reaching orgasm with a partner. That's absolutely the ultimate loss of control.

As Meg spoke about her sexuality and her incest history, several connections became much more powerful for her. In closing she stated, "I just wasn't aware that his doing what he did to me was really going to affect me as an adult, that that was going to affect my sexuality."

Discussion

What is most striking about these three "lucky" women is the perspective they have on the incest with regard to the issue of responsibility. The absence of self-blame in these narratives is unusual, as will become apparent in the remaining narratives. Esther clearly sees the incest as a series of acts of violence on the part of her brother. Nancy recognizes the contribution of learned patriarchy, sexism, and misogyny within her family. Meg understands that her parents failed in their obligation to teach her that she had rights as a child and was of value as a person. As a result of correctly perceiving the "cause" of the incestuous abuse as outside the self rather than within the self, each of these three women has effectively eliminated guilt as a major source of sexual discomfort.

In addition to the absence of self-blame in these narratives, there is a relative absence of anger, an additional source of sexual difficulty. The theme of anger, which will appear repeatedly in the remaining narratives, is not particularly prominent here. While all three women experience anger over the incest, it is expressed for the most part in an appropriate sense of outrage directed at the offenders and those who failed to protect them. The displacement of anger onto partners or onto themselves, and the "acting out" of anger sexually is thus minimally in evidence here relative to the other narratives.

Also of note in relation to these "lucky" women is the manner in which they approached rather than avoided problems related to sexuality. Esther speaks of the "excitement" of discovering new areas to work on, Nancy speaks of still having fear at times, but of "doing something about it", and Meg speaks of being sexual with men again, saying, "There was no way I could continue to be alive and not do that, not deal with it."

Through approach rather than avoidance all three women learned to take pleasure in their bodies and all three women altered their body perception over time. This implies a process of repeatedly inviting the feelings related to the incest to surface, and repeatedly tolerating the feelings for whatever period of time is possible. While the process would seem most evident in the instance of Nancy, who changed her body perception with an activity that placed her in the precise environment she had been abused in, all three women clearly had strong feelings related to their bodies to confront and overcome. By being willing to give consistent attention to the painful issues involved rather than ignoring them, these women opened themselves to corrective experiences and reclaimed one whole aspect of their sexuality.

A final note that seems important to make in relation to this series of narratives specifically concerns Esther. It is interesting, given that she is the most contented with her sexuality of the ten women interviewed, to observe that she instinctively utilizes some of the cognitive techniques described further on in the treatment chapters. She successfully separates the past from the present in four important instances in the narrative. To paraphrase the "corrective cognitive statements" that appear in Esther's narrative, they are:

Then was abuse; now is sex.

I hated my brother's semen on my legs; I don't hate my thighs.

Me initiating sex is not my brother forcing sex.

Me entering me (masturbation) isn't him entering me.

The significance of these simple "separations" will become apparent as the next series of narratives unfolds.

8

"Uncomfortable" Women

THE TEN WOMEN INTERVIEWED for the study reported a range of variation in the degree to which the incest was felt to have influenced their sexuality. The four women who represent the middle of that range are presented in this chapter. Their chosen pseudonyms are Claudia, Eva, Juliane, and Natalia.

Claudia

Claudia is a 30-year-old woman who is occupationally involved in the media and the arts. She is heterosexual and has been married since early adulthood. She and her partner have two children.

Claudia is from an upper-class Catholic family of French and Italian descent and is the second of four children. From early childhood to the age of 19, she was sexually abused by her father.

Claudia perceives her sexuality as something she has always been "uncomfortable" about and traces her discomfort "all the way back to the incest." From very early on, Claudia suppressed her sexuality.

I went to Catholic girls' school and there were no boys and I really liked it. Then that closed and I went to junior high. When my two best friends got interested in boys I couldn't deal with it. I ended up being really mean to these two girls. I cut them off because I thought "Oh, they're just real promiscuous."

During later adolescence Claudia continued to develop a neuter sexual identity that "felt safe."

It was sort of asexual. I never dated. I never went to dances. And I never really talked to men. When I was in high school, I was in plays with men who I think were probably gay although at the time I didn't realize it. But they weren't asking me out.

Claudia's partner is the only person she has ever dated and, then too, safety was an issue.

I went out with my husband in high school, but it was just walking home from school. I never dated all through college 'til my last year when I dated my husband. And I think what kept me in the relationship was that he wasn't physical at all. I felt safe with him. I knew he wasn't going to attack me.

During adolescence and young adulthood, Claudia never felt like the other girls.

I always felt different and I never felt attractive. I didn't feel pretty enough to be one of those girls with nothing on their mind but boys. And I never would have dressed to attract boys.

Claudia has always dressed to conceal her sexuality and to avoid notice.

I sort of feel ashamed that I have breasts. I always wear white blouses and I realize how stupid I must look at 30 wearing white blouses. All my life I wore one-piece bathing suits when they really weren't in style. And I used to wear men's clothes. Even today I never wear high heels or rarely.

This she sees as directly related to the incest experience. "It really affected me fashion-wise. I'm afraid to dress as if I'm proud of my body." Claudia is also afraid to hold herself as if she is proud of her body.

I have really bad posture and I think I'm covering up my breasts. I'm afraid of standing with my shoulders square. And I kind of put my head down as well. I always hold my head to one side and I never stare at someone directly. That has to do with the incest too 'cause it's a way of being timid.

Claudia's perception of her body is both negative and distorted. She is unable to see her tall, broad-shouldered, muscular body as attractive.

I feel really uncomfortable about my body. I feel like a geek. I feel like my arms are too big and my shoulders are too big. I feel like my body is all contorted, like my spine is all twisted. I don't know if it really is or not, maybe it is from having bad posture.

Some of these negative feelings are related to concerns Claudia has about gender identity.

I have this feeling that I'm not really a woman. I feel like I'm just sort of a transvestite or something. Maybe if I were small-boned and petite I wouldn't have these feelings about not being a woman. I have an obsession about being thin and that's because that can make me feel feminine. To be small, to be feminine. Maybe it's harder being a tall incest survivor.

Claudia's doubts about her gender identity can be traced back to puberty. At that time Claudia experienced difficulty embracing "womanhood" due to the incest.

When I first realized that I was getting breasts I prayed that if I was really good that they wouldn't get any bigger. To be female was to be pretty. Except being female meant you were going to be—you know, somebody's going to rub your breasts. To be female means to be attacked or something—it's such an easy correlation.

Other negative feelings Claudia experiences regarding her body are related to an identification with her father.

Genetically I'm built in some ways like my father. I'm very muscular like my father. And he has bad posture, too, and I feel like I have the same back as he does. When I was 15 or 16 he would take me swimming at night and have me ride on his back and he would do this water play that was real inappropriate. I feel like my back is his back and that's part of the incest, part of me.

Claudia's difficulty making clear distinctions related to body boundaries and sensations has influenced reproduction as well as body perception.

I started nursing with both my children, but I stopped because I couldn't stand that sucking feeling. It felt like my father was sucking on me. It was like he was aware that I was nursing and he could feel the way I felt having him suck by this baby.

Claudia also wanted to return to having small breasts because she felt "self-conscious" around others with large breasts.

Another element of reproduction that has been influenced by Claudia's incest history is birth control.

I hardly ever use my diaphragm. My husband uses condoms because I cannot tolerate the sperm. The first time I saw sperm was during manual sex with my husband when he ejaculated on my stomach. The smell of it made me physically sick and I threw up.

This Claudia traces to the smell of sperm in her father's bed throughout childhood. "It was really strong, the bed just reeked of sperm."

Claudia has considered having her tubes tied rather than continuing to practice birth control but doesn't really feel this is an option. "To have my tubes tied would mean that I wasn't producing an egg and that, again, would be that I wasn't a woman."

In addition to influencing reproductive decisions, Claudia's uncertainty regarding her gender identity has also contributed to confusion over her sexual preference.

That feeling I have of not really being a woman, I've had that for a long time. And my sister is gay and my oldest brother is gay and I thought, "Gee, maybe that means I'm gay because I don't feel like a woman." But then I was having this fine sex life and this good marriage.

Claudia has additionally been confused about her sexual preference in the past because she finds women attractive. More recently she has begun to separate the issues of gender identity and sexual preference. "Many times I still don't feel like I am a woman, but I know I am attracted to men."

Claudia's attraction to men tends to be limited to men who are "safe," generally gay men.

I work with a lot of gay men and I prefer to work with a gay. We hired a new person about two months ago and I know he's not gay. I check the lunch schedule to make sure I don't have to eat with him because I really almost suffocate when I'm with a male who's not gay.

With heterosexual men Claudia feels inadequate, exposed, and anxious almost to the point of "an anxiety attack."

Claudia's fear of men contributes to inhibition. Her adult sexual "lifestyle" has primarily been predominated by inhibition and secondarily been predominated by aversion consistently over time. Compulsion has never been predominant.

As with sexual "lifestyle," Claudia's sexual functioning has been characterized by inhibition and aversion. Most of the "interference" Claudia experiences with sexual functioning is due to her father's "presence" in the room.

It always felt like my father was watching me. From the time I got married and started having sex I've always felt that he was in the room and that he was getting off on the fact that I was having sex.

At times Claudia feels as if her father has taken her partner's place (just as she felt her father had taken her baby's place during nursing).

The other night my husband and I had sex and I couldn't tolerate my husband caressing my clitoris. I felt like it was my father's finger. My father has this really big finger and being a gynecologist, fingers are part of his job.

During Claudia's childhood and adolescence, her father performed anal and breast "exams" on her. "Because he was a gynecologist, he was able to cross over those boundaries instead of having my mother examine me."

Father's "presence" during sexual activity between Claudia and her partner sometimes brings things to a total halt. At other times "the feeling that there may be a third party there" contributes to "self-consciousness" and detracts from arousal and orgasm, although Claudia is able to continue to engage in sexual activity.

Claudia always has an orgasm when she and her partner have sex, which is gratifying, although she is unable to tolerate penetration until after she has had an orgasm. She attributes her orgasmic frequency to the sensitivity of her partner and to being very selective about when to engage in sex.

My husband is very patient. And he gives me a lot of control. When I want to stop, he'll stop. So that's part of it. And I think it's because when

I do have sex, it's when I'm able to. Many times I just won't have sex because I can't.

As Claudia spoke about the ways in which the incest has influenced her sexuality, she became aware of the degree to which shame and fear related to the incest are still operating today. In closing she stated, "The interview was fine. I really thought I would cry, but it was fine. It was really very validating and enlightening."

Eva

Eva is a 36-year-old Hispanic woman who is a doctoral candidate. She is a lesbian and has been in a significant relationship with a partner for a year and a half. She has one adopted child.

Eva is from a Roman Catholic working-class family and was raised in Puerto Rico and in New York City. She is the fifth-born child of seven, with two siblings and four half-siblings. From the age of 2 until the age of 12 she was sexually abused by her father.

Eva perceives her sexuality as "an issue" she will "probably be working on for a long time."

It's not a "here today, gone tomorrow" kind of thing. The incest is there and I can feel the effects. With sexuality, it's like you just don't know what to expect sometimes until it happens. But now when things get stirred up I know what it is. I know what it is so clearly. I know where it comes from.

During adolescence and early adulthood Eva did not understand that much of her discomfort and confusion regarding sexuality was related to her incest history.

The incest stuff never came up. It was totally blocked. But becoming a sexual person was very difficult for me. I just couldn't handle it. It was completely beyond me. I didn't even know what to do with myself. I was totally intimidated by boys and I repressed like crazy.

When Eva went off to college her "weight shot up," something she now sees as "connected to sexuality and the incest."

It was a way of hiding away. It was like if I get as fat as possible and unattractive, maybe they'll leave me alone. It wasn't conscious, but it was there, I think. I dressed like a Jehovah's Witness at the time. And the kids were wearing miniskirts. I looked so severe.

Eva has remained heavy since and, although she now feels "less awkward" in her body, she still experiences a sense of shame sometimes in relation to her body.

Eva is also "very conscious of control as an issue" in relation to her body, particularly as it has pertained to pregnancy in the past.

I definitely did not want to have kids. There was always a concern about not having any control. It's like at least I had control over my body to some extent. Even if I got heavy or whatever, I had some control over my body. And having a baby, definitely it would have more control over my body than I would.

Eva's concern about control also extended to the parenting partner.

The baby having control over my body was one thing. The other thing was pregnancy as something that would make me vulnerable, that would put a person in control over me because of the baby. To be pregnant would be to have something taken away from me. Somehow it would mean being left powerless.

Eva now feels a certain sadness about her past reproductive decisions.

At 12 I knew that I wasn't going to have any kids. I don't think I knew why. This past year part of me has been feeling a kind of loss, realizing that I had made such an intense decision at such a young age and that I had made it probably around the incest stuff, never rethinking it afterward.

The "incest stuff" that influenced Eva's reproductive decisions included a powerful element related to her self-perception.

The other piece of it, it's like that movie Alien. *There's this one scene where this monster sort of bursts forth from this guy's stomach. The imagery was all up there on the screen. Part of me was feeling that because I was a monster I would bring forth a monster. I would bring forth something that was not good. And that came into my deciding not to have any kids. I couldn't do it.*

Eva's "way out" was to adopt as a single parent. At the time of the adoption she was in a relationship with a woman, but the relationship was ending.

I always thought I'd wind up being a single parent. The initial commitment when I adopted him did not include a partner and I think because of my own lifestyle I didn't expect to have a co-parent there for him. So he knows I'm the parent. Ours is the primary relationship, we're the team. And I'm careful about letting somebody else in because I don't know where things are going to be five, six, two years from now. And knowing that, I can't make it any more confusing for him than it is.

Eva herself has been confused by the changes that have occurred in her relationships over time. She has been in long-term relationships with both men and women during her adult years, and while she is now very certain and satisfied with her sexual preference as a lesbian, many questions accompanied her shifts from heterosexuality to bisexuality to lesbianism. Throughout most of Eva's twenties she was exclusively heterosexual. In her late twenties she entered a short-lived "bisexual phase" before she "wound up declaring" herself a lesbian.

At that point if I had tried to handle my sexuality as a bisexual person, I would have gone nuts. And being with men at that point was just bringing up a lot of issues around my father. It was just too intense, too much of a freakout. It was getting safer for me to just deal with women at that point and I felt I needed to declare myself one way or the other. But the questions around my incest—they confused the issue a lot.

While "trying to sort out the question" of sexual preference, Eva's sexual "lifestyle" also underwent changes. At one point Eva "just stopped dealing with sexuality, period." From the age of 24 to the age of 26 Eva adopted celibacy as a "lifestyle."

I didn't do anything with anybody for about two years. I made sure I was in a position where I didn't have to because I did not want to have a sexual encounter of any kind at that time. I just needed to take a break to try to figure things out.

Earlier in Eva's twenties her sexual "lifestyle" had been predominated by compulsion.

After I first had sex at about 20 I went from having no sex to being hypersexual. If I was doing it, I was doing it too much because I think it gave me this sense of control. It was like you come when I say, you leave when I say. I had total control when I acted out my promiscuousness. It was a way to have power over men.

"Promiscuity" also allowed Eva to express her "rage toward men."

There was a lot of contempt. A lot of contempt for men. There was an angry quality to it. It was like, "Fuck you. If this is what you want, take it. You can have it." And when it was finished it was like, "Don't touch me or hug me." If it was my bed, get out. If it was their bed, I was gone. The rage was right there. Looking back I can see that it was part of the acting out of my incest history, although I don't think I thought about it at the time.

"Promiscuity" was additionally related to the negative sexual identity Eva had assumed.

There was a part of me saying, "Well, if I'm bad, let me be bad all the way." The whole Latin thing of the virgin/whore and if you were not the virgin then you had to be the whore. So if I was a whore, I was going to enjoy it.

Casual, nonmonogamous relationships were in some respects easier for Eva to deal with as well.

I couldn't be emotional and sexual at the same time. I could be sexual but then there was no intimacy. And there was no wanting that intimacy with someone I was sexual with because being sexual tends to make you feel more vulnerable anyway. So I would have lovers, I would have sexual partners.

When Eva did allow herself a degree of emotional intimacy, sexual intimacy was difficult.

The one person that I had a relationship with at that time was supposedly a safe person—he was older, he was married, he was no threat. I could be emotional with him. And our sex life was like zip. I really wanted to see somebody else to satisfy my sexual urges. I could not deal with sexual urges with him.

For Eva the "split" between sexual intimacy and emotional intimacy was related to the issue of commitment. Emotional intimacy with a sexual partner, Eva feared, might be construed as commitment, and commitment implied a "loss of control and power" to Eva.

> I spent a lot of time between 21 and 28 walking out of relationships with men because when the time came for me to make a commitment, I wasn't able to do it. The married man I mentioned separated from his wife at one point and it was time to run. I left the country! That whole idea of giving yourself up, of allowing someone to own you, of losing yourself—particularly as we talk about it in my country when we speak of love—was like I just couldn't do it.

Over time the "split" between sexual intimacy and emotional intimacy narrowed for Eva, resulting in sexual "lifestyle" changes.

> In the beginning of the relationship I'm in now, definitely because there was a wish for intimacy, all my issues around the incest came up. My fears about being close. I was terrified. But because we had this friendship and this trust, we were able to give ourselves the six months it took for things to even out and settle down.

Commitment remains problematic for Eva, although over time it has become less so.

> I don't think about running so much now. And we have talked about living together. If I were to move into her house the power/control issue would be too much. I'd be too vulnerable. But we're considering finding a neutral place, a place that would be ours. I just want to give myself time.

If Eva does move in with her partner, she is aware that they will "have to look at" their sexual relationship and "how it is developing."

> Part of this whole thing about moving in together points to the fact that our sex life is going to become more evident than when we were not living together. Because it's one thing popping in on the weekend, and it's another thing when you're there every day.

Already Eva feels it is evident that their sex life could be better. "Things are satisfactory, but they're not great. There's a potential for it to get better." Eva's reluctance to "push on the issue" she sees as connected to the incest.

> *It's hard for me to push on those kinds of things. I don't know how far to push. Since I don't like being pushed myself, I don't like to push others. I'm almost too respectful about giving people room. I just don't want to put out any kind of energy that could be construed as being intrusive. But then you turn around and two months have gone by because you just didn't want to deal with the issues.*

Part of not dealing with the issues and of accepting a sexual "lifestyle" predominated by inhibition Eva views as "self-protective."

> *It's a really safe thing to sort of decide not to be the assertive one because then I don't have to deal with being sexual. Or sometimes it's easier to just masturbate because there's no person on the other side, no discussion about it. It makes it simpler. So I end up trying to figure out how much of it is her and how much of it is just me being protective.*

"Being protective" of herself Eva sees as directly related to the incest.

> *It's hard not to associate sexual desire with a lot of bad things rather than good things. And it's hard to allow the arousal instead of trying to control it, to respond to it instead of detaching. It's hard to really be there, to not disconnect during sex.*

By controlling her desire and arousal, Eva avoids feelings of shame and guilt associated with the incest.

> *It took me a while to think about that there was possible arousal going on with the incest. It brought up too much shame, too much self-blame. Responsibility, intense feelings of responsibility. Like I should at least have been able not to respond. What does it mean that I didn't disconnect enough? I should have been able to sort of split off.*

The interference that this causes with regard to sexual functioning both saddens and angers Eva.

> *It's so hard to have that turned around on you and brought into the present day. To be there with your lover, somebody you care about, somebody you trust, and to have all those feelings. You should be able to*

be sexual. You should be able to be spontaneous. You should be able to just be there.

Eva expects, however, to have the feelings remain. "The feelings are going to be there no matter what, I think, so it's really a question of figuring out how to have them not make an impact in the same way."

In closing, Eva stated that she had found the interview "easier" than she had anticipated. While emotionally "difficult," the interview left Eva with a sense of the healing she has already achieved.

It took a lot for me to acknowledge being an incest victim. I mean, that was — ugh. And it's hard work trying to deal with the impact of it. But I've gotten to a place where I don't get all tight in the chest anymore, where it's not so scary. And it isn't detachment, either. There are moments when your voice cracks and your eyes water or you start crying, period. But it's okay. It's like it's part of the story of who I am. It's that integrated.

Juliane

Juliane is a 37-year-old woman who is occupationally involved in counseling and education. She is a lesbian and has been living with a life partner for many years. She and her partner have no children.

Juliane is from a Protestant working-class family of Polish and Eastern European descent and is the youngest of two children. From infancy to the age of 10 she was sexually abused by her father, and from infancy to the age of 16 she was sexually abused by her mother.

Juliane perceives her sexuality as something that "has been through a lot of different phases and has changed a great deal over time." Some of the changes in Juliane's sexuality have been consciously brought about.

I was so self-conscious and ashamed of my body. I grew up with the notion that you hide your body and I'm sure the incestuous experiences didn't help that any. When I saw how comfortable other people were with their bodies, with being nude in front of other people, that's when I realized I needed to change that around. I consciously would pretend to be comfortable and that was how I got over a lot of those inhibitions. But it was work, a really conscious thing.

Juliane now feels "basically good about" her body, although she still is "more comfortable in lots and lots of clothes."

One of the reasons I prefer winter to summer is you wear sweaters and coats and things like that. I feel safer. I do wear shorts and T-shirts and go to the beach. I do those things, but if you ask me what my preference for dress is, it's to be out on a cold day with my coat on. It's funny.

Part of feeling "basically good" about her body for Juliane is associated with having it be "connected." During much of the past and at times still in the present, Juliane physically cannot feel her body or physically cannot feel that she is in her body.

I think that comes from the incest and also the physical abuse in my family. At times I lose sensation or I can't feel my body and at times it's as if I might just disappear from my body. I think I developed not feeling as a lifestyle. I did that throughout my life. Now when a doctor says to me, "This is going to hurt," I think, "Okay, let me see if I can try to feel it."

Juliane has also had to overcome a perception of herself as "ugly" that was "caused by the incest."

I never had a sense of myself as a cute little kid. I never knew I was cute. I was never aware of that because there was always this feeling of being an ugly person. I guess I thought because I wasn't loved, because I wasn't liked, that I was ugly and that that was why.

Juliane's concept of herself both physically and emotionally has grown much more positive over time. She only recently has been able to think about herself as a potential parent.

I didn't really think I wanted to become a parent for a long time. With my history I'm such a high-risk person for abusing a child. And that scared me. But I think I'll be a much better parent than most people because I've had to think about it all. And I'm sure I'll be constantly checking out with myself and with other people what's appropriate because I didn't grow up in a home where you could learn that.

Juliane plans to become pregnant in the very near future and will be co-parenting with her life partner. She and her partner have been together for over ten years, having met a couple of years after Juliane came out as a lesbian.

Juliane's shift from heterosexuality to lesbianism was relatively struggle-free, and her coming out was a "huge relief" despite the "lack of support" at the time.

Things were about to change, but they hadn't. There wasn't the sense then that you could be healthy and be a lesbian. I spent a lot of time reading all the literature and all of it said you were sick. So there I was with no way to be lesbian and to be OK, too. It was really awful. At the same time, I was reevaluating everything from this new perspective, looking at my whole life, and suddenly everything was making sense.

Juliane's sexual preference as a lesbian has remained a source of satisfaction and comfort. "Being a lesbian is very consistent with who I am. It fits."

Finding a sexual "lifestyle" that "fits" has been somewhat more complicated for Juliane. Aversion has never predominated in Juliane's "lifestyle" and she has "never defined" herself as celibate. Swings, however, between compulsion and inhibition have been evident over time.

When I was younger—18 to 25—I had many, many heterosexual relationships. I was really destructive then and I got so sick of what I was doing. At some point, when I was getting more self-respect, for a long time I couldn't sleep with people. It was like a safety valve. I just couldn't have that many relationships. I couldn't continue to do the more casual kinds of sex I was doing earlier on.

Juliane sees her early lack of "self-respect" as related to the incest.

When all that promiscuity was going on and the alcoholism, that came from the abuse, from being violated. One thing kids need to get from their parents when they're young is the sense that their body is sacred, respected. And I never got that. I couldn't say no because I really didn't have that self-respect. If somebody wanted something, I'd give it to them.

Juliane's "promiscuity" was also related to the incest in other ways.

Another thing is that somehow being promiscuous gave me more control. It's like, "Well, I'm going to get abused anyway, so let me do this a whole lot so I'll have some control over it." I think what I was doing was saying, "If this is my decision, I can't be exploited." And there was this feeling of I'm an awful person and it makes sense that that, too, came from the incest.

Juliane also hadn't learned to distinguish between sex and affection and "didn't have any idea what love was."

I really didn't know how to form relationships. So sex was, well, it was in the right direction. I was so vulnerable and wanted so much to be loved. I needed others because there was so little self there, because I was so incredibly lonely and so far away from myself and any kind of fullness. If I'm real honest, that's probably what those more driven times were about.

At the time Juliane never acknowledged her vulnerability or her emotional needs. "I was probably thinking how really cool I was to be collecting men like Boy Scout badges, having that illusion of power."

In contrast to Juliane's early adult "lifestyle," her sexual "lifestyle" in later adulthood has been predominated by inhibition. During one period Juliane's sexual inactivity was directly related to the incest.

My partner and I do meditation and we went to this event. It was also a woman's retreat, and there was a group there for incest survivors—a one-hour or two-hour discussion. And after that, I started getting so much fear. It was really awful. And the fear didn't get dealt with in a positive way, it got repressed. For a while I just couldn't be physical. It was so painful to be exposed. And even casual contact, touch felt awful.

Juliane's relationship with her partner has been sexually inactive for some time and they now "sleep together maybe a few times a year." Juliane has had "brief affairs" over the past nine years which "have not been a big issue" between her and her partner, who has chosen to remain monogamous. Juliane feels that "the incest stuff" has influenced their sexual relationship in several ways:

Sexually things between us initially were really good. It seems like maybe as the relationship deepened it got more frightening. I feel afraid of being overwhelmed, of crossing some levels of intimacy where you might lose yourself and I think that comes from the incest stuff.

I'm afraid somehow I'll be a baby again and there will be this huge person who has all the control. It's like anything could happen, I could open my eyes and it could be somebody else, I'd be with the monster again.

I'm afraid not to be the one initiating and controlling all the time. That's changed, but I've had to work on that.

There was a time when a lot of anger would come up and the sexual encounter would get really bummed out. I'm sure that anger was from the incest and it just had a false name.

Juliane and her partner have come to accept their pattern of infrequent sexual activity for the most part. "I think probably we unconsciously found each other because we knew we weren't going to threaten each other after a certain point. My guess is that she's an incest survivor as well. She's wondered about it herself."

Juliane meanwhile is sexually active in her fantasy life and in masturbation and is generally open to desire and arousal. She is "baffled," however, by her sadomasochistic fantasies and sometimes feels "very discouraged and confused about it."

My feeling about the fantasies is to let them be there. Fantasies don't hurt anybody. At the same time it feels like an aberration to have these violent, sadistic fantasies. I can live with them, but I'd much prefer to have romantic, sensuous fantasies I'm totally comfortable with.

As a child Juliane was exposed to sexual sadism on the part of her mother. "The sexual abuse by my mother was more frightening. She was more crazy. I had such a bizarre orientation to sex as a baby." Juliane "doesn't completely understand how that may be connected," but she finds that the more she works "on the abuse and the incest," the less frequent the fantasies are.

Juliane's only adult experience with sadomasochism was at the age of 18 and "wasn't at all satisfying."

It really came from being 18 and not having a whole lot of experience and it really didn't last very long. There was this pornography showing sadistic stuff that lesbians supposedly did with one another, but it was written for men. So we were trying to copy it and that just didn't make it.

Juliane "would like to experiment with sadomasochism again," but "the thought of finding someone else to experiment with frightens" her.

I guess it's something that I would like to try, but it doesn't seem very safe. I think you really have to trust the person you're doing it with or it could be too scary to be in that situation with somebody. So I don't know. My guess is that acting it out wouldn't really be as arousing as the fantasies might be.

In her closing comments, Juliane stated that she hadn't found the interview as difficult as she had expected it to be.

I knew it was probably going to be painful because focusing on this stuff hurts. I guess I thought it might be a lot more awkward. It seemed easier to talk than when I was thinking about coming here ahead of time.

Juliane also stated that she felt there were things she would take away with her from the interview to "go over in my mind and see what I come up with."

Natalia

Natalia is a 35-year-old Hispanic woman who is completing her doctoral dissertation. She is a lesbian and has been living with a life partner for several years. She and her partner have no children.

Natalia is from a Roman Catholic working-class family and was raised in Santo Domingo and in New York City. She is the youngest of four children, with three half-siblings. From the age of 6 to the age of 16, Natalia was sexually abused by a maternal uncle who was a father figure. From the age of 7 to the age of 10, she was sexually abused by her mother who was psychotic during much of her childhood and adolescence.

Natalia perceives her sexuality as something that "belongs to the incest," something she has been unable to fully reclaim. She continues to ask herself, "Why has so much in my life contrived to spoil what can be such a beautiful thing?"

Allowing herself to feel the rage associated with the incest has sexually "freed" Natalia to some extent.

I have an awareness of my humanity in sex sometimes now. I realize I'm not so terrible after all. I'm not a monster, I'm not disgusting, I'm just a person, that's all I am. Not a miracle, not an imperfection, just a person.

In conjunction with her growing sense of her "humanity," Natalia has become "more forgiving" with regard to bodily limitations and imperfections. At one time Natalia felt that her body "needed to be pushed to tolerate discomfort, needed to be taught." She "fantasized" that with hard enough work on her body she would "somehow undo everything that had been done to it" and would "somehow become impregnable." While Natalia is no longer "fanatical" about exercise, she continues to be fitness-motivated by an acute awareness of her physical vulnerability to attack.

I've often wondered just how heavy a person I could push off my chest if I had to. Exercise is an anxiety-reducing ritual that provides enormous satisfaction and peace of mind. I feel good about my body, and I enjoy what my body can do.

Natalia's positive body perception includes a respect for her reproductive functioning and capacity. She is planning to become pregnant in the near future and feels physically well-prepared for this event.

Natalia is also very excited (despite self-doubts regarding her parenting capacity due to her history) about having a child in the context of her present relationship. At the age of 16 Natalia was impregnated by her uncle. She miscarried during the first trimester without the pregnancy having been disclosed to anyone. "It was really grim and painful. I was in the girl's bathroom at high school and I was all bloody and it was horrible. It was horrible! And I was all alone. No one knew." Natalia subsequently terminated two pregnancies because she "did not wish to have a child with a man." Ironically, Natalia had consciously decided to be heterosexual in part due to the fact that children were an option only in that context at the time.

Natalia's rejection of lesbianism as a young adult was additionally due to feeling "unable to brave the ostracism." While she felt that "something had been spoiled" by her uncle such that she "couldn't accept men being close" in her life, she also "couldn't tolerate living in hiding with a woman, not being public, not being socially approved of." Having experienced the accumulated stigmas of "illegitimacy," cultural difference, and incest, Natalia was unable as a young adult to embrace lesbianism. When she later accepted lesbianism as her sexual preference, she experienced "an enormous feeling of relief."

A sense of sadness remains, however, over not having been able to "do things the right way."

Having experienced that abuse, that craziness, I still feel a little bit less good, a little bit less normal. It's painful to hear about normal families. It's the time when I feel my cultural differences most too. I wonder if there's ever going to be a time when there isn't some corner of my life that doesn't fit. Is there any leaving it behind, is there any not being who I am? I've certainly worried about my sexual preference enough and it's still hard to believe that I'm okay, that I'm accepted. I've watched heterosexual couples walk down the street with their children and I've thought, "God, what a blessed legitimacy! What a relief to be just right!"

As with sexual preference, Natalia has struggled over time with sexual "lifestyle" choices. As an adolescent Natalia "made a decision to use that which nobody worthy could want," her body, which was "worthless because of the incest." She became a prostitute.

> *It was a matter of taking care of men's needs—just as I had done all along with my uncle. It was caretaking through sex. I felt disdain for the neediness of men and their channeling of their needs into sex—the same disdain I felt for my uncle. So if anyone was stupid enough to want my body and to pay for it, well, they could have it.*

Through prostitution Natalia confirmed her sense of worthlessness and her negative identity.

> *I was going to teach myself that I was in no way important. I would get rid of any lingering notion that I had a right to certain things. I would humble myself. I wasn't a person anyway. I was a thing. I tried very hard to be the bad person that I was treated like. I tried real hard to be a slut. I tried real hard to be crazy and succeeded at it for a time.*

Natalia also punished herself for the incest via prostitution.

> *For a period of time when I was young I was adoring of my uncle. In a way he saved my life. If he hadn't interfered with my mother things would have been much worse. He gave me some shred of self-esteem, he taught me little pieces of love, however misguided and exploitive. I was horribly ashamed later to realize that I had been attracted to my uncle in a way and had been physiologically aroused by him. It was important to somehow do penance for that. I used prostitution to teach myself not to feel anything, part of that being not to feel sexual.*

Natalia "succeeded" in experiencing no sexual pleasure from that time until she reached the age of 24.

Following her one-year period of adolescent prostitution, Natalia went away to college. During young adulthood her identity and worth remained dependent upon her sexuality. She dressed to attract sexual interest and "scanned the environment for others' reactions and responses." She wanted to affect others sexually and "felt a certain amount of power and control in that arena." Her sexual "lifestyle" was one in which compulsion predominated at the time. She was nonorgasmic during this time in casual relationships but enjoyed the "prowess that was involved." She was sexually "apt," concerned with being "a good technician" and pleasing others.

In later adulthood, Natalia's sexual "lifestyle" became more characterized by inhibition. An expectation remained that sexual pleasure would be followed by "punishment" for having been "a bad person." Natalia explained, "Someone asking me to be sexual was asking me to betray myself, asking me to do the things, feel the things that made me hate myself."

Inhibition has also been more recently favored in Natalia's "lifestyle" due to incest issues related to commitment. As a child and adolescent Natalia was repeatedly told by her uncle that they would marry when she was 18. She was terrified that she would be "trapped by sex into taking care of him forever." In several adult relationships Natalia has experienced a loss of sexual feeling with the development of commitment.

Sex can begin to feel oppressive, demanding, unreasonable. It's not that I don't want sex, but that I don't want to be trapped. The refusal to be trapped can get translated into a refusal to have sex. In fact, in the past the only way I knew how not to be trapped was to leave the relationship altogether.

Fears of entrapment associated with the incest also influence Natalia's sexual functioning. Permitting herself to physically feel pleasure in sexual interaction with a partner is difficult.

It's so much easier with no partner. Allowing anyone to affect me sexually is related to going down the tubes. If I just lay there and let somebody love me it will be the beginning of trouble. To be passive, to allow things to be done to me like I did with my uncle involves too much trust. I wonder what terrible thing is going to happen if I don't maintain sexual control.

Guilt associated with the incest also affects Natalia's sexual functioning.

I first became orgasmic with oral sex, but that doesn't happen now so much. It's as if it's too nice to me, too self-focused. And if I allow it now, does that mean that I was to blame for then?

As Natalia spoke about her sexuality and the ways in which it "belongs to the incest," she felt "very saddened and a bit dissociated." At the same time she felt that the interview left her with an awareness of her strengths. "Looking back I can see how much things have changed and that makes me feel remarkably new."

Discussion

The "uncomfortable" women presented in this chapter differ from the "lucky women" presented in Chapter 7 in several important ways. To return to the issue raised in the previous chapter's discussion regarding "separations" and their significance, the narrative on Claudia presented here contrasts sharply with the narrative on Esther highlighted in the previous series. Here, there are no "corrective cognitive statements" to separate Claudia's past from the present. The following paraphrased "beliefs" operate unchallenged:

To be female is to be attacked.

My back is my father's back.

My child's sucking is my father's sucking.

My husband's finger is my father's finger.

These "beliefs" continue, in the absence of "separations," to affect Claudia's gender identity, sexual "lifestyle," body perception, reproduction, and sexual functioning.

Although less immediately obvious, similarly uninterrupted "beliefs" related to the incest can be seen in the other narratives as well. For example, when Juliane speaks of being sexual with her partner of many years she says, "It's like anything could happen, I could open my eyes and it could be somebody else, I'd be with the monster again." The absence of "separations" between her present partner and her past offenders allows her fear to remain unchallenged.

More in evidence among the "uncomfortable women" presented here than among the "lucky women" presented in Chapter 7 is the theme of anger. The displacement of anger onto partners and the expression of anger though a period of "promiscuity" and/or prostitution is a pattern shared by Eva, Juliane, and Natalia. Their narratives speak to the satisfaction derived (whatever the costs) from having power sexually over men, from controlling them in turn, and from treating them with contempt and disdain. While "promiscuity" was mentioned in the previous series of narratives, the motivation in Meg's instance was not anger-based but self-esteem-based. In this set of narratives those very same self-esteem issues are present, but they exist in conjunction with the anger.

Some shared themes also emerge in comparing the two groups of women. Most salient here, as with the earlier series of narratives, are the themes of fear, power, and control. A subtheme that appears more strongly here in association with the theme of fear is boundaries, with concerns expressed in differing ways by Claudia, Eva, and Juliane. Another repeated subtheme is entrapment, which appears in association with the theme of power, most noticeably, and with heightened cultural meaning, in the narratives of Eva and Natalia, the two Latina women.

Also significant, as in the previous set of narratives, is the theme of shame. The potential for shame to permeate every aspect of sexuality is particularly well-illustrated here in the instance of Claudia.

Lastly, the theme of guilt can be seen to be more apparent among the "uncomfortable" women presented here than among the "lucky" women presented in Chapter 7. Self-blame is clearly evident, particularly in the narratives of Eva and Natalia as they struggle with the confusing issue of having experienced physiological arousal during the incest. Echoes of this struggle will be heard in the next, and final, series of narratives.

9

"Damaged" Women

OF THE TEN WOMEN INTERVIEWED, three experienced the incest as having had relatively more pervasive and persistent effects on their sexuality. Those three women, whose chosen pseudonyms are Katherine, Pat, and Angie, will be presented in this chapter. Their narratives illustrate both the intensity and the complexity of issues that may arise for women with incest histories in relation to their sexuality.

Katherine

Katherine is a 27-year-old woman who is occupationally involved in the media and the arts. She is undecided about her sexual preference and is not significantly involved in a relationship with a partner. She has no children.

Katherine is from an upper-class Jewish family of Eastern European descent and is the second of four children. From the age of 2 to the age of 6 she was sexually abused by her father. Throughout her tenth year she was also sexually abused by her older brother.

Katherine perceives her sexuality as "really damaged" by the incest and is uncertain how she will recover. "I don't know, it just seems really impossible. And I feel very angry about that." Part of Katherine's experience of the "damage" is through bodily sensations and physical symptoms she has had since the emergence of her incest memories almost three years ago.

I have chronic vaginal infections and I don't think terminal vaginal infections are out of thin air. I feel like it's memories. Most days of the week I get shooting pains in my vagina because it feels like somebody's entering me who doesn't belong there, who doesn't fit. And orgasm physically hurts. I don't know how long that's going to go on. I feel like as long as I have these sensations I'm damaged.

Since medical professionals are unable to explain Katherine's symptoms, she is left in a position not unlike that of her childhood, when her disclosure of incest was dismissed as "fantasy" by a psychiatrist.

I go to the doctors and they say, "Oh, nothing's wrong." And it's horrifying, because if nothing is wrong, what in hell is going on here? Nobody finds anything! Well, what is this all about then if nothing is going on? It makes me feel crazy!

Prior to the process of retrieving her incest memories, Katherine "didn't even notice" that she had a body.

I literally did not even consider that a person has a body. I didn't eat. I barely ate. I didn't understand why people eat. There was no emphasis on it. I just didn't consider that I had a body. I wasn't aware of it at all.

In the early part of the process of remembering her incest experiences, Katherine gained 30 pounds in one month.

As my body got bigger, my bones and even my features started disappearing. I was literally burying myself in flesh. And it was a way to cover up, to cover up this incredibly horrible thing that I had participated in, that I must have caused. I wanted to hide my body. I consciously decided, "I don't want a body." And so I made it into a blob. And it was nonsexual. I didn't have a gender.

Katherine then became aware of her body, but in a negative sense.

It was as if I had devised a scheme to get fat so I could notice my body more and notice how much I hated it so I could work that through and not always have to hate it forever.

Katherine started losing the weight she had gained after deciding that she "hated living in that body" and that her "self-destructiveness had come so close" that she "really had to work it out."

Having often experienced her body as "out of control," Katherine enjoys exercise as a way to feel "in control" and "in charge" of her body.

I get to physically shape my body like a sculpture that I'm making. It's a project that I oversee. I get to decide when I can do it and when I can't. I know where it begins and where it ends and that's very comforting. I accomplish something and in the course of it I've been in control.

Exercise also appeals to Katherine almost as an antidote to the incest.

I feel like I have so much anger in me that that's one way that I get to burn some of it off or channel it. I actually get to beat someone up in a way. I think of my father and use a kind of imagery and I can get into a good motion like pedaling real hard and fast. It's like purging the incest; you actually sweat it out of your body. If I can't do something physical it feels like my incest is sitting in me very heavily, stagnating.

The more Katherine works on the incest, the better able she is to appreciate her newfound body and her newfound gender.

Through this incest stuff I decided for the first time in my life that I was really female and that a lot of shit goes with that but a lot of nice things, too. And I wanted to be a woman.

In the past Katherine has always thought of herself as "an honorary boy."

Before my incest memories I always thought I was this lucky person who was by accident born a girl although I was really sort of a boy and that I was kind of special that way. That that was why I could hang out with all these guys, because I was an honorary boy. And that was very safe to be a boy. Boys are much safer.

As Katherine gave up being an "honorary boy" she realized she "didn't know how to go about becoming a woman."

So as I started losing weight I started looking at women to see what women look like. I started looking to see what their bodies look like so I could make my body look like that. And so that's what I did.

Up until the time of Katherine's weight gain the only time she was even briefly aware that she had a body was when she was pregnant.

I really liked being pregnant. I felt very vital. I could not believe that I had a body. I mean, pregnancy gave me a chance to realize that I had a body. I felt this sense of elation, as if I knew about myself a little more. I felt a little more connected to myself. It was a really thrilling feeling. In fact, I think that's why I got pregnant the second and third time. I really wanted to recapture that feeling, that connection.

Katherine chose to terminate all three of her pregnancies partially in response to feelings associated with the incest.

It's as if every time I was impregnated, these men became my father, that's what it felt like. And I would hate them. I would be disgusted by them, repulsed by them. And I wouldn't want anything more to do with them ever. It was a way they could possess me—"If I get her pregnant, then I own her, then I possess her." I've always had those feelings about both my brother and my father, that they possess me, they own me, they own my body. And I didn't want to be possessed.

Katherine also didn't want to be "found out" as a sexual person and "having a baby is the proof that you had sex, that you're sexual."

While Katherine now feels that she would eventually like to have a child, she reports feeling discouraged about achieving the context in which she would like to have that happen.

One of the hardest things for me is realizing that I may not be a mother because I'd like to do that someday. I feel like I could be a great mother. I feel like I mother people that I know and they turn into wonderful children. I guess I'm scared that I'll never find this person who is sane enough to do that with. It would be really hard to find a man that I would feel safe leaving a child with for 15 minutes. I've heard they exist, but I'm really mistrustful. And the idea of being a single mother is not appealing to me. That's just financially really stressful and emotionally really isolating.

Katherine is also uncertain at the present time whether that "sane enough" person she is looking for is male or female.

I feel like I wish there was a sexual preference category for incest. I feel like I don't have a sexual preference. I feel lots of pressure sometimes from women who say, "Come on. Why don't you just admit that you're a lesbian and that's it." But it isn't that easy. Everybody wants me to claim something. "Oh, you mean you're bisexual?" "No, I didn't say that!" I feel I don't know. I don't know what's going to happen to me.

Katherine was exclusively heterosexual until approximately a year ago when she became involved in a relationship with a woman she was working with. Her entry into this first lesbian relationship was preceded by "two solid years of hanging around with women really closely."

I used to go out with lots of men all the time. And I really had no female friends. I was mostly attracted to men and slept with a lot of men. Then I started this incest stuff and completely let go of that. That was something I just couldn't do anymore. And as I started being with women all the time, working closely, there was a huge shift in consciousness for me. I suddenly was taking women into my life.

When Katherine "started feeling like being sexual was maybe a possibility," she was surprised to find herself considering women.

When I started feeling like I wanted to be sexual again, I was terrified of men. I mean I'm really scared of men. I'm scared of their bodies as a weapon. It feels like a weapon to me. So I would sit on the train and I'd say, "Now who's attractive to me on this train?" And I'd spot somebody and sort of look at them and, oh my God, they were a woman!

Katherine then had to deal with her "own homophobia" and "how much" she "really didn't want to be a lesbian."

It was horrifying to me because I never thought of myself in those terms and didn't want that. I feel like incest is enough to deal with, and deciding to become a lesbian is a whole other thing. It feels like being a lesbian is just another way to be an outsider and to really be removed from what everybody else is doing in the mainstream and what's acceptable and what's normal—just like the incest.

There were other incest associations for Katherine as well.

Somewhere in the back of my head I heard my mother saying, "Somebody who suffers a trauma like this grows up and becomes a lesbian because there's no other choice." And I heard my father on the night I confronted him about the incest saying, before I could even speak, "What do you have against me? Are you a lesbian?"

Katherine also heard herself asking whether her attraction to women could be "trusted" since it "never came up before the incest stuff" and since she had "an absolute terror of men and male sexuality."

Shortly thereafter Katherine made "one last-ditch attempt to be normal" by having a sexual relationship with a man and "it didn't work out really well." "It was really too scary for me to have a man be excited with me. That was really terrifying. It reminded me a lot of my father basically."

Katherine's first lesbian relationship followed but left her "still pretty confused."

I was working at a place and there was this woman who was just the most stunning woman I've ever seen in my life. And that's the person who became my lover. It was probably the most nonsexual relationship I've ever had in my life, which is also kind of weird to me because I'm not quite sure what makes a lover a lover. Is it somebody who can hold your hand while you're going through the terror? Certainly there weren't a lot of men willing to do that with me. I don't know, I'm still pretty confused.

Another source of confusion for Katherine in her relationship with this woman was an association she made to the incest.

At the beginning of this relationship I said, "This is so interesting. I get to have a secret relationship." Which is like what I had with my father, basically, and my brother. It's another chance to have a sexual relationship in secret. And that was a little disturbing because it felt a little bit in some kind of way like acting something out. I felt a little bit out of control, I guess.

The relationship ended for Katherine just prior to the time of the interview, and Katherine remained undecided about her sexual preference.

I don't know what's going to happen next. I dream about having sex with men. But by day I'm hanging around with women because I'm getting filled emotionally from women. I feel like I'm entering another period of celibacy to clear out again, to clean out.

Celibacy has been "helpful" to Katherine when she has "needed to get clear, needed to make sense of things" in the past.

I had done a lot of traveling, gone to some faraway places and was being molested right and left. And I didn't even know it because I was an honorary boy so, hey, that's okay. When I came back, there were some really serious repercussions. I realized all these hands were always on me. And it felt shitty, it felt bad. So I stopped going out with anybody. That was it. Celibacy happened because I just needed clear space to figure out what in hell was going on.

When Katherine adopted celibacy as a sexual "lifestyle" at age 23 she knew she "didn't want anyone touching" her although she didn't know why. Within a year her incest memories surfaced, and she has since continued to lead an inhibited sexual "lifestyle."

Prior to age 23, Katherine's "lifestyle" had been characterized, for the most part, by compulsion.

I sexualized everything. Sex was something I wanted to be close to people. That was a way for me to feel like I was loved. It was compulsive. I didn't know any other way to get attention or to feel loved. I sort of had an equal sign between physical contact and love. If somebody loves you they want to sleep with you. If they sleep with you, it means they love you. I got lots of attention through sex and so I thought I was loved.

This equation Katherine "learned" from the incest. She also learned that sex was all she was good for.

When I was a really little kid, while the incest was going on, I used to think that I was chosen by God, that I was put on Earth for a special task. My mission was to comfort men who were really alone in the world and felt unloved. It was my duty to sleep with them and make them feel loved and accepted and okay. It was my purpose, it was the only thing I could do well, the only thing I was good at. My brother was really smart while I was really good at sex. I could do that. I could be important in some way.

With Katherine's identity and self-worth based so much upon sex, her attraction to prostitution was not surprising.

I wanted to grow up and be a prostitute. I thought, "Gee, what a great way to be powerful in the world." They're allowed to be sexual. It's even applauded. And they get to wear nice things. And since it was my mission already to take care of men, it was perfect! So the idea of being bad became interesting. I was already bad and here was this way to be very good at being bad.

Katherine never did adopt a sexual "lifestyle" of prostitution, but she was "promiscuous" for a period of time and doesn't "really believe that that's power."

I felt very powerful at the time. I felt like, "Oh, this is interesting, what I can accomplish with this, what I can make happen." I felt mobile, I felt light. I felt like I was always an inch off the ground. I got real thrills out of it. But to actually culminate in sex was a destructive act that sort of deflated all the power. In sex I lost my power.

The loss of power for Katherine was related to no longer feeling "in charge of" herself "and other people."

I felt like a sports car and I was the driver. I was very much in charge of myself and very comfortably in charge of others. Everything was fine until it actually culminated in sex. I became a Dodge Dart after sex and that was scary. Because I felt I had lured people in under these false pretenses and I couldn't really come up with the goods.

Having presented herself as a very sexual person, Katherine then wouldn't know how to deal with the fact that she "didn't even like sex."

It's so ironic. I had lots of sexual energy and it felt like a really creative energy to me. I mean, the sexual energy was fun, but sex was not fun to me. It was more a ritual and a compliance than something I really wanted. And that would be found out. I would be found out. They didn't see it, I saw it. I was found out by myself.

To "be found out" meant that somebody might realize Katherine was "a fake or a liar," a fear reminiscent of the time when the incest had to be hidden. "I'm scared somebody will see inside my body. They'll discover what's horrible about me. They'll find this tiny piece of rot right in the middle of me."

Katherine's fear of being "found out" has contributed to a "split" between sexual intimacy and emotional intimacy which has sometimes encouraged a more casual sexual "lifestyle."

Being obsessed with a person who is committed to someone else is ideal. Since you can't have them it's safe. They won't find you out so it never will get ruined at the end. And you get to feel like an honorary lover even though it's just so lonely.

To be emotionally intimate where there is no sexual intimacy and vice versa is preferable because it is not threatening. When Katherine attempts to integrate the two, she is unsuccessful.

I start getting these urges to carouse on a person. I start thinking, "Boy, it would be so much fun to go out and find someone and sleep with them. It would be dirty. I'm dirty. It would go together."

The urges to "sleaze around behind someone's back" Katherine can relate to the incest.

Either I'm going to be found out—that little piece of rot is going to be discovered—or I've made myself vulnerable by saying how I feel about them and now they're going to say they don't feel that way about me. So I'm going to get stepped on and feel stupid and used. So much of incest is about being tricked. People you put your trust in trick you over and over again.

To "sleaze around" on someone, Katherine has come to understand, is to "betray before I get betrayed, to zap before I get zapped." Katherine's expectation of discovering that she's been "had" or been "used" has influenced her sexual functioning as well as her sexual "lifestyle." "I'd worry that the person really didn't care about me, that sex was just something that they were doing that was sort of recreation and I could just as well have been a fire hydrant." Katherine's fears of being "used and thrown away" she relates directly to the incest.

I think about how rejecting my father was in the daytime, as if he didn't even know me. But in the nighttime we were intimate, and how confusing that was. To feel like you were only useful for sex and disgusting in that too. There was just rejection afterwards.

Rejecting, verbally abusive men sometimes intrude into Katherine's sexual fantasies, interfering with masturbation. Also disruptive, when Katherine is able to have more pleasurable fantasies, is her sense that others "know."

It's almost as if anyone who wants to see inside of me can see. And if I'm having a fantasy about someone, they're going to know. They'll find out and then I'll be bad again. I just assume that everyone can see inside of me although I can't see inside of them. Which is another part of having been tricked.

When Katherine tries to be sexual with a partner, the offenders often intrude.

It's very hard for me to stay in my body. It's very hard for me not to feel molested by somebody touching me. Even if I don't get pictures of my father and my brother, it's like this creepy, skin-crawling feeling. So I have to go up into my head to concentrate on staying in my body. It becomes this really intellectual process and the arousal just fades.

Katherine's arousal is also inhibited by guilt related to the incest.

I get this panic like I'm bad for wanting to be sexual. And if I want to be sexual, then that implies that I wanted to be sexual. If I wanted to be sexual, then I was complicit in the incest. I'm to blame. I'm to blame for the incest myself if I want to be sexual.

Even when Katherine is able to overcome these interferences and achieve orgasm, she is left without a sense of satisfaction after sex.

Orgasm is this horrible alone feeling. It's like being abandoned. It's like having an orgasm with my father, being touched and having my body responding and me not having any say in it and being out of control and then being abandoned. Him getting up and leaving me all alone there with a pillow over my face. I don't know how to be with somebody after sex. I just stop talking and feel frightened and hate myself.

As Katherine spoke about her sexuality and the many connections she sees with her incest history, she became both angry and sad.

I feel deeply wounded and I don't know how I can have any kind of sexual relationship. And that makes me so angry. The only two ways I ever knew my father were sexually and physically abusive. I guess I really make sex into this physically abusive thing as well. There's a part of me that thinks if you love somebody you won't have sex with them because sex is such a violent thing.

Despite the difficult emotions associated with the interview, Katherine felt it was "really helpful."

I feel like I got to some new places today. I feel like when I did the questionnaire I got to some new places. And today I did. Today there have been little sparks going off about things that I can think about. And that's really useful to me.

Pat

Pat is a 49-year-old woman who is occupationally involved in counseling and education. She is celibate and has not been in a relationship for over two years. She is twice divorced and has two adult children by her first marriage.

Pat is from an upper-middle-class Jewish family and is the second of two children. From the age of 3 to the age of 10 she was sexually abused by her father. From the age of 3 to the age of 8 she was sexually abused by her stepgrandfather.

Pat perceives her sexuality as "marked" and recognizes in retrospect that problems were evident as far back as her first marriage.

There were indications even then although I had no memories of the incest at the time. There were feelings of déjà vu—a lot of them, but I didn't know what was happening. My first husband would label me frigid. It was always such a fight about frequency. I realize today that he raped me all the time.

Pat's inability to protect herself within her marriage she sees as related to the incest.

There was never a sense growing up of being respected, of feeling that my body was my own. My objections were laughed off or totally ignored. It was as if my body didn't belong to me and I had no right to do what I wanted to with it.

Pat's attitude toward her body was also influenced by the incest. As an adolescent she feared her father's sexual attention and would dress early in the morning before he was up. His looks and comments regarding her sexual development contributed to a sense of shame as well as fear. This led Pat to devalue both her body and her gender.

It was as if my body was disgusting because it was sexual and it was sexual because it was female. It was almost as if it grew without my permission. It just developed. I didn't even know what my genitals looked like until four or five years ago. Just the thought of taking a mirror and looking created too much anxiety.

Pat's body devaluation was also due, in part, to involuntary arousal during the incest.

I got confused by the physical sensation of pleasure. Did that mean that I wanted the sex? It made me really angry that my body responded even though I didn't want it to. When I have sexual feelings now I think that my body is betraying me.

Pat's body image as an adult has remained negative and distorted. She is unable to perceive her body proportions realistically and is unable to gauge when her body weight is within appropriate limits. A dramatic increase in weight, which followed upon separation from her second husband, she sees as related to the incest.

There's always a feeling that people are going to look, that people are going to have control over me somehow. If they see something they like they're going to be able to have access to it. See, it was all right when I was married because that husband was going to protect me from all the others who were waiting on my doorstep to rape me.

The excess weight provided Pat with a sense of safety that allowed her to be sexual. "The fat felt real comfortable. I could feel sexy, sexual. Then when I'd get my weight down, something would happen. The minute I get down it's that fear of 'What are they going to do to me?'"
For similar reasons Pat has always been very careful about her style of dress.

There was always an issue of what was showing. I couldn't wear shorts. I did, but it was very difficult. Shirts had to be pretty big, never anything too sheer. 'Cause if I exposed myself too much, then that was a sure sign that I was asking for it.

Pat's body shame and fear carried over into the realm of reproduction. Being exposed during childbirth was very "embarrassing" for Pat, and nursing was experienced as discomforting.

I tried nursing her and I ended up giving up on it because I was afraid. It felt too sexual. I was uncomfortable with the vaginal contractions. It felt like if I allow a little piece of sexual feeling out into the world, is it going to be out of control?

Today Pat sees those feelings as associated with the incest and the fear of sexualized touch between parent and child. With her son during his adolescence Pat also sometimes experienced difficulty distinguishing between physical and sexual touch. That confusion remains today. "I forget that you can touch without it being sexual or without having it become sexual, that it can be just touching. It's hard not to confuse the two."

Another area of confusion that Pat associates with the incest is sexual preference.

It's left me very confused about my sexual preference. I know I'm at-tracted to men but a feeling starts to come in. And the fear is so intense that I think, "Why don't you just forget about men and get into a relationship with a woman, concentrate on that? Not just an emotional one but a sexual one." And yet I'm not even sure that a woman's touch would feel safe.

While Pat finds the female body very sexual and is sometimes confused by her attractions to particular women, she feels she is generally more attracted to men. She thus doubts that she is "really lesbian." "It's not like I've had a sense all along or knew early on that that's where I belong. It feels more recent and it feels more like giving up on men."

Pat is additionally aware of the difficulties encountered in today's soci-ety as a lesbian from having listened to lesbian friends. "It's hard to live as a lesbian. I have to be really sure of the facts, sure that's where I want to go before I experiment."

For now, celibacy allows Pat a chance to explore the issue of sexual preference further and allows her a sense of sexual safety. As a sexual preference, however, celibacy does not feel to Pat like a real choice. "It's very conscious and yet it feels like it was out of my control."

As a sexual "lifestyle," celibacy was adopted by Pat in response to the emergence of her incest history.

It's been three years since I've remembered the incest and it's been almost that long since I've been with anyone. Just the thought of some-body touching me is real scary. And there's a lot of fear of flashbacks and those feelings of déjà vu I've had in the past. I'm afraid that I'll just freak out on somebody.

Although Pat was never formally celibate during her marriages, for the most part she "avoided sex as much as possible." Her sexual "lifestyle" over time has been strongly influenced by both aversion and inhibition. Compulsion has never been predominant, and Pat has never adopted a "lifestyle" of "promiscuity."

The possibility of "acting out" sexually is a source of great anxiety to Pat because of her perception of her own sexuality as potentially unrestrainable and ungovernable.

> I feel like there's this volcanic activity like with sexuality. Will it just erupt out of control? If I let it out will it spread out all over, contaminating everything? It feels like, remember the shmoos that kept multiplying? That's exactly what it feels like. Or like mercury in a thermometer that escapes and keeps fragmenting. You just can't scoop it all up.

Pat fears she might become a "wayward woman," that she might "go on a sexual binge," and that her sexuality might "ruin" or "take over" her life. She fears if she were to allow herself "to be out of control" and to act on a sexual compulsion or to become "promiscuous," that she would "somehow end up powerless." "I can't believe that they won't have that power and control over me and that they won't use that power to hurt me." As a result of such fears, inhibition has often characterized Pat's sexual "lifestyle."

As with sexual "lifestyle," inhibition has been notable in relation to Pat's sexual functioning. Similar power and control issues are involved.

> I have this feeling that if I let somebody touch me, if I let somebody make skin contact, then I will be powerless and abused, I will have to do what they want me to do. I forget that I have a choice, that I can say no.

Worse yet for Pat is the prospect that she might find the touch pleasurable.

> And then there's the ambivalence and the confusion in this because it [touch] feels good and is that okay to like it? That seems like the incest. If you touch me and I enjoy it in any way, I'm a goner. You'll have total control over me. And I feel like I haven't had a strong sense of self, my sense of self feels very, very weak. So if you don't touch me, then I'm safe, then I'm still in control of my life.

Inhibition in sexual functioning for Pat extends to her fantasy life as well. She experiences fears that she may "act on" her fantasies and is particularly troubled by sadomasochistic fantasies.

My father got very abusive after a while with the incest although things started off loving and gentle. When I think about what might have happened that I can't fully remember and get turned on by that—I mean, it makes me crazy that I can be aroused by sadistic stuff.

Having experienced pain and sexual arousal concurrently during the incest "maybe explains" Pat's masochistic orientation in fantasy, but Pat is left very "uncomfortable" thinking "maybe that's the only way I can be aroused."

While multiply orgasmic, Pat often inhibits masturbation because she experiences "this intense, raw emotional pain" with orgasm.

Sometimes no matter how many orgasms I have, I'm not satisfied. And what stops me is it's too painful to go on. Just the anxiety—I can't handle the orgasmic feeling. Sometimes I've heard myself say, "He's gone and left. He's brought me to orgasm and now he's left." It almost feels like it's happened before. It's confusing to me and it's just over-whelming.

As Pat spoke about her sexuality and the ways in which she perceives it as "marked" by the incest, she found herself protectively withdrawing. In closing she stated, "I don't know how I feel yet about the interview because I think I really shut down. Partly I'm not here. I thought I could talk about it but I guess I wasn't prepared to have all the feelings."

Angie

Angie is a 31-year-old woman who is employed in a secretarial capacity. She is heterosexual and has been married since the age of 19. She and her partner have no children.

Angie is from a working-class Protestant family of Western European descent and is the eldest of five children. From the ages of 11 to 13 she was sexually abused by her father, and from the ages of 13 to 16 she was sexually abused by her stepfather. On several occasions during a one-week period when she was seven years of age, she was sexually abused by an uncle. At the age of four, she was also sexually abused once by her grandfather.

Angie perceives her sexuality as something she has been "gypped out of." She continues to experience her sexuality as "painful," as something she finds it "easier to try to avoid." She explained:

I don't give a great deal of thought to my sexuality. Most of the time I don't give any thought at all to it. I prefer not to feel any sexual feelings, not to feel myself as a woman even, notwithstanding any type of sexual feelings, just being a woman.

Angie does find it comfortable to be in touch with certain aspects of her sexuality through fitness.

Exercise allows me to respond to my body instead of ignoring it. I can listen to my body when I exercise and pay attention to it. I was always so disconnected from my body. All the time, all the time. I had to. That's how I survived.

Fitness also contributes to a more positive body perception for Angie. "Exercise really improves my body image. Most of the time with my body it was just a reflection of how I felt about myself. I neglected myself terribly. Terribly."

Angie perceives other forms of body neglect in the past as also having been associated with feeling undeserving due to her childhood abuse. "I didn't eat on any regular basis, I wouldn't give myself enough sleep, I just didn't have any rights. I was surprised I didn't have to ask anybody for permission to breathe. That's how low my self-esteem was."

Issues of self-esteem and body ownership related to the incest and compounded by Angie's childhood history of physical abuse by her mother were also associated with marital rapes Angie later experienced.

I had no control over my body—anything could be done to it that they wanted. My body was never mine, nothing was mine. My home was a set-up for incest. I was just free game. Later, with my husband, even if I was experiencing any kind of pain I just didn't think I had the right to tell him to stop.

Angie has abused her body herself in the past through substance abuse. She is a "recovering alcoholic and drug addict" and a member of Alcoholics Anonymous. She has more recently joined Overeaters Anonymous as well in order to control "these really destructive Hate Angie Binges."

Angie's body hatred is evident, too, with illness. "When I'm coming down with something, I'm very negative on my body and I'm really annoyed and angry, really just very, very negative."

When physically ill or injured, Angie associates the body with emotional as well as physical pain.

It's that feeling of powerlessness that I just cannot stand. I get so de-pressed if I'm in pain. I just crawl into the depths of despair. Sometimes I've been so sick that I couldn't do anything about it so I haven't even bothered to despair. I've just waited for it to get over. And I think that, too, could be the feelings similar to my stepfather—I just lay there and wait for it to get over with.

A generalized self-hatred similar to that which Angie experienced with the incest sometimes accompanies the body hatred.

I get very, very upset with myself for being sick. I think, "I have control over my body and why can't I stop these outside forces from attacking me and taking advantage of me and hurting me?" I can't control the outside forces.

Because of this self-blame, Angie reports feeling "guilty" about being sick. The guilt is exacerbated by Angie's assumption that others will deny or minimize her illness. "I have this thing, 'No one will believe me.' And that's probably a lot to do with the incest. 'No one's going to believe that I was that sick. Why talk about it with anybody, anyway?'"

Angie often thus experiences herself as isolated and unsupported dur-ing times of physical discomfort or pain. This feeling was most heightened during the second of two unwanted pregnancies.

I had to share my body with the baby all by myself, even though it wasn't my fault. I was fit to be tied! I felt lousy, really horrible! And I was so angry that my husband didn't have to share any of that. And the abor-tion was physically painful, very painful.

The same feeling of powerlessness that Angie experiences with ill-ness accompanied this pregnancy. She felt that the child had taken away her control over her body and she resented the child for that. Angie doubts that she will have a child although she often feels that she wants one.

I don't think that I could go through pregnancy. I don't think so in terms of my body being out of control and not being able to do anything about it. I hated being pregnant. I felt like such a victim. I hated it. I just felt overwhelmed, powerless. And I hated the child. I scared myself with my feelings of hate.

Angie also is aware that she would experience difficulty with the medical care necessitated by pregnancy. She is "extremely paranoid" in doctors' offices and "terrified" of gynecological exams.

I think somebody's going to hurt me. And I don't know what they're going to do and I don't know how long it's going to last or anything like that. I hate being alone with a male with nothing on but a johnny. That really, really frightens me.

Heterosexual relationships with men other than her husband are, for the most part, difficult for Angie and, in some instances, reminiscent of the incest. Males in authority are particularly threatening to Angie. She described a dissociative response to an interaction between herself and an unreasonable boss:

We went into a room and we talked. And I got out of the room after the meeting and I wanted to run away. I felt an incredible anxiety and my head was racing and my eyesight, my perception was off. And I wasn't on any drugs—this was after I quit drugs. And it dawned on me, this little voice inside me said, "That's your incest. You've been through this before." And after I got that voice, I calmed down, after I was aware of what was going on with me.

Angie experiences other problems related to the incest in peer heterosexual relationships.

If a guy offends me in any way sexually, with a joke or whatever, I feel like I've asked for it. I must be doing something to make them feel that way. I sometimes don't have the distance from the incest to not feel that shame, that guilt, that feeling that something I've done has evoked that behavior.

Angie tends to be "careful" about her dress, her speech, and her manner because of her concern that if she doesn't "restrain" herself, "some man will take it the wrong way."

If Angie does not inhibit herself in these ways she experiences "an awful feeling of being out of control." She feels she is about to "flip over to the other side" where she'll feel "incredibly sexy and like such a sexual object." This is a feeling that Angie is "very ashamed of" and that "feels very infantile" to her. She explained the associations that arise if she engages in sexualized behavior with men.

I visualize a little girl that wants to be hugged and kissed, that wants attention, that wants someone to play with. I guess that's how I feel in terms of men. I want the men to feel like I'm their girl, there's nobody else, and I'm really special. And I'm very needy and I feel really stupid—I hate those moods.

When Angie is in one of "those moods" she experiences a sense of compulsion sexually. "It's almost like I've taken a drug or something. It's like a disease kicking up in me that makes me feel like I have to sell myself to all the guys." Her response is to swing back to inhibition. "That's usually when I clam right up and go the other direction."

Swings have been very evident in Angie's sexual "lifestyle" over time, while her sexual preference has remained unchanged. During various periods, compulsion, aversion, and inhibition have predominated.

During Angie's early years of sobriety, compulsion was more predominant. After a period of two years, Angie reached "a bottom in terms of embarrassing" herself.

I would be very inappropriate with men in front of my husband. It didn't matter. Later I got very tired of sick men. I was attracting sickos by acting that way. It took me a while to realize that. It took me a while of getting burned by all these sick men who treated me like a French poodle.

During this period of time, Angie felt that her sexual fantasies were "out of control" and were "driving" her to behave in certain ways, even in the workplace. "I'd sexualize constantly and think that men would think I was sexy and would play along. Sometimes they would and that would usually bring an about-face because I didn't want that kind of attention."

More recently Angie's sexual "lifestyle" has been predominated by inhibition. She considers her present lack of sexual feelings to be "an extreme" and considers her "sensitivity around touch" to be related to the incest. Angie is sexually inactive with herself and less active than she would like to be able to be in her relationship with her husband.

While not predominant to the degree it has been in the past, aversion continues to influence Angie's "lifestyle."

I don't so much now or as often as I did, but I tend to think of sexual organs as being disgusting, and really ugly, and unattractive, and dirty. I had to build up to masturbation. I still sometimes find it hard to imagine having sex. I just think it's dirty, it's gross—I get a little warped with it sometimes.

Periods of sexual inactivity including abstention from masturbation have occurred throughout Angie's marriage. She has never formally adopted a "lifestyle" of celibacy, however.

Angie did, for a period of time at her partner's urging, adopt a "lifestyle" of prostitution. This was during the early years of Angie's marriage, from the time she was 19 until she was 23. Angie views her years of prostitution as reflective of "low self-esteem" and "an identity built so much around sex." In many respects the prostitution was but a continuation of Angie's experience of men during childhood and adolescence.

The prostitution was a duty, something I felt I had to do for my husband. The only way he was going to love me was if I performed for him and did for him. I thought my world would crumble if he wasn't in it. And my identity revolved around sex so much that it wasn't abnormal for me or I didn't think it was abnormal.

Like the incest, the prostitution was imbued with "the power of the secret." Angie "felt like a part of some kind of underworld, something glamorous." This, too, was not unfamiliar. As a child Angie was taken into bars by her father where he would have her dance the twist to the jukebox for all the male patrons. "The scary part," Angie commented, "was that my father would often say, 'Hey, you wanna take her home?'"

Aside from "the power of the secret," Angie experienced a personal sense of power (however brief and illusory) in relation to the prostitution.

I usually just thought men were controlled by their dicks and that I could switch them on and off if I wanted to. I look back now and I think it's pretty pathetic to have felt superior to somebody that was exploiting me, that didn't give me any sense of self. Maybe it did in the short term give me some feelings of power, but in the long term I felt very, very ashamed and guilty.

Angie "survived" the prostitution by "feeling superior" to others and by relying on familiar dissociative states. "I would distort, my body would disconnect, and I wouldn't see him [stepfather] even though my eyes were open. The same with being a prostitute."

While dissociation has provided a measure of relief at times that Angie has "needed to get through," it has also been a source of "pain." Angie often experiences dissociative reactions while engaged in sexual activity with her partner. If she does not stop as these are "coming on," she experiences a secondary reaction.

I physically feel like I've gone into a black hole. I feel like a shroud of blackness is coming over me and it's just the eeriest, creepiest feeling and I have to stop, and sometimes I'll cry. It's just such an awful, awful feeling. Sometimes it's so bad that I feel suicidal. I just want to reject whatever that is. And I know it has to do with being so frightened because I don't have any limits. My boundaries were totally destroyed. I'm just so frightened of being a nothing. And that's what the incest did to me. It turned me into a nothing. It robbed me of personhood.

Since it is "very rare" that "the blackness" does not intrude during sexual activity, Angie's functioning is affected at all of the sexual phases of desire, arousal, and orgasm. She thus has to "work on" herself before she can engage in sex.

I feel like I've got to stock up on emotional energy beforehand. I've got to go to my A.A. meetings, I've got to pray, I've got to talk to people, I've got to get some other needs met and really feel good about myself for at least four or five days in a row before I can do that.

Even then, Angie fears she will "disappoint" her partner. "I'll tell him I want to make love, and then he'll make advances to me, and then I'll get very, very turned off and tell him I've changed my mind. It causes a lot of conflict." It also causes a great deal of sadness for Angie.

We are, at some point in time, going to leave this world and I'll think of how I could have loved him. And I don't want my incest to prevent me from loving somebody else, from being tender and compassionate and sensitive to him.

As Angie discussed her sexuality and the influence of the incest on her sexuality she became "profoundly aware" of her "sense of sexual inadequacy" and her "feelings of worthlessness." She found the interview "painful," but stated, "I'm glad I did it. And I'd do it again because it gave me a lot of insight into myself, and validated a lot of things for me."

Discussion

As is true for the "lucky" women in Chapter 7 and the "uncomfortable" women in Chapter 8, the most significant themes for the "damaged" women presented here are fear, power, control, and shame. The subtheme of boundaries appears, as it did in the previous series of "uncomfortable" women, in association with the theme of fear, but the absence of self experienced by Pat and Angie add a deeper dimension here.

The theme of trust and the related subthemes of betrayal and abandonment wind their way through all three sets of narratives. But nowhere is the potential for trust issues to affect all aspects of sexuality better illustrated than here in the instance of Katherine.

Much more in evidence among the "damaged" women presented here than in the two previous series of narratives is the theme of confusion. While Nancy in the first series and Claudia in the second series struggle with confusion related to gender identity, they do so in the context of a consistent sexual preference and consistent sexual "lifestyle" over time. Here in the narratives of Katherine and Pat can be seen the layered confusion that survivors sometimes experience as they reexamine and sort out issues of sexual preference, sexual "lifestyle," and gender identity simultaneously.

Self-esteem appears once again as a strong theme in this particular series, but noticeably more so in relation to its role in the repetition of abuse through revictimization. Katherine "was being molested right and left" and "didn't know it." Pat "realizes today" that what she experienced "all the time" with her husband was "rape." Angie "didn't think, even in pain" that she had the "right" to tell her husband "to stop." All three women felt that their bodies belonged to others, and that the only way to get attention, protection, or care was through sex.

As in the previous set of narratives, the theme of self-esteem also appears in relation to "promiscuity" and prostitution. Here, both Katherine and Angie speak of how sexually based their identity and self-worth were.

The theme of anger is present but less so in this series of narratives than the last. Only Angie shares the pattern described by Eva, Juliane, and Natalia in the previous series of expressing anger through a period of "promiscuity" and/or prostitution. While Katherine discusses "promiscuity" here, it appears that her motivation, like that of Meg in the first series, was more self-esteem-based than anger-based.

Guilt and self-blame are clearly apparent in all three narratives in this series. Katherine and Pat, like Eva and Natalia in the previous series of "uncomfortable" women, associate physiological arousal with complicity. What is different here is the degree to which the self-blame is accompanied by self-hatred. Katherine speaks of wanting "to cover up this incredibly horrible thing I participated in, must have caused" and of having others discover the "rot right in the middle of me." Pat speaks with self-disgust (as well as fear) about her sexuality, which she envisions almost as a kind of toxic energy that could "spread out all over, contaminating everything." Angie expresses self-loathing as she describes a "little girl that wants to be hugged and kissed, that wants attention, that wants someone to play with her." Unlike the "lucky" women in Chapter 7, the "damaged" women presented here still perceive the "cause" of the incestuous abuse as somehow within themselves.

10

Treatment Recommendations: Cognitive and Behavioral

VARIOUS SERVICE PROVIDERS, including educators and health educators, clergy, nurses and physicians, counselors, social workers, psychologists, and psychiatrists, come in contact regularly, by design or by chance, with women with incest histories. In some instances women may not identify themselves as such to service providers, and their shared thoughts and feelings may be less understandable. It is hoped that the information generated by this study will better equip helping professionals and others to effectively support and treat both women who disclose an incest history and women whose problems suggest an incest history.

Clearly, it is essential for helping professionals today to be knowledgeable about the effects of incest on sexuality, as well as on many other areas of a woman's life. As sexuality has come to be accepted as an important aspect of women's lives, women have become more and more open about discussing problems related to sexuality. Women with incest histories are apparently more likely to have sexual problems to discuss; in addition, they are seemingly unlikely to seek formal sex therapy. While sex therapists treat many women with incest histories, those women would appear to be but a small percentage of the women with incest histories who experience sexual problems.

Of the 43 participants in this study, all of whom reported problems with sexual functioning, 40 percent of whom reported greater dissatisfaction than satisfaction during sex, and half of whom reported dissatisfaction after sex, only two (5 percent) had ever been in sex therapy. Several reasons were consistently given by the participants of this study as to why they would not seek sex therapy for sexual problems.

1. An inability to trust the motivations of people who would enter the field of sex therapy, that is, a fear that the therapist would be voyeuristic or exploitive.

2. An expectation that sex therapy would feel coercive, that is, that assignments and exercises would be experienced as demands for compliance and performance.

3. A tendency to minimize or deny sexual problems so as to avoid the shame and anger that would accompany the acknowledgment of serious sexual problems.

4. A sense that the sexual problems in evidence were really not sexual problems per se, but problems of trust, intimacy, and so on that would best be worked out in individual psychotherapy or couples therapy.

The participant comments from the study suggest that traditional sex therapy could, indeed, be inappropriate, ineffective, and even potentially countertherapeutic for some women with incest histories. Treatment modifications and special strategies need to be developed for incest survivors who seek sex therapy.* This study underscores the need for sex therapists to view the sexual problems of women with incest histories in the context of their experiences and for particular sensitivity to the potential for problems in the therapeutic relationship. Specific recommendations (encompassing those of McGuire & Wagner, 1978) would include:

1. Minimize the "doctor"-"patient" power dichotomy.

2. Adopt a nonparental, nondirective, gentle manner.

3. Assist the client in overcoming self-blame regarding her sexual problems by validating that the incest was a serious violation.

4. Empower the client by applauding her for "taking charge of things" by seeking sex therapy rather than avoiding the problems and thereby eliminating the chance of corrective experiences.

5. Give the client control over the pace at which exercises proceed.

6. Assist the client in perceiving her participation in the exercises as a choice she herself has made.

7. Give the client control over the initiation of sensual or sexual activity.

*Maltz (1991), released since this book was written, has been very confirming in this regard.

8. Give the client control over the degree of sensual or sexual activity engaged in.

9. Assist the client in recognizing when displaced anger is undermining treatment.

10. Assist the client in recognizing when guilt is undermining treatment.

The latter two items involve the separation of past and present, an important element of work on sexuality with women with incest histories. It is important to construct strong boundaries between the offender(s) of the past and the sexual partner(s) of the present, and it is equally important to construct strong boundaries between the offender(s) and the woman herself in terms of identity. A treatment model for problems related to sexuality in women with incest histories should thus include a strong cognitive component.

The Cognitive Component of Treatment

In order to achieve effective separations of the sort mentioned above, it may well be necessary for a woman with an incest history to develop a personalized set of formal cognitive statements (Beck, 1976; Ellis, 1962; Lazarus, 1971). Personalized cognitive statements related to anger, guilt, shame, fear, and/or confusion may be developed by women with the assistance of any helping professional. Women need only to identify the problematic thoughts and beliefs that need to be interrupted and corrected. Exploration with the helping professional would, in most instances, readily reveal these. The following statements, for example, might be used to interrupt the displacement of anger that may occur if and when the role of sexual initiator becomes shared with the partner.

1. John hasn't taken control from me just because he expressed a desire to be sexual. I can say "no," "wait," and "stop" at any time.
2. I know it's my right to refuse John if I want to. Therefore, I don't have to always say "no."
3. If I'm automatically saying "no," then I'm not really exercising a choice.
4. If I'm just being oppositional where it's safe to be (with John), then I'm not really empowering myself, I'm just disempowering John.
5. It's not fair for me to punish John for what my father did to me. John deserves more from me than that.

6. John is not pressuring or forcing me to be sexual. This is my choice.

7. John is not engaging with me sexually just to gratify himself the way my father did. John cares about me; his sexual desire has to do with me as a person.

8. I am a woman, I am not a child. This is John, this is not my father. (A trusted partner might gently make similar statements to a woman aloud, and this may prove more effective, in this particular instance, than a woman speaking to herself.)

All of these statements assume, of course, that the partner and the offender are, in fact, dissimilar in their attitudes and behaviors. Where real similarities exist, changes would need to be made by the partner.

As another example, the following cognitive statements might be used to interrupt interference from guilt.

1. It's OK for me to have sexual needs. It means that I'm human, that I'm normal. I like feeling human and being normal.

2. Just because my brother's needs made him act inhuman and abnormal with me doesn't mean I'm like that. It wasn't even his sexual needs but other needs that he was expressing that way.

3. My brother is the guilty one who should feel ashamed. I'm not going to feel the guilt for him!

4. It's OK for me to feel sexual pleasure with Susan. She isn't my brother. Sex with Susan is right, it's good.

5. Just because my brother's sexual desires and needs seemed disgusting to me doesn't mean mine are disgusting to Susan. She's as accepting of my sexual expression as I am of hers. She's being sexual with me by choice and wants to know my desires and needs. If I verbalize them, I'll be taking responsibility for my own sexual pleasure.

6. Sex with Susan is nice, and I deserve nice things. I have a right to receive sexual pleasure, not just give it like in the past. It's even OK to concentrate on my own sexual pleasure rather than Susan's sometimes. If I put myself more in control of my sexual pleasure, I'll feel more powerful.

7. If I'm a sexual person it doesn't mean I'm to blame for the incest. Bodies respond to sexual stimulation; that's the way they're made. Mine responded, and all that means is that it was working like it was supposed to.

8. If I don't stop feeling guilty, my brother is still running my life. I'll show him!

From each of these sample statements several others might be generated, tailored to the woman's particular needs. A few key words or a meaningful phrase is all that is really necessary. While using cognitive statements requires energy and may be distracting during sexual activity, it can prove effective in dealing with thoughts and affects that are themselves energy-consuming and distracting. Several of this study's participants described "talking" to themselves as an important self-help technique. Women reported the use of this technique in relation to body perception, reproduction, sexual preference, and sexual "lifestyle," as well as sexual functioning.

Corrective cognitive statements may also be used in conjunction with thought-stopping or image-stopping techniques (Bain, 1928; Lazarus, 1971; Wolpe, 1973; Wolpe & Lazarus, 1966). For example, if troubled during sex by thoughts that a partner might injure her physically, a woman can be taught to shout "Stop!" to herself and to then make corrective cognitive statements, such as: "David is very gentle. He is not my uncle. He would never hurt me. He would stop if I ask. I am safe with David." Likewise, images may be interrupted by teaching a woman to shout "Stop!" to herself or to place a huge red "Stop" sign over the image and to follow this with such statements as, "I'm not in danger anymore. I'm a grown woman now."

Image-altering techniques (Beck, 1976; Lazarus, 1971; Wolpe, 1973; Wolpe & Lazarus, 1966) may also be used. Offenders can be marched out of the bedroom when their presence intrudes. Tearful or terrified little girls (self-representations from the past) can be held and comforted until ready to leave the bedroom. Women can be taught to yell at or to talk back aloud to offenders whose images appear on the scene. While this latter technique requires a woman to be relatively uninhibited in the presence of the sexual partner, the partner enjoys the benefit of having the survivor's anger aimed at the appropriate target rather than displaced. A couple willing to try this technique may find that fear is defused as well as anger. This may relax things appreciably and even encourage moments of playfulness.

The use of image-stopping and image-altering techniques to manage flashbacks should generally be accompanied by a discontinuance of sexual activity and an explanation to the partner of what is occurring. By talking with the partner and stating aloud that what is happening has nothing to do with the partner, a woman can pull herself out of the past and into the present and can further differentiate the partner from the offender.

If the partner is aware that a flashback is occurring, s/he should speak calmly and make eye contact with the survivor as soon as possible. A reassuring statement that includes a time or place reminder, such as, "It's all right. No one's going to hurt you now." or "It's OK. Look around. You're in your own bedroom," will help the woman to connect to the partner and to the present.

Generally, partners have no idea, however sensitive they may be, of what to say or do during a flashback. For this reason, and also because control is such an important issue, the woman should take responsibility in these instances to indicate to the partner what kind of comfort, if any, she would like. She may want to be held or she may be unable to tolerate more than having her hand held. She may want to curl up in a ball and cry while her partner lightly rests one hand on her shoulder, strokes her hair, or gently rubs her back.

If at all possible the woman should allow herself to receive physical comfort from the partner at these moments. This will contrast with the abandonment she experienced as a child following her abuse and will encourage her return to the here-and-now. It will also indirectly involve her in reparenting and nurturing the child part(s) of herself, an important aspect of self-help for women with incest histories.

After a flashback the woman should also indicate to the partner what her other needs and wants are. Would she like the partner to turn on all the lights or at least a nightlight? Does she need to put on a comforting flannel nightgown? Does she want to talk about the flashback and any new information it may have provided? Does she need some space for herself to just think about it while her partner is silent? There are many ways a partner can help if a woman takes responsibility for asking.

The importance of a trustworthy and understanding partner should not be underestimated. Learning to choose appropriate, nonexploitive partners was mentioned by a number of this study's participants as key to their efforts to alleviate sexual problems. If a gentle, patient partner is chosen, a woman will be better able to separate the past from the present, since the dissimilarities between the partner and the offender will be obvious. If a woman is allowed to take her time to become involved sexually, she will be less likely to fear that she will be hurt or used, her body will feel like her own, sex will feel like a choice, she will be better able to communicate any fears or reservations she has, and she will be better able to risk revealing her sexual self by verbalizing her needs and desires. That is, power, control, and trust issues will be minimized in a sexual relationship of this sort.

Increased and improved selectivity of partners may only develop, however, after substantial work on self-esteem and trust issues. To enter a sexual relationship with an appropriate, nonexploitive partner, a woman must both be able to believe that she deserves such a partner and be able to trust that the partner is real. The latter may prove more difficult with a male partner. Several heterosexual participants in this study felt that the reworking of trust issues with a caring, nonsexist male therapist had played a significant role in enabling them to achieve satisfactory relationships. Some women consciously chose to do this work specifically with a male therapist after having worked with a female therapist on various issues, including mistrust of women related to having been unprotected or "sacrificed" by mother.

The selection of an understanding male or female partner may tremendously enhance the self-help efforts of a woman with an incest history. A partner who is willing to and interested in reading about incest can develop an appreciation for the problems that might arise in the relationship and can encourage open communication with a woman about her particular experience. A woman will be less fearful of revealing herself if she knows a partner is "educated" about incest and will be neither shocked nor judgmental. Some books to consider for partner education are listed in Appendix F. If a woman is able to discuss her history in some detail with a partner, further separation of the past and the present may be achieved.

When appropriate, a partner should also be involved in any self-help methods employed. This differentiates the present partner from the past offender(s) by placing the partner in the role of ally; in addition, it encourages the partner to direct his or her own frustration, resentment, and anger at the offender (or at the incest experience) rather than at the survivor. Such self-help methods would include the use of cognitive statements, thought-stopping, image-stopping, and image-altering techniques discussed earlier. A woman and her partner can also be encouraged to develop their own creative solutions with the help of the cognitively based self-help books listed in Appendix F, which are recommended for both helping professionals and women with incest histories.

The Behavioral Component of Treatment

The behavioral component of treatment serves primarily to alter dysfunctional responses related to sexuality through the application of systematic desensitization principles (Lazarus, 1971; Wolpe, 1973; Wolpe & Lazarus, 1966). A list of sexual activities that produce discomfort may be prepared by the woman, with each activity recorded on an index card. Cards are then arranged in a hierarchy, from those causing the least discomfort to those causing the greatest. For example, walking toward the bed undressed may be at the bottom of the hierarchy, and performing oral sex on a partner at the top.

While a woman is constructing such a hierarchy, deep muscle relaxation (Jacobson, 1938; Wolpe, 1973; Wolpe & Lazarus, 1966) is introduced. Over several sessions the woman is trained to be aware of body tension by having her tighten, release, and further release various muscle groups. The woman is instructed throughout to regulate the rhythm of her breathing, letting go with each exhale to augment relaxation. In between sessions, relaxation should be practiced twice daily for a total of 20–30 minutes. Time does not increase as muscle groups are added, since practice makes efforts that much more efficient. (For a summary guide of the series of relaxation sessions about to be described, see Appendix G.)

The first session begins with the arms, since they are easy to demonstrate and to check for relaxation. First the woman, while seated, drops her hands to her sides, arms straight, and notes any sensations of tingling, numbness, or warmth. She is asked to imagine the tension draining down her dangling arms and flowing out her fingers. She is instructed to regulate her breathing, relaxing with each exhale. Once aware of sensations that generally accompany relaxation, the woman is asked to grip the arm of the chair in which she is seated and to note the tightening in the forearm. She is then instructed to release and to attempt to recapture the sensation of her arm dangling by releasing further. The woman is next asked to pull the arm of the chair toward her with bent elbow and then with straightened elbow and to note the contraction of the biceps and the triceps, respectively. Again, she releases and, after releasing, is instructed to release further. She continues by shrugging her shoulders, releasing, and releasing further; pulling back her shoulders, releasing, and releasing further; and, finally, hugging herself, releasing, and releasing further.

The second session focuses on the muscles in and around the head, since these are, from an emotional standpoint, the most important. The woman is warned that she may feel silly doing this series and is encouraged to indulge in unrestrained laughter rather than containing its release. First she raises the forehead up and releases it in increments. When she feels she has relaxed it fully, she is instructed to release further. Then she frowns, simultaneously wrinkling her nose, releases, and releases further. She smiles, releases, and releases further; then purses her lips, releases, and releases further. She pushes her tongue into the roof of her mouth, releases, and releases further; clenches her teeth, releases, and releases further; and finally presses her chin to her chest, releases, and releases further.

In the third session, the focus is on the lower body and legs. The woman is told to tense her stomach as if anticipating a punch, then release, and release further. She tries to raise herself off the chair by tightening her buttocks, then releases, and releases further. She lifts her legs, turns her toes in, tightens, then releases, and releases further. She lowers her legs, points her toes in, tightens, releases, and releases further. She does the same with her toes pointed out. Finally, she curls her toes in, releases, and releases further.

In the fourth session, after sufficient preparation, the woman is guided into as deep a state of relaxation as possible while seated in a chair with her hands on her lap and her eyes closed. This is achieved without first tightening any of the muscles. The woman is instructed to regulate the rhythm of her breathing and to relax further on each exhale. She is told to imagine the tension draining out of the muscles and flowing out of her body. She is instructed to feel the heaviness of the muscles as they relax, to feel the sense of calm coming over her as muscle groups are progressively relaxed. When fully relaxed, the woman is asked to visualize herself in a real or fantasied place representing safety, beauty, and peace. When visualization is complete, the woman is instructed to return to this place as she continues to practice the relaxation techniques she has learned. Relaxation is practiced in a variety of settings and in a number of body positions. Since sexual activity may occur under varied circumstances and in differing surroundings, learning should take place accordingly.

During relaxation practice the woman is instructed to alternately feel her breath moving in her chest, moving in her abdomen, and moving in her pelvis. This encourages greater body awareness and connection, and promotes self-focusing skills.

As a woman becomes proficient at relaxation, she is assigned the task of imagining the least discomforting activity on the constructed hierarchy of sexual activities while in a state of relaxation. Cognitive statements such as those described earlier are used to counteract any negative thoughts that might occur. Visualization of each activity proceeds in steps from less threatening to more threatening images. For example, a woman visualizing oral sex with a partner could proceed from imagining looking at the genitals, placing her cheek against the genitals, to imagining placing her lips on the genitals, placing her mouth or tongue on the genitals, and finally performing oral sex. The woman would continue to envision the activity, building on previous images in this manner, until she felt she had mastered her dysfunctional response to the activity. She would then move on to the next item on the hierarchy. In similar fashion, desensitization principles are used to achieve transfer from imagined activities to real activities.

As skill with relaxation and cognitive management techniques develop, women are encouraged to increase their exposure to sexual stimuli, such as books, magazines, movies, and the like. Several resources for erotic materials are listed in Appendix F.

The use of pornography, which has sometimes been suggested as an aid to sexual arousal in women, is not recommended. If the distinctions between erotic and pornographic materials are unclear to a survivor, these should be elaborated. Fortune (1983) offers, for example:

Pornography is sexually explicit material which portrays abuse, violence, and degradation for the purpose of arousal and entertainment. Erotica describes sexual materials which may or may not be sexually explicit and are used for the purpose of arousal and entertainment. Erotica does not include any violence, abuse, or degradation of a person. (pp. 232–233)

The portrayal in pornography of sex as coercive or violent may reinforce survivor associations between sexual activity and sexual abuse when, in fact, these associations need to be broken. Pornography should thus be avoided.

As relaxation and cognitive skills grow, a woman should also be encouraged to increase her level of sensual and sexual self-pleasuring in a graduated fashion. The self-help guides to orgasm listed in Appendix F are, in fact, gradation-based, describing programs (for orgasmic as well as nonorgasmic women) involving a series of hierarchically ordered steps. So, too, are programs for the treatment of vaginismus, which involve the use of progressively larger vaginal dilators over time and which benefit from the formal introduction of relaxation techniques.

The concept of a hierarchy may be informally adopted in a self-help fashion as well. For instance, a woman who has difficulty with physical closeness or body contact of any kind may wish to develop a list of activities to eventually carry out, such as:

1. Sitting close to a friend on a couch instead of in a separate chair.
2. Kissing a friend hello and goodbye.
3. Hugging a friend hello and goodbye.
4. Leaning against a friend while listening to music or watching TV.

The items on the list may be ordered from least to most difficult; the survivor then applies a series of steps to each item, such as:

1. Watching someone else carry out the activity on the list.
2. Imagining herself carrying out the activity on the list.
3. Proceeding with the activity with a distance limit or time limit built in.
4. Repeating the activity again and again with a gradual reduction in the distance limit or expansion of the time limit.

The pacing and sequence of the exercises are the survivor's own, and the hierarchical ordering may be adjusted, if necessary.

An example of a well-known, formally developed series of progressive exercises is sensate focus, developed by Masters and Johnson (1970). Sensate exercises are routinely used with couples by sex therapists and can be appropriately used by properly trained psychotherapists. Sensate focus consists of graduated assignments in giving and receiving touch, which proceed from physical and sensual activity to more overt sexual activity over a period of time.

Several modifications may be made when using sensate focus with women with incest histories. Specific recommendations (encompassing those of Maltz & Holman, 1987, and McGuire & Wagner, 1978) would include:

1. Expansion of the number of general sessions before beginning the sensate focus exercises to ensure establishment of a trusting therapeutic relationship.

2. Expansion of the overall period of time expected for completion of the exercises, anticipating dealing with guilt, displaced anger, and feelings of coercion.

3. Incorporation of survivor-suggested modifications to increase safety during both nonsexual and sexual touch assignments. (The significance of safety modifications is beautifully illustrated by Maltz and Holman's (1987) incorporation of a clothes-on period of activity when using sensate focus with survivors.)*

4. Instruction that the survivor begin with the role of giver during the initial touch assignments to increase her sense of control.

5. Instruction that the survivor begin with the role of receiver during the later assignments in teaching and learning stimulation techniques to increase her sense of control.

6. Anticipation with the survivor of possible difficulty with the role of giver during the later assignments due to associations with having been "instructed" by the offender. (Should such associations arise, they would best be addressed with the cognitive techniques described earlier in relation to promoting separation of past and present.)

Each of these simple modifications conveys an important message to the survivor. One is that you expect her trust to be earned, not given. Two is that you are aware of the complexity of the incest issues and will respect her pace. Three is that she may know things about herself that you don't know that are important to incorporate. Four is that you want her to be as comfortable as possible from the start. Five is that her comfort will remain a priority with you. And six is that you will remain aware of the complexity of the incest issues.

The sixth, final message may need to be conveyed again and again, for

---

*Maltz (1991), released since this book was written, includes an excellent series of exercises for survivors in relearning touch.

that complexity is often experienced by the survivor on a daily basis as she contends with a variety of triggers. The sights, sounds, tastes, odors, and sensations that can elicit incest memories, evoke affective connection with the past, or produce flashbacks may seem limitless to the survivor, and all such associations are problematic, particularly with regard to sexual functioning.

It is important to realize, however, that not all dysfunctional responses to triggers require the application of cognitive and behavioral techniques. Where avoidance is an option, it should be stated as such. If the taste of semen makes a woman sick, she can choose not to engage in fellatio to the point of ejaculation. This may seem obvious, but a woman with an incest history may need permission to make this choice.

In addressing the issue of triggers with a survivor, it is important to point out that partners are often willing to make changes that a woman might consider too much to ask, such as shaving off a mustache or changing the decor of a bedroom. The partner may have been thinking about a change or at least have no investment in whatever the trigger may be. Although the partner's feelings obviously need to be taken into account, women with incest histories often make assumptions about partners' needs and often honor those assumed needs, even at the expense of their own. While it is important to avoid partner concessions that might later produce resentment, it is equally important to raise possibilities of which the incest survivor may be unaware. The survivor should not be made to feel that she must extinguish all dysfunctional responses, however ideal that might seem.

In some instances, once triggers are identified they can be eliminated with a minimal amount of effort. Triggers such as coffee, alcohol, or tobacco on the breath and/or body odor, paint, grease, or smoke on clothing can be eliminated by toothpaste, mouthwash, detergent, a shower, and fresh clothing. Nontriggering odors can be introduced by the use of perfumed soaps and lotions, scented candles, lamp oil, or incense. Partners can avoid the exact phrases or tone of voice that the offender used. The problem is that the survivor often doesn't know that she has a right to request (or even demand) certain terms and conditions in a sexual encounter or relationship. Again, permission may be needed for her to institute the changes necessary to eliminate triggers.

Of course, in some instances the triggers may be unavoidable. If loose flesh is a trigger, for example, partners cannot simply tighten it up overnight or keep it covered at all times. But desensitization, as described earlier, can be accomplished through the combined use of relaxation and a graduated series of exercises in approaching the trigger.

Nonsexual approaches may be used with particularly difficult triggers, and these may even be childlike and fun. In the instance of loose flesh, it can be kneaded into breakfast rolls, it can invite the outlining of elephants and rhinos on the skin, it can hide pennies or jelly beans. The incest associations can thus be broken and new pairings established. Other examples, including altering the meaning of heavy breathing through the development of a new association with music, are described in Maltz and Holman (1987).

Given patience, commitment, creativity, and a sense of humor, survivors and their partners can (and do!) free themselves from the past. The uneven progress experienced by many survivors can be discouraging, but healthy sexuality is constructed piece by piece and, for survivors, with as much unlearning as learning involved.

Integration of Treatment Components

In working on sexuality with women with incest histories, the cognitive and behavioral components of treatment described in this chapter are essential. This is particularly true in the realm of sexual functioning.* The cognitive and behavioral components are not, however, sufficient in and of themselves to address the myriad problems survivors may experience related to sexuality.† In the chapter that follows, the physical and educational components of treatment, which, if needed, should be carried out concurrently with the behavioral and cognitive components, will be discussed.

*Recently discovered work by Jehu, Klassen, and Gazan (Jehu, Klassen, & Gazan, 1985–1986; Jehu, 1988), carried out in Canada during the time of this study, has been very confirming in this regard.

†An article by Sprei and Courtois (1988), acquired since this book was written, has been very confirming in this regard.

11

Treatment Recommendations: Physical and Educational

COGNITIVE AND BEHAVIORAL TECHNIQUES have been around for many years; we need only adapt and apply them to women with incest histories (as well as other populations). There have been few such physical and educational techniques to formally draw upon until quite recently. The recommendations in this chapter, in fact, are grounded primarily in an "oral literature" that began to develop in the late 1970s and early 1980s among pioneers in the treatment of women with incest histories. That "literature," largely informed by survivors themselves, outdistanced published information on treatment for a number of years.

The programs and techniques described here evolved in large measure from the self-help discoveries of survivors and the pragmatic experiences of the early therapists assisting their recovery. When the cognitive and behavioral components of treatment described in the previous chapter are combined with the physical and educational components described here, the problems that incest survivors so often experience in relation to sexuality can be more systematically addressed.

The Physical Component of Treatment

The physical component focuses primarily on those aspects of sexuality that are related to body perception, including body hatred and devaluation, body "ownership," body estrangement, body distortion, and body shame. Any program developed to provide a physical component of treatment should offer nonverbal emotional release, an experience of power and control associated with the body, a lesson in self-care or self-appreciation, and natural antidepressant and tranquilizing effects. Descriptions of some model programs follow.

I.R.*obics

I.R.*obics, Therapeutic Aerobics for Incest Survivors (*Incest Resources), was created in 1986 in response to the need for a physical program for survivors in the Boston-Cambridge area. Program adaptions of I.R.*obics are now offered through survivor organizations and individuals in a number of states, as well as in Canada and several European countries.

In developing a physical program, an all-survivor group format was considered desirable, since entering a room full of other incest survivors may, in and of itself, be therapeutic. In addition to reducing the isolation that women with incest histories often feel, such a format offers a sense of relative comfort, shared purpose, and collective enthusiasm.

Aerobic dance was intentionally chosen as the physical activity for several reasons. These included the high degree of structure, which contributes to a sense of safety for the participants; the inclusion of pulse-taking, which teaches the participants to trust in their bodies over time as well as to honor direct feedback from their bodies; and the exclusion of any pairing or physical contact requirement, which allows each participant to work in her own protected physical and emotional space.

Additionally, sustained aerobic activity is known to release endorphins (that is, endogenous morphine) into the blood stream. These naturally occurring opioids, which assist the individual during trauma or painful injury, have anxiolytic, tranquilizing, and antidepressant properties and can reduce feelings of rage, aggression, paranoia, and inadequacy (Verebey, Volavka, & Clouet, 1978).

Endogenous opioids may be released under a variety of healthy and unhealthy circumstances. For survivors, the unhealthy circumstances may include sexual revictimization (Van der Kolk & Greenberg, 1987) and self-mutilation (Coid, Allolio, & Rees, 1983).

For some years now it has been generally observed that individuals with post-traumatic stress disorder, incest survivors among them, have a particular vulnerability for repeated abuse. It is now speculated that the biochemical changes that accompany post-traumatic stress disorder play a role in this vulnerability, and the opioids have been implicated due to their addictive qualities (Van der Kolk & Greenberg, 1987). The fact that self-mutilation can be halted by the use of drugs that block the release of these opioids (Richardson & Zaleski, 1983) would seem to confirm this suspected connection.

This should not be interpreted, however, to imply that survivors are putting themselves in danger or injuring themselves in order to "get high." The purpose of such behaviors is to relieve unbearably painful internal states. Inasmuch as such behaviors may result in the release of endorphins, they may successfully fulfill this purpose. Thus, the behaviors will be reinforced over time. This does not mean that the survivor should be viewed as an individual suffering from "an addiction." Rather, the "compulsive" quality of such behaviors should be viewed as a reflection of the reliable relief they provide and the absence of alternatives in the survivor's repertoire of self-soothing methods.

Unlike the immediate but short-lived sense of control the opioids produce with self-mutilation or sexual revictimization (Van der Kolk & Greenberg, 1987), the gradual release of endorphins during aerobic activity can contribute to a reduction in stress and a more lasting sense of well-being (Flannery, 1987). In its more heightened form, this sense of well-being may approximate what has commonly been referred to as "runner's high." Dr. Murray Allen of Canada's Simon Fraser University has suggested that the actual effect of sustained aerobic exercise would be better labeled "runner's calm," and indeed, this is more in keeping with the objectives of the aerobics program described here.

Another factor in choosing aerobic dance as the activity around which to develop a physical program was the built-in opportunity to incorporate the affective power of music. Women with incest histories, who may be skilled at "numbing" and other forms of dissociation, often experience difficulty accessing their feelings. Music can enable survivors to tap into feelings otherwise unavailable to them through the lyrical significance or emotional mood of particular songs. Some survivors, in fact, use the music from the I.R.*obics program without physical activity for this purpose.

The songs used for the I.R.*obics program, while not specifically written about sexual abuse (with the exception of one), were selected on the basis of meaningful themes and heightened affective quality. The music for the program moves from keeping the secret to disclosing the secret, feeling the sadness and anger, gaining perspective, self-acceptance, self-love, belonging, and faith. The songs are purposefully sequenced in this manner to empower the participants by mirroring the movement they seek to create in their lives as they recover from the incest.

As with any aerobics program, an appropriate warm-up, a minimum of 20 minutes of aerobic workout within the targeted heart rate zone, an appropriate cool-down, focused muscle strengthening (the abdominals in this instance), and final stretching are included. Varied aerobic dance routines suitable to the workout sequence and relevant to the tone and theme of each song were choreographed. Only dance/movement steps that could readily be modified down or up to allow women of all fitness levels to participate were incorporated. Special attention was given to including movements that would address body shame and postural problems and movements that would enhance the expression of anger in a safe, controlled, enjoyable manner. For example, a routine of kicks, shoves, punches, swings, and the like accompanies a song "dedicated" to the offender for its appropriate lyrics and tone.

An instructor who herself has an incest history is best equipped to "track onto" the incest in movement and in commentary so as to emotionally capitalize on each song; in addition, she provides an important role model for the participants. A survivor is also best able to relate to the feelings the participants experience about the incest and about their bodies during the program. These should be briefly shared in group fashion at the end of each session. This helps the participants make the transition back to present time, to a state of relatedness with others, and to a concurrent awareness of body and mind.

The I.R.*obics program takes approximately 80 minutes to complete, allowing for pulse checks and group discussion time. The music tape, which is 60 minutes long, is available from Incest Resources (see Appendix F). Female and male survivors have used the I.R.*obics tape for jogging, stationary bicycling, weight lifting, and fitness training in addition to aerobics.

Inside Out

Inside Out, Therapeutic Bodywork for Incest Survivors, is a program of exercises created in 1987 to help survivors focus on issues related to body hatred and devaluation, body estrangement, and body "ownership." The Inside Out program walks (talks) the survivor through seven different exercises aimed at increasing body connection, knowledge, and appreciation. Generally the exercises are carried out at home on an individual basis, but it is helpful to discuss reactions afterward, particularly in a group format if this is available.

The first half of the Inside Out series begins with a relaxation piece and moves into a body awareness exercise using chest, abdominal, and pelvic breathing combined with sensing of inner body dimension and space. Two exercises in recognizing body boundaries and limits follow, in which the participant observes the reactions in her body to a set of imagined situations.

The second half of the Inside Out series begins with an exploration piece in which the survivor identifies how her body is "housing" the offender, the nonoffending parent(s), and the incest emotions. An inner purification exercise follows, in which breathing and color imagery are used to cleanse and expel the incest. The series ends with a final body transformation piece based upon a spiritual connection with nature.

The exercises can be completed one at a time, in a half series manner as described, or in a full series manner. The Inside Out program tape, which is 45 minutes long, is available from Incest Resources (see Appendix F). It is appropriate for both female and male survivors.

Picture This!

Picture This!, Rage Release for Incest Survivors, is a program of exercises created in 1988 to help survivors direct their anger outward through physical activity. This program can be carried out individually or, with modifications, in a group.

In relation to sexuality, the Picture This! exercises may help to diminish survivor displacement of anger onto partners. When a concrete pictorial representation of the offender or the incest is used as a "target," anger is focused and directed where it belongs. Some women, in fact, have their partners join them in the exercises as their "ally," further differentiating the partner (on whom the anger has been displaced) from the offender.

Survivors who feel more frightened of their anger and those who have difficulty fantasizing harming the offender may use something as simple as a large piece of paper with the word "PERPETRATOR" or the word "INCEST" on it as the "target" or may use a symbolic representation of the incest, such as a drawing of a bedroom doorway or a set of cellar stairs. Survivors who are comfortable expressing their anger and who are able to maintain sufficient distance may use an actual photograph or sketch of the offender. If this seems too "personalized" or too "real," the survivor may use a representation that includes an object associated with the offender, for example, a magazine or catalogue clipping of a pair of men's work pants, a pipe, or a woman's apron.

Whatever representation is used as a "target," it should not include the survivor or suggest the survivor's presence. A drawing of the survivor's childhood bed, for example, would not be a good choice.

Photocopies of the representation are made on heavyweight paper to serve as the incest "pictures" in the exercises. The original is preserved for when additional copies are needed. Some survivors laminate their "pictures" for "more intense" rage release sessions.

The Picture This! exercises include a progressive series of safe, physical

activities in which the incest "pictures" are defaced, damaged, and destroyed. All six of the exercises utilize inexpensive "props" and materials
generally found in the home, for example, spices, the Yellow Pages, and ice
cubes. The exercises rely primarily (although not exclusively) on facial and
upper body movement and are adaptable for use by survivors with a variety
of physical disabilities. Each exercise can stand alone or be completed in
combination with others, depending upon how much time the survivor
wishes to spend. A formal "cool-out" and relaxation exercise is included to
end each session.

The Picture This! program packet, including written instructions for
each of the exercises, is available from Incest Resources (see Appendix F).
All exercises are appropriate for male as well as female survivors.

The development of these three physical programs for Incest Resources
was assisted by the author's self-help discoveries during her own years of
recovery as well as an undergraduate degree in health sciences. Health
educators could readily develop a number of exercise and activity programs
for women with incest histories. Particularly needed are prenatal and postpartum programs combining appropriate exercise, group discussion, and
support.

Participation in exercise and activity programs often promotes better
nutritional, sleep, and other lifestyle habits in individuals. These benefits
are important to consider for women with incest histories, whose tendency
may be to abuse or neglect the body in a variety of ways.

The Educational Component of Treatment

In addition to incorporating a physical component of treatment to primarily address body perception and/or the reproductive aspects of sexuality, an
educational component of treatment is advisable. The objectives of the
educational component would be to:

1. Reduce guilt and self-blame related to the incest experience.
2. Establish a sense of "normalcy" and appreciation regarding the
body and regarding sexual feelings and behaviors (as they exist among
women in general as well as among women with incest histories).
3. Correct "magical thinking."
4. Consider partner issues.
5. Provide reassurance.

Reducing Guilt and Self-Blame

The first objective of the educational component would probably best be met in a group environment. Perspective on the incest experience, particularly perspective on the responsibility of self and other(s) for the events of the past, is often gained only through the perception and validation of others. In a group situation, the nonblaming attitude women adopt toward the other group participants may extend to the self.

An exercise that is useful in reducing guilt and self-blame, and that is adaptable to a group or individual format, is the review of childhood photographs. Women can be questioned as to whether they found themselves "seductive," "provocative," or otherwise "deserving" or "inviting" of what happened to them. Women can be asked to describe their reactions and thoughts as they reviewed their photographs. This is an excellent way to connect women with their earlier selves, with their histories, and with their emotions. Images from childhood can be very powerful and may engender an appropriate sense of outrage. Such images may promote self-care, self-protection, and self-love.

A similar exercise is the observance of young children. For women who have no childhood photographs, this is a suitable substitute for the first exercise. For others, this may be used as an adjunct to the first exercise. Children should be observed who are the approximate age(s) that women were at the time of their abuse. Again, this can prove very powerful and may evoke self-protective and self-nurturing instincts and behaviors.

Another helpful exercise in reducing guilt and self-blame is the assignment of reading materials related to child sexuality. Women often do not know that physiological arousal is a natural response to sexual stimulation in all children, and that what was unusual in their instance was that the sexual stimulation was in the control of someone other than themselves. Women must be assisted in recognizing that they were initiated into sex prematurely by inappropriate, exploitive caregivers who renounced their responsibility to the child, and that the experience of positive physiological sensation during the incest does not alter that fact.

It is important to point out to women who report that they sought out the sexual contact for a period of time that this was in response to their premature initiation into sex and early sexual awakening. Appropriate, nonexploitive caregivers who had not abandoned their role would have taught them as children that such activity was not "socially acceptable," not "age-appropriate," not "safe," or whatever, and would have explored the meaning behind their behavior as children.

In a group situation, those women who are parents may be able to describe how their own children express their natural sexuality and how others respond in an appropriate fashion. Or reading materials may be used to demonstrate examples. In an individual format, similar description by the woman if she is a parent should be encouraged, or reading materials may be used, or the helping professional may share relevant observations about children. Several books on the development of child sexuality that might be used to generate discussion on this issue are listed in Appendix F.

Establishing a Sense of "Normalcy" and Appreciation

The second objective of the educational component, establishing a sense of "normalcy" and appreciation regarding the body and regarding sexual feelings and behaviors, also involves reading assignments and discussion. Some books to consider for this purpose are listed in Appendix F. It should be pointed out that the general population of women includes women with incest histories, and thus the reading assignments will include the voices of survivors, unidentified or otherwise. If women are specifically seeking information about sexuality in women with incest histories, they should be referred to Maltz and Holman (1987) or to this book.* It is helpful, however, for women with incest histories to read about sexuality among women in general. This assists survivors in recognizing that, although the meaning they may assign to feelings and behaviors related to sexuality may differ, their sexuality per se is not so very different from other women.

If discussion is to take place in a group format, the group should be limited to women with incest histories to provide a safe environment. The advantage of an all-survivor group format is that common patterns or themes related to sexuality emerge under such circumstances and may immediately alleviate feelings of "abnormality" and/or "inadequacy" related to the incest. If discussion within such a group cannot take place, a reading of Maltz and Holman (1987) or portions of this book might serve similarly.†

Exercises to consider in relation to establishing a sense of "normalcy" and appreciation regarding the body and regarding sexual feelings and behaviors might include selected steps from one of the self-help guides to masturbation and orgasm listed in Appendix F and/or exercises from one of the body books listed in Appendix F. The steps included in the self-help guides to orgasm are adaptable to orgasmic as well as nonorgasmic women for purposes other than the attainment of orgasm. The purpose of assign-

---

*Maltz (1991), released since this book was written, should also be referred to.
†Again, see Maltz (1991).

ing and the goal of carrying out any of these exercises should be to increase body acceptance and enjoyment over time. The body books listed in Appendix F describe a variety of exercises, many of which are applicable to establishing a sense of "normalcy" and appreciation regarding the body and some of which are applicable to establishing a sense of "normalcy" and appreciation regarding sexual feelings and behaviors.

Experiential assignments to be carried out individually at home should cover the following three areas:

1. Body exploration exercises, including full-body mirror work and genital mirror work.
2. Sensual awareness/self-nurturance exercises, including self-massage with soap during bathing and self-massage with oil or lotion.
3. Sexual awareness/"ownership" exercises, including self-stimulation without orgasm and self-stimulation with orgasm.

All of these exercises will gradually increase a woman's tolerance for attention on self, which can increase her comfort with partner attention during sensual or sexual activity.

In addition to assigning appropriate exercises, women should be instructed in the use of affirmations. These are positive statements about the self that are recited aloud or silently to counteract and reduce negative thoughts about the self. In this instance, affirmations would be self-appreciations related to the woman's body, her sexual feelings, or her sexual behaviors. These would be verbalized by the woman in front of a mirror. Women do not need to believe the statements for them to become effective, and this should be explained when the use of affirmations is assigned as an exercise. Always state the affirmation in the positive and always in the present tense.

Examples of such affirmations are:

1. I have a body.
2. I like my tummy.
3. I'm beautiful when I'm sexually aroused.
4. I deserve sexual pleasure.

Women should be assigned the task of developing their own personal set of affirmations to use and should share these with the group and/or the helping professional(s). They should also type up their affirmations and post them in a place at home where they will be seen daily to reinforce their use.

Correcting "Magical Thinking"

The third objective of the educational component is to correct "magical thinking." In some sense women with incest histories may continue as adults to believe in their own omnipotent power or the omnipotent power of others. Without awareness, women may be operating with a set of yet-to-be discarded beliefs from childhood. Such beliefs may include:

1. If I have a sexual thought or fantasy, I'll make it happen. (To a child, thinking and doing are often synonymous.)
2. If I have a sexual thought or fantasy, others will know. (To a child, adults appear to be able to read minds.)
3. S/he might "take over" my body. (As a child, others did, indeed, do just that.)
4. S/he might be "contaminated" by my "evilness." (As a child, the self—the "hollow inside" as perceived by the child—may have been "contaminated" by semen.)
5. If I feel sexual pleasure, I'll disintegrate or explode. (As a child, "disembodiment" or "disappearance" may have been experienced through dissociation.)

"Magical thinking" of this nature may interfere with sexuality in a number of ways, as previously described, and thus needs to be interrupted. Women may be unaware that all children demonstrate "magical thinking" and that there may be reasons related to the incest experience that such thinking has remained with them.

An exercise to consider in relation to correcting "magical thinking" is having the woman dialogue with the child within her about such beliefs. She should respond to the child's "magical thinking" with a clear statement that the belief is not really true, followed by an explanation of why it might appear to be so to the child. This encourages positive self-contact, self-reflection, and self-modification of thought processes.

Considering Partner Issues

The fourth objective of the educational component is to consider partner issues. This is an essential piece because most survivors experience their problems with sexuality in a relational context. Additionally, the routine focus on what partners are doing or not doing for survivors can totally overshadow the fact that survivors need to consider the same, in turn, if they are half of a couple. Assuming the survivor wishes to remain coupled, she will need to accept that the partner also has a set of feelings about the incest and about being victimized indirectly. She will need to develop some empathy for the partner, as well as look to the partner for this for herself.

The first step is for survivors to think about the phrase "victimized indirectly" in relation to their partner and the sexual relationship they have. The language may seem rather strong initially, but after exploring how the partner may be affected by the incest, most survivors can appreciate the phrase.

To fully explore partner issues, the following questions need to be asked:

1. Is your partner waiting?

Does your partner fear that you might never be sexual again? Do you verbally acknowledge and express understanding of that fear to your partner? Do you support your partner's masturbation and, more generally, your partner's sexuality? Is that support spoken? Do you share that you have sexual thoughts and feelings, at least, even if you can't act on them? Do you talk to your partner about what's going on inside you sexually and how your awareness of the impact of the incest is growing? Do you discuss how that awareness will ultimately help you both?

2. Is your partner feeling controlled?

Are you able to let your partner express resentment that the when and how and where of sex depend on you without personalizing it? If not, are you personalizing it because your partner is blaming you instead of the incest? How can you help your partner see that both of you are being controlled by the incest, and that you know how your partner feels? How can you also acknowledge that it is different for your partner (assuming s/he is not a survivor) because it is *your* history, not your partner's that is affecting both your sexual lives?

3. Is your partner feeling helpless?

How can your partner learn to tolerate being unable to "fix" things? How can you emphasize the ways in which your partner *is* effectual? What specific things does your partner say or do that actually help you sexually? How can you express appreciation so your partner will know these things really make a difference?

4. Is your partner feeling abandoned?

Are you more withdrawn physically than you need to be? How can you connect on an affectionate level with your partner? Can you go for a walk holding hands? Can you offer a hug now and again? What kinds of nonsexual exercises can you do together? What kinds of sensual touch can you engage in? How can you communicate your limits in advance so you will feel safe initiating physical contact? How can you take responsibility for preventing undesired kinds of touch?

5. Is your partner feeling angry?

Are you able to listen to your partner's frustration with your sexual relationship and depersonalize it? If not, are you personalizing it because your partner is expressing anger at you instead of at the incest or at the offender? What can you and your partner do together to physically release some of this anger and to direct it appropriately? Have you encouraged your partner to join (or start) a partner support group to create a space where these feelings can be freely ventilated? Can you appreciate your partner's isolation, lack of support, and lack of information in the midst of all that is available for survivors?

6. Is your partner feeling fed up with your relationship?

Can you understand your partner's wanting to quit the relationship? Can you hear your partner's feelings, knowing you can't "fix" the situation or do you expect to be spared at all times from feeling anxious or guilty about your partner? Can you relate to your partner's feelings of not wanting to have to work so hard at it? Do you recognize that your partner is really expected to be understanding and supportive all the time? Do you realize what an unrealistic ideal that is?

7. Is your partner feeling unloved?

How can you express your caring in nonsexual ways? Do you ever bring small presents to your partner like flowers or a favorite pastry? Do you ever leave cards or notes for your partner? Do you ever plan a romantic meal or offer to do a bothersome errand for your partner? Do you verbally compliment your partner on looking nice, having a fit or comfortable body, being sexually attractive to you?

8. Is your partner feeling sexually inadequate?

Do you tell your partner what you want and need sexually? Do you express your needs and wants as requests rather than as demands? Do you try to be as consistent as you can about your sexual limits? Do you try to be sensitive if you need to stop sexual activity? Do you alter your partner's touch rather than pulling away abruptly or pushing your partner away? Do you provide alternative ideas for sexual giving or receiving when you need to say "no" to something?

9. Is your partner feeling guilty?

Do you identify your partner with the offender because your partner wants sex? Do you make your partner feel bad for expressing sexual desire? How can you convey that you accept having your partner feel differently about sex than you do? How can you communicate that you understand your partner's dissatisfaction with what you offer instead of sex? Would it help to consider that sex for your partner may be equivalent to talk for you? Would it help to consider how you would feel if your partner couldn't talk to you and didn't know when s/he would be able to? Would it help to consider how you would feel if your partner offered to have sex to compensate for being unable to talk?

10. Is your partner feeling uncertain that you're trying?

Do you share how you're working on your sexuality? Are your struggles visible to your partner? Can your partner see ways that you are being active rather than avoidant about your sexuality? If not, *are* you being avoidant? Do you accept that you cannot always escape discomfort around your sexuality? Do you continue to talk about "not feeling safe" when the issue is really one of not feeling comfortable? In concrete terms, how are you challenging yourself? How can your partner see that you are committed to improving your sexual relationship? What changes have taken place in the past six months, the past year, the past 18 months that you can talk about together?

The final series of questions included in item 10 are the most confrontive and therefore the most difficult to address. They require the survivor to be honest with herself in acknowledging negative contributions she may be bringing to the sexual relationship. Before exploring these particular questions it must be emphasized that they are not intended to blame the survivor, nor are they intended to demand that she change her behavior. Whatever avoidance may be present is understandable, but it does represent a major block to reworking sexuality. As such, avoidance is important for the survivor to identify. If she is unable to change the avoidance, she will nonetheless have gained a new perspective on her relationship with her partner. She will be less likely to blame her partner unfairly for the status of the relationship, and she may develop a more compassionate, less angry view of her partner.

After these questions are fully explored, a written list of actions the survivor can take to address her particular set of partner issues should be constructed. This list should be posted in abbreviated form where the survivor will see it daily. A commitment to carry out at least one action per day should be made, and the survivor should evaluate herself on a weekly basis. The number of actions carried out daily can be increased over time, and the partner can be made aware of these conscious efforts by the survivor.

An action-oriented approach to partner issues can reduce feelings of helplessness and hopelessness experienced by both the survivor and the partner. If resistance to "caretaking" the partner in this way is present, it is important to determine whether this is due to displaced anger that belongs to the offender or to resentment over an existing imbalance of nurturing in the relationship. In the first instance, "separations" (of past/present and offender/partner) and interruptions of misdirected anger can be achieved through the development and use of appropriate cognitive statements (described in Chapter 10) and through joint (survivor/partner) participation in the Picture This! rage release exercises (described earlier in this chapter). In the second instance, the partner can be assisted in constructing a list of actions to be taken daily, as with the survivor. It would be important, however, to first examine how the imbalance of nurturing in the relationship had developed and been maintained.

It is not uncommon for survivors to ask for nothing and to then be angry when they get nothing in return. Some survivors don't know what they need because they haven't given any thought to themselves or don't know how to go about figuring this out. Other survivors know what they need, but don't want to have to ask for it. They expect others to pick up on nonverbal cues or behavioral hints, and they feel they shouldn't have to "spell it out." Still other survivors know what they need, and expect others to know also. They anticipate and fulfill the needs of others and look for the same in return. They feel that, if they have to ask for something, it "just isn't worth it."

All of these attitudes may have roots in the survivor's experience within the incestuous family. In the first situation (not knowing what one needs) can be seen a reflection of the self-sacrifice encouraged by the family (even at the expense of the survivor's development). In the second situation (not wanting to have to say) can be seen a reflection of the wish to be spared from the shame and vulnerability associated with revealing the incest (by having someone guess). In the third situation (knowing and expecting oth-

s to know) can be seen a reflection of the survivor's childhood role of
edicting and satisfying the emotional needs of the offender (for the
nefit of a family that remained unknowing and thankless). Since the
rvivor's experience of giving and receiving is so imbalanced in the origi-
l family, it is important to examine how she may be contributing to
rrent imbalances in the partner relationship.

None of this is to imply that the partner's contributions should not be
imined as well. Clearly they should, but the emphasis in this piece of the
educational work is on identifying what is directly under the survivor's
control to alter or assess differently in relation to her partner.

Providing Reassurance

The fifth and final objective of the educational component is to provide
reassurance. This is accomplished primarily through the conveyance of
knowledge regarding the incest experience and the healing process. Examples of the type of reassurances that might be necessary are:

1. Reassurance that "negative" fantasies and flashbacks related to the
incest or to the offender will diminish and likely disappear as the
incest is worked on, but often first become more active.
2. Reassurance that the flashbacks that often accompany newly established sobriety will become less "intense" and will recede over
time.
3. Reassurance that body sensations including gagging, constriction
of the throat, difficulty breathing, nausea, vomiting, lower abdominal
cramping, urinary immediacy, genital numbness, and vaginal and/or
anal pain that may not be medically understood are sometimes experienced as the incest is worked on. In the absence of clear memories,
these body sensations may provide clues as to the nature of the
incestuous abuse that occurred. Reframing these as body memories
(when no medical explanation can be provided) is important to the
survivor's healing process.
4. Reassurance that gynecological and reproductive dysfunctions
and disorders that may not be medically understood are sometimes
experienced as the incest is worked on. These can be treated sympto-
matically in the same manner that other not fully understood medical
conditions are treated.
5. Reassurance that a period of discomforting hypersexuality and/or
compulsive masturbation frequently accompanies the reworking of
the incest but generally is not lasting.

6. Reassurance that a period of sexual aversion and/or total loss of sexual desire frequently accompanies the reworking of the incest but generally is not lasting.

7. Reassurance that confusion regarding sexual preference often accompanies the resolution of incest issues.

8. Reassurance that *nobody* knows the why of one's sexual preference.

Discussion among women with incest histories who are at varying stages in their recovery process is most helpful in terms of fulfilling this objective. Participation in self-help discussion groups for women with incest histories, such as those developed by Incest Resources, should be encouraged to address this aspect of the educational component. Where such support groups are not available, survivors may be interested in creating their own. A useful training/preparation manual for this purpose is *Starting from Scratch: The I.R.* * *Group Model*, which is available from Incest Resources (see Appendix F).

Integration of Treatment Components

The manner in which the physical and educational components of treatment outlined here are combined with the cognitive and behavioral components of treatment described in Chapter 10 depends upon a number of factors. The needs of women with incest histories relative to these components may vary widely. While the feelings associated with the incest experience and the issues arising from the incest experience may often be similar, responses to those feelings and issues in terms of adult sexuality may be highly individual and complex. Additionally, the treatment resources of women may vary. One woman may be engaged in individual therapy, group therapy, and periodic self-help workshops. Another woman may attend only a monthly drop-in discussion group for women with incest histories and periodically share her problems with a female physician she trusts. The components discussed here may thus be integrated very differently depending upon the system of services available to any given woman. Many of the treatment ideas described here and in Chapter 10 are, however, appropriate for use by a variety of helping professionals and many techniques may be self-taught.

EPILOGUE

THE FINDINGS OF THIS STUDY testify to the power and complexity of the incest experience and the long-term nature of its effects. Clearly, in the realm of adult sexuality the effects of incest may be quite pronounced.

It was the intent of this study to offer an integrated and complete description of the manner in which the development and expression of sexuality in women with incest histories might be altered by their childhood sexual experiences. The information generously provided by the participants of the study will enhance our knowledge and enrich our understanding of women with incest histories. Keeping in mind the unrepresentative nature of the sample, and noting the very deliberate use of the word "may," the findings of the study related to adult sexuality can be summarized as follows:

Body perception may be influenced by the incest experience. Negative and/ or distorted body perception, body hatred and/or devaluation, estrangement from the body including detachment and/or dissociation, and false convictions of physical abnormality and/or ugliness may be attributable to the incest experience. Attitudes toward fitness, illness, and gender identity may be affected. Body perception may be influenced by feelings of guilt, shame, fear, anger, and confusion that are associated with the incest experience. Significant issues arising from the incest that may have an impact on body perception are trust, control, power, and self-esteem.

Reproduction may be influenced by the incest experience. An intolerance for reproductive dysfunction, negative and/or distorted self-perceptions related to reproduction and/or parenting capacity, and interference with the joys of pregnancy, birth, and nursing in women with incest histories may be attributable to the incest experience. Reproduction may be influenced by feelings of fear, shame, and confusion that are associated with the incest. Significant issues arising from the incest that may have an impact on reproduction are control, self-esteem, and trust.

Sexual preference may be influenced by the incest experience. Sexual preference in women with incest histories may, in some instances, be associated with the incest. The data from the study reported on in this book specifically suggest that women who are celibate or undecided may be likely to attribute their sexual preference to fear or control issues related to the incest. The data from the study do not suggest that women with confirmed heterosexual, lesbian, or bisexual identities may be likely to attribute their preference to the incest. The study further suggests that confusion over sexual preference may be experienced by a substantial minority of incest survivors. Women with incest histories of all sexual preferences may experience self-doubts over their preference and may anticipate that others will automatically attribute their choice to trauma. The double stigmatization of an incest history and a societally devalued sexual preference may discourage women with incest histories who are not heterosexual from declaring their sexual preference for a period of time.

Sexual "lifestyle" may be influenced by the incest experience. A variety of sexual "lifestyles" may be adopted by women with incest histories including "lifestyles" predominated by aversion, inhibition, and compulsion. The data from this study suggest that in later adulthood sexual "lifestyles" predominated by inhibition may be more common than "lifestyles" predominated by compulsion or aversion. "Lifestyle" changes or a pattern of alternation between "lifestyles" over time may be common among women with incest histories. Feelings of fear, shame, anger, guilt, and confusion that are associated with the incest experience may encourage the adoption of particular "lifestyles," including celibacy, "promiscuity," and prostitution. The data from the study suggest that a period of "promiscuity" may be rather common among women with incest histories, but that a period of celibacy may be even more common. The study further suggests that prostitution may be relatively uncommon as a "lifestyle" among women with incest histories. "The split," the nonintegration of emotional intimacy and sexual intimacy attributed by some women to the incest experience, may encourage "promiscuity," inhibition, or compulsion. Significant issues arising from the incest that may have an impact on sexual "lifestyle" are self-esteem, power, control, and trust.

Sexual functioning may be influenced by the incest experience. An absence of sexual fantasy, desire, arousal, and/or orgasm in women with incest histories may be attributable to the incest experience. The data from the study reported on in this book suggest that an absence of arousal may be more common than an absence of sexual desire and much more common than an absence of orgasm. Interference with sexual fantasy, desire, arousal, and/or orgasm in women with incest histories may also be attributable to the incest experience. Again, the data from the study suggest that arousal may be most commonly affected, followed by difficulties with desire and orgasm. "The split," the nonintegration of emotional intimacy and sexual intimacy attributed by some women to the incest experience, may influence sexual desire, arousal, and/or orgasm. Orgasm may occur in women with incest histories in the absence of felt desire and/or arousal, and orgasm may be experienced by women with incest histories as nongratifying. The study suggests that it may be more common for several aspects of sexual functioning to be affected than one discrete area. An unexpected suggestion from the study is that vaginismus and dyspareunia may be more commonly experienced by women with incest histories than previous reports would indicate. Sexual functioning may be influenced by feelings of fear, shame, guilt, anger, and confusion that are associated with the incest experience. Significant issues arising from the incest that may have an impact on sexual functioning are control, power, trust, and self-esteem.

The data suggest that of the five aspects of adult sexuality that may be influenced by the incest, sexual functioning may be most commonly influenced and sexual preference may be least commonly influenced.

Briefly, the clinical implications of these findings are:

1. That helping professionals in a variety of fields need to be knowledgeable about the effects of the incest experience on adult sexuality in females.
2. That traditional sex therapy needs to be substantially modified to be generally appropriate and effective with women with incest histories.
3. That psychotherapists working with women with incest histories focusing on their sexuality need to be well-versed in the practice of cognitive and behavioral therapy techniques.
4. That psychotherapists working with women with incest histories

focusing on their sexuality need to familiarize themselves with educational resources related to sexuality and with exercise/movement programs available in their area to clients.

5. That led group, facilitated group, and self-help group resources need to be significantly expanded to best meet the treatment needs of women with incest histories.

6. That more comprehensive group treatment models need to be developed to best meet the treatment needs of women with incest histories.

7. That self-help is an important element in the treatment of sexuality in women with incest histories and should be encouraged and supported.

The willingness and openness with which the study participants approached the sensitive topic of sexuality speaks to the significance of sexuality as an issue for women with incest histories. It is also a testimony to the impressive strengths that women with incest histories, individually and collectively, so often bring to their own healing. It is my hope that women with incest histories will derive both direct and indirect benefits from this book, for their life experience is my life experience but for the details, and I would wish each one the resolution and recovery I have been blessed with.

APPENDIX A

Methodology

AN OVERVIEW OF THE STUDY on which this book is based is presented to all readers in Chapter 2. This appendix is intended to provide interested readers with a detailed description of how the study was designed and carried out. It is also intended to educate readers unfamiliar with qualitative research about the nature and purpose of exploratory phenomenological study and how it differs from quantitative research.

Qualitative and Phenomenological Research

Qualitative research is concerned with understanding a given phenomenon from the subject's own perspective. The main focus of the phenomenological approach is the individual's subjective reality (Lofland, 1971; Patton, 1980; Taylor & Bogdan, 1984). Qualitative research methods enable us to enter and explore the inner world of the individual, and allow us to describe individual experience in depth.

> When we study people qualitatively, we get to know them personally and experience what they experience in their daily struggles in society. We learn about concepts such as beauty, pain, faith, suffering, frustration, and love whose essence is lost through other research approaches. (Taylor & Bogdan, 1984, p.7)

Since the personal meaning given to experience is of primary interest, qualitative research methods do not involve the formulation of precise research hypotheses. No assumptions are made in advance about linear or correlative relationships among variables. The qualitative methodologist does not presuppose what the important dimensions will be, but allows these (and their multiple interrelationships) to emerge from the data.

Although qualitative research makes no attempt to provide statistically valid statements pertaining to a given phenomenon, it does attempt to provide a clear conceptualization of the organizing patterns among a group of participants. This expanded context or structure enlarges the rich and varied specifics of each individual experience and produces greater understanding.

There are several reasons why a qualitative approach was considered most appropriate for this study:

1. Quantitative data could not adequately capture the complexities of the incest experience and its felt influence on adult sexuality. The need for descriptive, exploratory research was evident.
2. With newly emerging research areas, the research method of choice is qualitative. Sexuality in women with incest histories has not been sufficiently explored to allow for the specification of variables required in quantitative research.
3. Quantitative research with women with incest histories is in some respects impractical. Due to the stigma and shame associated with incest, the population is an "invisible" one, thus impossible to sample systematically.
4. With areas of investigation as shrouded in myth as incest and sexuality, it is essential to approach the individuals to be studied as the experts. Qualitative research allows the subjects to identify the variables, thus encouraging greater discovery.
5. Qualitative methods particularly suit the author as a researcher. As an experienced clinician and interviewer, the author's skills and "style" are compatible with qualitative methods. Thus, a qualitative approach in this instance best utilized the personal resources the author brought to the work.
6. Therapeutic potential for the subjects was also a consideration. A qualitative approach increased the benefit for the subject in terms of the "trade" between researcher and subject. A woman with an incest history is rarely asked to tell her story or to discuss her sexuality, let alone invited to explore and express related feelings. Because most women with incest histories maintain silence for many years, speaking about their lives is often experienced as both healing and empowering.

Sampling

As is often the case in exploratory research, the selection procedures for this study were based on purposive rather than random sampling (Mayer & Greenwood, 1980). No attempt was made to obtain a representative sample of women with incest histories willing to discuss their adult sexuality in depth. Rather, the limitations of a nonrepresentative sample (discussed in Chapter 2 in the "Limitations" section) were accepted.

Likewise, no attempt was made to obtain a large sample. Since the intent of qualitative study is to inquire about the properties of a given phenomenon, not the distribution of those properties, sample size is a relatively unimportant matter in exploratory research (Mayer & Greenwood, 1980). In this particular study the samples were purposefully limited so as to provide sufficient data to undergo in-depth analysis without the research becoming unmanageable, prohibitively time-consuming, or less focused than desired. This was in keeping with the objective of the research, which was, as with all qualitative research, to present "the vividness of 'what it is like' with an appropriate degree of economy and clarity" (Lofland, 1971, p.7).

Data Collection

Questionnaire participants were recruited from the self-help support groups facilitated by Incest Resources in Cambridge, Massachusetts during 1985. Prior to group meetings the author introduced herself, announced the study, provided the rationale for the study, assured confidentiality, and provided all volunteers with a letter of introduction and a statement of informed consent. As a precaution the consent form did not include language which revealed that the signatory had an incest history.

Following group meetings the number-coded informed consent was signed by the volunteer, presented to the author, and exchanged for a matching number-coded questionnaire (Appendix B). The construction and testing of the questionnaire are discussed in Chapter 2 under "The Questionnaire." Matched coding assured anonymity while allowing the author to construct a master list.

Included with the questionnaire was a tear-off on which the subject indicated (after completing the questionnaire) whether or not she was also willing to participate in an interview. Also included were two self-addressed, stamped envelopes, one for return of the questionnaire and the other for return of the tear-off. This precaution ensured that the subject's telephone number was kept physically separate from the highly revealing questionnaire responses in the event that materials fell into inappropriate hands prior to return. Unreturned questionnaires were followed up on through the use of the master list, and requests for return were made by mail at four-week and eight-week intervals.

Ten women were selected as interview subjects from among the questionnaire respondents who volunteered to be interviewed. Women were contacted by telephone to arrange an interview time. An interview place that was convenient and perceived as "safe" by the subject was agreed upon. In two instances this was the Cambridge Women's Center, in five instances the subject's home, and in three instances the author's office.

The interview began with a brief review of the purpose of the study and an expression of appreciation for the subject's willingness to participate. The subject's right to control her participation in the study was discussed and the safeguards to confidentiality built into the study were elaborated. Each participant was asked to choose a pseudonym of meaning to her. This initial discussion provided an opportunity for the author to establish rapport and for the participant to be put at ease.

Permission to use a tape recorder was requested following an explanation of the purpose of this procedure. Assurances were provided to the participant that the recorder could be stopped at any time, that the tape would be listened to only by the author (and by a transcriber other than the author, if agreed upon), and that the tape would be erased by the author or given to the participant, if preferred, after transcription. A separate statement of informed consent for the interview was read and signed.

The author conducted the interview in an open-ended style, initiating discussion with a single interview question (Appendix C). The design of the "focused interview" question is discussed in Chapter 2 under "The Interviews." Areas of inquiry identified by analysis of the questionnaire responses were covered using a prepared interview guide (Appendix D). The construction of the "focused interview" guide is also discussed in Chapter 2 under "The Interviews." Pertinent areas to cover in each interview were highlighted on the guide in advance, individualizing the guide for each interview. During the interview, brief note-taking (on the guide) was used for the purpose of keeping track of what had been discussed and what remained to be discussed. Areas not addressed in the interviewer's spontaneous response were inquired after, and the interview ended when the respondent had nothing further to report in the identified areas.

A discussion of the participant's feelings regarding the interview experience and an expression of appreciation for the participant concluded each interview. An assurance that the author would be accessible to participants and would offer appropriate referrals for psychotherapy if needed or desired was provided. After the interview the author immediately wrote process notes in an interview journal to record impressions and observations.

Data Analysis

The material to be analyzed included the data from the questionnaires and from the interviews. The open-ended data from the questionnaires underwent qualitative analysis with three objectives in mind. The first was to identify emerging patterns and themes. The second was to establish the range of variation within the respondent group with respect to sexuality, in part for the purpose of planning the interviews. The third objective was to generate an interview guide based upon the questionnaire responses.

Analysis was an ongoing reflective process beginning with receipt of the first completed questionnaire. Interviews were informally analyzed and organized throughout the period during which they were conducted. Insight and understanding gained from each stage of the research were integrated into subsequent stages and analysis was continually refined.

Analysis of the open-ended portions of the questionnaire was based upon an adaption of the method of qualitative analysis described by Lofland (1971). Themes identified in the analysis of the questionnaires were those apparent in the statements of the respondents.

> Participants under study are themselves analytic. They order and pattern their views and their activities. . . . In order to capture the participants "in their own terms" one must learn their analytic ordering of the world, their categories for rendering explicable and coherent the flux of raw reality. That, indeed, is the first principle of qualitative analysis. (Lofland, 1971, p.7)

Participant statements were first coded by theme within each questionnaire and then catalogued in file folders by category. For example, a statement might be coded "F" for fear and be catalogued in the file folder for the category "Reproduction." A second statement might be coded "G" for guilt and be catalogued in the file folder for "Sexual Functioning." A third statement might be coded "A" for anger and be catalogued under "Sexual Lifestyle." Subcategories emerged as materials in each category file were reviewed. For example, the "Sexual Lifestyle" folder might be found to include statements pertaining to the theme of anger and the lifestyle subcategory of "promiscuity," the theme of fear and the lifestyle subcategory of "celibacy," the theme of trust and the lifestyle subcategory of inhibition, the theme of power and the lifestyle subcategory of compulsion, and so forth.

Analysis of the data from the transcribed interviews was based upon an adaptation of the method of thematic analysis described by Taylor and Bogdan (1984). This involved a series of steps aimed at identifying, labeling, and interpreting significant themes. The steps were as follows:

1. Transcripts were re-read and compared with initial impressions and observations recorded in the interview journal. The author remained open and receptive to newly emerging themes.

2. A code and highlighter color were assigned to each theme discovered in the interview data. For example, the code for shame was "S" and the highlighter color was yellow; the code for self-esteem was "SE" and the highlighter color was pink.

3. Each participant's important statements were catalogued by theme by recording the code in the transcript margin and by highlighting in the appropriate color.

4. The material was analyzed on the basis of the major and minor themes that emerged. Commonalities and differences among the participants were visually revealed by color predominance.

5. Themes were synthesized and organized into a larger pattern and structure that included all interviews.

As a reliability check on the analysis of the data, a colleague from Incest Resources who has an incest history and a colleague from outside Incest Resources who does not have an incest history but who has expertise in the area each read five transcripts selected at random. They then reported independently on the themes and subthemes they felt were significant within and across the interviews. This served to confirm or disconfirm the author's identification and interpretation of themes. A summary of the salient themes from the analysis of the interview data is provided in Table 9 (Appendix E). The narratives on the interview participants appear in Chapters 7, 8, and 9.

Reflections on the Methodology

The thoroughness of the responses to the questionnaire seemed to indicate that items were generally pertinent and clear, and that respondents were comfortable with the language used. Several respondents spontaneously commented on the "relevance" or "importance" of the questionnaire items, and several others expressed appreciation for the "thoughtfulness" and "sensitivity" they felt went into the questionnaire. This underscored the importance of having refined and revised the instrument after testing. Of course, in use with other populations of women with incest histories, the language in the questionnaire might well need to be altered to reflect the particular locale or community and its values.

It would seem that the "cues" used on the questionnaire (as described in Chapter 2) were also generally appropriate and meaningful, since the very same words were regularly used by the respondents in the open-ended portions of the questionnaire. It remains essential, however, to question the reliability and validity of the instrument, given that it was developed specifically for this study and has not been otherwise used.

As with the questionnaire participants, the interview participants spoke about their incest history and their adult sexuality without apparent censorship. It was generally agreed among the participants that the author's gender, the author's identity as a women with an incest history, and the participants' prior knowledge of the author's "mind set" (via the incest survivor community or previous publications) all contributed to a sense of safety that permitted a high level of disclosure. Illustrative comments by the interview participants included:

I could never imagine this interview with a man — oh, God, never! No! No! And if it had been with a woman who wasn't a survivor I would have written a little paper for her — aloud. I would have done a presentation and tried to educate her and given her little symptom categories and done a lot more clever interpretation. And I wouldn't have talked about the prostitution and I would have been extremely careful how I conceptualized my positive feelings for my uncle.

I'd have to know someone was really sincere in trying to do something for incest survivors to interview with them. It definitely made a difference that you're an incest survivor and that you've been around working on this, that you didn't just pop out of a void. I think just having that little bit of history, just knowing that you're an incest survivor, says a lot to me. It's like being an alcoholic. Alcoholics don't have to go over each other's history to know where they've been. And it's the same way with incest survivors.

To do an interview like this it would have to be with someone like you, someone who really knew. And I'd have to know that they looked at incest from a certain perspective. I've read things that you've written so I know enough about you and your thinking that I can trust you.

These and other comments by the interview participants underscored the advantageous aspects of the author's own life history and unique position in the incest survivor community.

There were, of course, related disadvantages as well. While the author's training as a psychologist was consciously enlisted to try to minimize the influence of her own frame of reference, as Giorgi (1970) states:

Once the data are obtained they are organized, interpreted, and written up according to the researcher's view of the situation. The major protection against bias is for the viewpoint itself to be made explicit, so that its validity may be circumscribed. (p. 189)

The author's own subjective experience of incest and her feminist orientation of necessity affected objectivity and influenced the documentation of the participants' experiences. Although care was exercised to avoid bias due to overfamiliarity and overidentification, this was inevitable. "It is impossible to avoid one's own commitments and biases. . . . Data are never self-explanatory. All researchers draw on their own theoretical assumptions and cultural knowledge to make sense out of their data" (Taylor & Bogdan, 1984, p. 142).

Given the potential for bias, the utilization of colleagues to provide a reliability check on the analysis of the data seemed essential. As differences were not observed between colleagues and were not observed between the author and either colleague, the reader can have somewhat greater confidence in the author's identification and interpretation of themes.

Several limitations related to the methodology should be mentioned here (in addition to the sample limitations discussed in Chapter 2), although all were apparent at the outset of the study and were accepted as such. First of all, the retrospective design of the study is a limitation. Memories that have undergone possible repression and retrieval as well as cognitive and affective processing over a period of many years may contribute to distortions of reporting. While such distortions constitute unintentional misrepresentation of "the facts," which must be accepted when we seek the respondent's phenomenology, they can be problematic. All self-report is in some sense "suspect," and only deliberate misrepresentation and omission can, in fact, be hopefully avoided. This was attempted in the study through careful construction of the questionnaire and through rapport in the interviews.

Secondly, this study is one of perception. Healing from the incest experience is a continually evolving process, as is a woman's sexuality. Perceptions can be ever-changing as individuals continue to grow, and thus studies of perception are always limited.

Finally, nothing was "proved" or "disproved" by this qualitative research. While this is true, by design, of all exploratory research, this, too, can be considered a limitation of the study.

APPENDIX B

Westerlund Incest Survivors Questionnaire

Date: _____

1. Questionnaire number _____

2. Age _____

3. Race _____

4. Ethnic background _____

5. Socioeconomic background of childhood family _____
   (working class, middle class, upper class)

6. Occupation of major breadwinner in childhood family _____

7. Religious affiliation of childhood family (if any) _____
   Practicing _____   Nonpracticing _____

8. Number of children in childhood family _____
   Age(s) of male(s) _____   Age(s) of female(s) _____

9. Position by age among children in childhood family
   (eldest, second eldest, etc.) _____

10. Present education (highest year completed) _____

INCEST SURVIVORS QUESTIONNAIRE

11. Present occupation _____

12. Present socioeconomic status _____
    (working class, middle class, upper class)

13. Present religious affiliation (if any) _____
    Practicing _____   Nonpracticing _____

14. Sexual preference (check one)
    Bisexual _____   Heterosexual _____   Lesbian _____
    Undecided _____   Celibate _____

15. Relationship status (check one)
    None _____   No current significant involvement _____
    Current significant involvement _____   Living with a partner _____
    Living with a life partner _____

16. Number of children _____
    Age(s) of male(s) _____   Age(s) of female(s) _____

17. Have you always remembered the sexual abuse?

    If no,

    a. At what age(s) did you recover your memories?

    b. What do you believe stimulated your memories to resurface?

    c. What do you believe assisted and encouraged the retrieval process?

    d. Please describe the progression of steps involved in recovering your memories.

Please answer the following questions to the best of your knowledge. If there is anything you cannot recall or anything that is not applicable to you due to sexual preference, please indicate this.

18. What ages were you when the sexual abuse began and when it ended?

19. What was the relationship of the offender(s) to you and what was the age difference between you?

20. Did the offender(s) use particular forms of coercion either to engage in sexual activity with you or to keep you silent? (Please specify which.)

    If yes, please describe under the appropriate choice(s).

    a. Force:

    b. Threat of force:

  c. Administration of drugs and/or alcohol:

  d. Bribes:

  e. Pressure:

  f. Threat of consequences to other family members:

  g. Threat of loss of love:

  h. Other:

21. Describe the offender(s).

  a. Personality:

  b. Coping methods:

  c. Alcohol abuse/drug abuse/other excesses:

  d. Attitude expressed in the home toward sex:

  e. History of having been emotionally, physically, and/or sexually abused (if yes, please specify which; if not known, please write "not known"):

  f. Adequacies and inadequacies:

  g. Health:

  h. Education:

  i. Occupation(s)/work history:

  j. Religious affiliation/religious practices:

  k. Social skills:

  l. Values:

  m. Features you liked and disliked:

  n. If deceased, time and circumstances of death:

  o. Other comments:

22. What factors do you feel played a role in that person's (s') sexually abusive behavior toward you?

23. What kinds of sexual acts did the offender(s) engage in with you? Please describe fully in your own words under the appropriate choice(s).

  a. Sexual activity not involving direct physical contact:

  b. Kissing and/or fondling:

  c. Manipulation of male and/or female genitalia:

  d. Oral-genital contact:

e. Simulated intercourse:

f. Vaginal intercourse:

g. Anal intercourse:

h. Other:

24. How often did the offender(s) engage in sexual acts with you? Please describe under as many choices as necessary to include variation based on differing sexual acts.

a. Once:

b. Several times a year:

c. Monthly:

d. Weekly:

e. Daily:

f. Other:

25. Did the offender(s) involve you in more "public" forms of sexual activity?

If yes, please describe under the appropriate choice(s).

a. Child pornography:

b. Prostitution:

c. "Swinging"/"swapping":

d. Cult or Satanic rituals:

e. Group sex:

f. Other:

26. Did the offender(s) involve you in sexual acts with animals?

If yes, please describe.

27. Did the offender(s) engage in sadistic sexual acts with you?

If yes, please describe.

28. Did the offender(s) impregnate you?

If yes, what was the outcome?

29. During the sexual acts what did you *do*?

30. During the sexual acts what did you *think*?

31. During the sexual acts what did you *feel*?

32. During the sexual acts how often did you experience physical arousal? Please describe under as many choices as necessary to include variation based on differing circumstances.

    a. Never:

    b. Rarely:

    c. Occasionally:

    d. Usually:

    e. Always:

    f. Other:

33. What feelings did you experience in relation to physical arousal? Please describe under the appropriate choice(s). (If you never experienced physical arousal, please write "not applicable.")

    a. Disgust:

    b. Shame:

    c. Fear:

    d. Guilt:

    e. Confusion:

    f. Acceptance:

    g. Pleasure:

    h. Other:

34. During the sexual acts how often did you experience orgasm? Please describe under as many choices as necessary to include variation based on differing circumstances.

    a. Never:

    b. Rarely:

    c. Occasionally:

    d. Usually:

    e. Always:

    f. Other:

35. What feelings did you experience in relation to orgasm? Please describe under the appropriate choice(s). (If you never experienced orgasm, please write "not applicable.")

    a.   Disgust:

    b.   Shame:

    c.   Fear:

    d.   Guilt:

    e.   Confusion:

    f.   Acceptance:

    g.   Pleasure:

    h.   Other:

36. Did you adopt particular coping mechanisms during the sexual acts?

If yes, please describe under the appropriate choice(s).

    a.   Pretended to be asleep:

    b.   Pretended to be waking up:

    c.   Fixed my mind on something else:

    d.   Went numb physically:

    e.   Detached myself emotionally:

    f.   Left my body:

    g.   Observed myself from nearby:

    h.   Other:

37. After the sexual abuse what did you *do?*

38. After the sexual abuse what did you *think?*

39. After the sexual abuse what did you *feel?*

40. Following the abuse did you experience changes in your sleep habits?

If yes, please describe under the appropriate choice(s).

    a.   Difficulty falling asleep:

    b.   Difficulty staying asleep:

   c. Sleeping more often:

   d. Nightmares:

   e. Night terrors:

   f. Sleepwalking:

   g. Nocturnal bedwetting:

   h. Other:

41. Following the abuse did you experience changes in your eating habits?

    If yes, please describe under the appropriate choice(s).

       a. Loss of appetite:

       b. Increased appetite:

       c. Less frequent eating:

       d. More frequent eating:

       e. Change in food preferences:

       f. Weight loss:

       g. Weight gain:

       h. Other:

42. Following the abuse did you experience bodily changes?

    If yes, please describe under the appropriate choice(s).

       a. More frequent illness:

       b. Sensitivity to cold:

       c. Frequent nausea/vomiting/stomachaches:

       d. Gagging/constriction of the throat/sore throats:

       e. Frequent urination:

       f. Headaches:

       g. Backaches:

       h. Other:

43. Following the abuse did you experience changes in your mood?

    If yes, please describe under the appropriate choice(s).

   a. Tearfulness/frequent crying:

   b. Irritability/temper outbursts:

   c. Increased energy level:

   d. Decreased energy level:

   e. Nervousness/apprehension:

   f. Vigilance/easy startle response:

   g. Emotional numbness:

   h. Other:

44. Following the abuse did you experience changes in your behavior?

    If yes, please describe under the appropriate choice(s).

    a. Changes in behavior related to school activities:

    b. Changes in behavior related to job activities:

    c. Changes in behavior related to social activities:

    d. Changes in behavior related to family activities:

    e. Changes in behavior related to religious activities:

    f. Changes in behavior related to sexual activities:

    g. Changes in behavior related to others' property rights:

    h. Other:

45. Following the abuse did you experience changes in your usual style of interacting with and relating to peers, children younger or older than yourself, family members, teachers, others?

    If yes, please describe.

46. As a child and/or adolescent, how did you explain the sexual abuse to yourself and try to make "sense" out of what had happened to you?

47. Did you adopt particular coping mechanisms over time to deal with the sexual abuse?

    If yes, please describe under the appropriate choice(s).

    a. Blocked out some or all of the memories:

    b. Denied or minimized the events:

    c. Self-medicated with alcohol/drugs/food:

    d. Developed avoidances (people/places/situations):

    e. Preoccupied self with activities and/or achievements (social/academic/household/other):

    f. Developed ability to enter trances and/or other states providing relief:

    g. Developed several personalities to alternate between:

    h. Other:

48. At the time of the sexual abuse did you tell anyone about it?

If yes,

    a. Who?

    b. What was the outcome?

49. At the time of the sexual abuse whom did you perceive to be responsible for protecting you from the offender(s)?

50. Describe this person.

    a. Personality:

    b. Coping methods:

    c. Alcohol abuse/drug abuse/other excesses:

    d. Attitude expressed in the home toward sex:

    e. History of having been emotionally, physically, and/or sexually abused (if yes, please specify which; if not known, please write "not known"):

    f. Adequacies and inadequacies:

    g. Health:

    h. Education:

    i. Occupation(s)/work history:

    j. Religious affiliation/religious practices:

    k. Social skills:

    l. Values:

    m. Features you liked and disliked:

    n. If deceased, time and circumstances of death:

    o. Other comments:

51. What factors do you feel played a role in that person's ability or inability to protect you?

52. Were any of your siblings also sexually abused? (If you do not have any siblings, please write "not applicable".)

    If yes, please specify sister(s) and/or brother(s); if not known, please write "not known."

53. What brought the sexual abuse to an end?

54. Have you ever confronted the offender(s) about the sexual abuse?

    If yes,

    a. When?

    b. Alone or in the presence of others?

    c. What were the offender's (s') reactions and responses?

55. Have you discussed the sexual abuse with members of your family?

    If yes,

    a. When?

    b. With whom?

    c. What were their reactions and responses?

56. Have you discussed your incest history with people outside your family?

    If yes,

    a. When?

    b. With whom?

    c. What were their reactions and responses?

57. In retrospect, do you believe the incest experience affected you in one or more areas of your life?

    If yes, please describe.

58. Do you believe the incest experience continues to affect you in the present?

    If yes, please describe.

59. After the sexual abuse ceased were you at any time involved in substance abuse (alcohol/drugs/food)?

   If yes, please elaborate.

60. After the sexual abuse ceased were you at any time involved in prostitution?

   If yes, please elaborate.

61. After the sexual abuse ceased were you at any time involved in pornography?

   If yes, please elaborate.

62. After the sexual abuse ceased were you at any time involved in sexual acts you considered to be deviant or perverse?

   If yes, please elaborate.

63. After the sexual abuse ceased, were you at any time involved in sexual self-abuse?

   If yes, please elaborate.

64. After the sexual abuse ceased were you at any time involved in sadomasochism?

   If yes, please elaborate.

65. After the sexual abuse ceased were you ever raped?

   If yes, please elaborate.

66. As an adolescent and/or adult, have you purposefully hurt or mutilated any part of your body by biting, cutting, burning, or other methods?

   If yes, please elaborate.

67. As an adolescent and/or adult, have you made a suicide attempt(s)?

   If yes, please elaborate.

68. As an adolescent and/or adult, have you had one or more unwanted pregnancies?

   If yes, please elaborate.

69. As an adolescent and/or adult, have you experienced any gynecological and/or reproductive problems?

    If yes, please elaborate.

70. As an adolescent and/or adult, do you feel the incest experience has affected your reproductive decisions?

    If yes, please elaborate.

71. As an adolescent and/or adult, do you feel the incest experience has affected your parenting? (If you do not have any children, please write "not applicable.")

    If yes, please elaborate.

72. As an adolescent and/or adult, have you been the mother of one or more victims of sexual abuse? (If you do not have any children, please write "not applicable.")

    If yes, please elaborate.

73. As an adolescent and/or adult, have you engaged in sexual acts with children?

    If yes, please elaborate.

74. How would you describe your sexual behavior and adjustment with peers during *adolescence* (ages 13 through 17)?

75. Do you believe the incest experience affected your sexual behavior and adjustment in *adolescence* (ages 13 through 17)?

    If yes, please describe.

76. How would you describe your sexual behavior and adjustment with peers during *young adulthood* (ages 18 through 22)?

77. Do you believe the incest experience affected your sexual behavior and adjustment in *young adulthood* (ages 18 through 22)?

    If yes, please describe.

78. How would you describe your sexual behavior and adjustment during *adulthood* (age 23 on)?

79. Do you believe the incest experience has affected your sexual behavior and adjustment in *adulthood* (age 23 on)?

    If yes, please describe.

80. What feelings do you experience in relation to your body? Please describe under the appropriate choice(s).

    a. Hatred:

    b. Disgust:

    c. Shame:

    d. Fear:

    e. Confusion:

    f. Acceptance:

    g. Appreciation:

    h. Pleasure:

    i. Pride:

    j. Other:

81. What is your attitude toward physical activity/exercise/fitness of your body?

82. Do you believe your attitude toward your body and/or toward physical activity/exercise/fitness of your body has been influenced by your incest history?

    If yes, please explain.

83. Have you ever been pregnant?

    If yes,

    a. What were your feelings about your body then?

    b. What were your feelings about pregnancy?

    c. What were your feelings about sex then?

84. Have you ever given birth?

    If yes,

a. What were your feelings about your body then?

b. What were your feelings about birth?

c. What were your feelings about sex postpartum?

85. Have you ever nursed?

If yes,

a. What were your feelings about your body then?

b. For how long a period of time did you nurse?

c. What were your feelings about nursing?

d. What were your feelings about sex during the nursing period?

86. How often do you experience sexual fantasies? Please describe under as many choices as necessary to include variation based on differing circumstances.

a. Never:

b. Several times a year:

c. Monthly:

d. Weekly:

e. Daily:

87. Who are the subjects of your sexual fantasies? Please describe under the appropriate choice(s).

a. Women and/or men you don't know:

b. Women and/or men you know:

c. Women and/or men you dislike and/or are repulsed by:

d. The offender(s):

e. Other family member(s):

f. Children:

g. Animals:

h. Other:

88. What are the themes of your sexual fantasies? Please describe under the appropriate choice(s).

a. Fantasies of romantic, tender sex:

b. Fantasies of forceful, violent sex:

    c.   Fantasies of forceful, nonviolent sex:

    d.   Fantasies of semipublic and/or public sex:

    e.   Fantasies of degrading and/or humiliating sex:

    f.   Other:

89. What feelings do you experience in relation to sexual fantasies? Please describe under the appropriate choice(s).

    a.   Disgust:

    b.   Shame:

    c.   Fear:

    d.   Guilt:

    e.   Confusion:

    f.   Acceptance:

    g.   Pleasure:

    h.   Other:

90. How often do you experience sexual desire? Please describe under as many choices as necessary to include variation based on differing circumstances.

    a.   Never:

    b.   Several times a year:

    c.   Monthly:

    d.   Weekly:

    e.   Daily:

91. What degree of sexual desire do you experience? Please describe under as many choices as necessary to include variation based on differing circumstances.

    a.   No desire:

    b.   Low level of desire:

    c.   Moderate level of desire:

    d.   High level of desire:

    e.   Intense desire:

92. What feelings do you experience in relation to sexual desire? Please describe under the appropriate choice(s).

a. Disgust:

b. Shame:

c. Fear:

d. Helplessness:

e. Desperation:

f. Guilt:

g. Confusion:

h. Acceptance:

i. Pleasure:

j. Other:

93. How often during sexual activity do you experience sexual arousal? Please describe under as many choices as necessary to include variation based on differing circumstances.

a. Never:

b. Rarely:

c. Occasionally:

d. Usually:

e. Always:

94. What degree of sexual arousal do you experience during sexual activity? Please describe under as many choices as necessary to include variation based on differing circumstances.

a. No arousal:

b. Low level of arousal:

c. Moderate level of arousal:

d. High level of arousal:

e. Intense arousal:

95. What feelings do you experience in relation to sexual arousal? Please describe under the appropriate choice(s).

a. Disgust:

b. Shame:

c. Fear:

    d. Helplessness:

    e. Guilt:

    f. Confusion:

    g. Acceptance:

    h. Pleasure:

    i. Joy:

    j. Other:

96. Under what circumstances and how often are you orgasmic and/or nonorgasmic? Please describe under *each* choice (for example, 60 percent orgasmic/40 percent nonorgasmic or 100 percent orgasmic or 100 percent nonorgasmic, etc.). (If you do not engage in the sexual activity listed in any of the choices, please write "not applicable.")

    a. During masturbation:

    b. During genital manipulation by a partner:

    c. During mutual masturbation:

    d. During oral-genital contact:

    e. During simulated intercourse/tribadism:

    f. During vaginal penetration/intercourse without additional clitoral stimulation:

    g. During vaginal penetration/intercourse with additional clitoral stimulation:

    h. During anal penetration/intercourse without additional clitoral stimulation:

    i. During anal penetration/intercourse with additional clitoral stimulation:

    j. During other activity (please specify):

97. Is your orgasmic capacity contingent upon any of the following?

If yes, please elaborate.

    a. Use of a vibrator:

    b. Alcohol and/or drug use:

    c. Erotic literature and/or pictures:

    d. Masochistic fantasies:

    e. Sadistic fantasies:

   f. Pornography:

   g. Humiliation:

   h. Pain:

   i. Sexual acts with children:

   j. Other:

98. Is your orgasmic capacity increased by any of the following?

If yes, please elaborate.

   a. Verbalization of fears to partner(s):

   b. Assurance that partner(s) will allow you to stop at any point:

   c. Separation in mind of partner(s) from offender(s):

   d. Establishment of trust with partner(s):

   e. Verbalization of needs to partner(s):

   f. Other:

99. How satisfied or dissatisfied are you *during* sex? Please describe those factors or feelings which contribute to your satisfaction or dissatisfaction under the appropriate choice(s).

   a. Totally satisfied:

   b. More satisfied than dissatisfied:

   c. More dissatisfied than satisfied:

   d. Totally dissatisfied:

100. What feelings do you experience in relation to satisfaction or dissatisfaction *after* sex? Please describe under the appropriate choice(s).

   a. Disgust:

   b. Shame:

   c. Guilt:

   d. Sense of having been used:

   e. Contentment:

   f. Fulfillment:

   g. Joy:

   h. Other:

101. Do you experience differences in sexual desire, arousal, and/or orgasmic capacity with changes in your relationship(s) to your partner(s)? (Please specify which.)

   If yes, please describe under as many choices as apply. (If you have not had experience with a partner listed in any of the choices, please write "not applicable.")

   a. Unfamiliar partner:

   b. Familiar partner:

   c. Partner committed to someone else:

   d. Partner you move in with:

   e. Partner you establish long-term commitment to:

   f. Other:

102. Do you experience inhibition in your sexual activity?

   If yes, please describe under the appropriate choice(s).

   a. Disgusted or repulsed by sex:

   b. Ashamed to have partner see sexual side of self:

   c. Afraid of losing control:

   d. Afraid of *feeling* sexual:

   e. Afraid of being *unable to feel* sexual:

   f. Afraid of *acting* sexual:

   g. Afraid of being *unable to act* sexual:

   h. Afraid of giving self over to partner:

   i. Afraid of failing as sexual partner:

   j. Other:

103. Do you experience "interference" during sexual activity?

   If yes, please describe under the appropriate choice(s).

   a. Have vaginal pain:

   b. Have vaginal "clamping" or closure:

   c. Have intrusive thoughts of the offender(s) and/or flashbacks:

   d. Associate certain sexual activities with the offender:

e. Become fearful of being sexually hurt:

f. Become fearful of being sexually used:

g. Start feeling "turned off":

h. "Shut down" physically and/or emotionally:

i. Start observing self like a spectator:

j. Other:

104. Do you experience compulsion in your sexual activity?

If yes, please describe under the appropriate choice(s).

a. Driven by sexual impulses:

b. Get momentary "high," relief, or release from sexual contact:

c. Repeat same sexual act(s) over and over again:

d. Sexualize friendships:

e. Compulsively become involved in brief sexual relationships:

f. Compulsively become involved in casual sexual relationships:

g. Compulsively become involved with numerous partners:

h. Compulsively become involved with people you don't trust:

i. Compulsively become involved with people you dislike:

j. Other:

105. What do you experience in relation to sexual control? Please describe under the appropriate choice(s).

a. Out of control sexually:

b. Unable to control sexual impulses toward children:

c. Unable to control sexual impulses toward strangers:

d. Unable to control sexual impulses toward partner(s):

e. Overcontrolled sexually by partner(s):

f. Unable to say no to partner's (s') wishes:

g. Overcontrolled sexually by self:

h. Unable to say yes to partner's (s') wishes:

i. Satisfied with sexual control:

j. Other:

106. What do you experience in relation to your sexual preference as identified in question 14? Please describe under the appropriate choice(s).

    a. Conflict:

    b. Confusion:

    c. Dissatisfaction:

    d. Uncertainty:

    e. Acceptance:

    f. Certainty:

    g. Satisfaction:

    h. Other:

107. With which gender(s) have you had sexual experience during your adulthood (age 18 on)? Please indicate under the appropriate choice.

    a. Men:

    b. Women:

    c. Both:

    d. Neither:

108. At present are you more satisfied than dissatisfied with your sexuality?

    If yes, what aspects of your sexuality do you feel are contributing to your relative satisfaction, and what factors and experiences do you feel have been helpful in attaining relative satisfaction?

109. At present are you more dissatisfied than you are satisfied with your sexuality?

    If yes, what aspects of your sexuality do you feel are contributing to your relative dissatisfaction?

110. Are there aspects of your sexuality that I've inquired about that you feel are particularly related to your incest history?

    If yes, please describe and explain.

111. Have you ever been in therapy?

    If yes,

    a.   Individual, group, or both?

    b.   Male or female therapist(s)?

    c.   How frequently (weekly, etc.)?

    d.   For how long (months, years, etc.)?

    e.   Are you presently in therapy?

112. Have you ever been involved sexually with a therapist(s) who was treating you?

If yes,

    a.   Male or female therapist(s)?

    b.   Please describe the involvement.

    c.   How did you feel about the experience at the time?

    d.   How do you feel about the experience now?

    e.   Have you spoken to others about the experience?

113. Have you ever been in sex therapy?

If yes,

    a.   What was your complaint when you entered sex therapy?

    b.   What attitudes did the sex therapist(s) convey regarding incest, sexuality, feelings, and treatment?

    c.   What did the sex therapy consist of?

    d.   How long were you in sex therapy?

    e.   What was the outcome?

    f.   Would you consider sex therapy again if you had a complaint?

    g.   Please state reasons for yes or no answer to preceding question.

    h.   Other comments about your experience with sex therapy?

If no,

    a.   Would you consider sex therapy if you had a complaint?

    b.   Please state reasons for yes or no answer to preceding question.

    c.   What are your beliefs and impressions regarding sex therapy?

114. Over time, have you developed techniques or methods of your own to alleviate sexual problems, improve sexual functioning, or enhance sexual satisfaction?

If yes, please describe.

115. Are there aspects of your sexuality that I have not inquired about?

If yes, please describe and, if related to your incest history, please explain.

*Is there anything you would like to say about the questionnaire or about how it was for
you to complete it? All comments are welcome.*

Thank you for completing the questionnaire. I hope you have found responding to
it a rewarding, if difficult, exercise. Please make sure that you have answered all
questions as *fully* as possible. Each person's unique experience educates others
about us as incest survivors and contributes to the eradication of the many myths
and stereotypes that surround us. Your participation is truly appreciated!
    Please return the completed questionnaire to me in the *large* self-addressed,
stamped envelope provided.
    Please fill out the tear-off below and return it to me *separately* in the *small* self-
addressed, stamped envelope provided. Please return the tear-off even if you just
check off "No."

THANK YOU.

- -

_____ No, I am not interested in participating in an interview.
_____ Yes, I am interested in participating in an interview as well.
    Questionnaire number: _____
    Telephone number(s): _____
    Best day(s)/hour(s) to contact: _____
    Special instructions, if any, with respect to telephone calls:

APPENDIX C

Interview Question

I'd like you to tell me about your sexuality and how you feel it has been influenced by your incest history.*

*An explanation regarding the general nature of the question is provided in Chapter 2 under "The Interviews."

· 211 ·

APPENDIX D

Interview Guide

1. *Body perception*

    Consider: Body hatred
    Body "ownership"
    Body control
    Body estrangement
    Fitness
    Illness
    Body and gender
    Physical appearance

2. *Reproduction*

    Consider: Reproductive functioning
    Reproductive decision-making
    Pregnancy
    Birth
    Nursing

3. *Sexual preference*

    Consider: Incest associations
    Dissatisfaction and preference
    Confusion and preference
    Assumptions and preference

4. *Sexual "lifestyle"*

    Consider: Aversion
    Inhibition
    Compulsion

Celibacy
"Promiscuity"
Alternation
Prostitution
"The split"
Masochistic orientation

5. *Sexual functioning*

Consider: Sexual fantasy
Sexual desire
Sexual arousal
Orgasm
"The split"
Sexual satisfaction
Self-help techniques

6. *The interview experience*

How was it for you to be interviewed?
Did it make a difference to you that I'm female?
Did it make a difference to you that I have an incest history myself?
Do you feel a need to talk further about your incest experience
   and your sexuality?
Whom would you want to talk with further?

APPENDIX E

Tables

TABLE 1

Demographic Data on the Questionnaire Participants

N = 43

Age	%	Socioeconomic Status	%
25–29 years	26	Middle class	65
30–39 years	56	Working class	33
40–49 years	16	Upper class	2
50+ years	2		
Mean Age (years)	34.3	*Sexual Preference*	
		Heterosexual	42
Race		Lesbian	35
White	95	Celibate	9
Hispanic	5	Undecided	9
		Bisexual	5
Religion			
None	30	*Relationship Status*	
Protestant	26	Living with life partner	42
Jewish	16	Living with partner	5
Catholic	12	Significant involvement	
Other	16	at time of study	16
		No significant involvement	
Years of Education		at time of study	12
High school	7	None	25
Some college	23		
Bachelor's degree	35	*Children*	
Master's degree	28	No	60
Doctoral degree	7	Yes	40
		Mean number of children	1.9
Occupation		Mean age of children (years)	12.9
Media and the arts	21		
Counseling and education	19	*Therapy*	
Secretarial	16	Ever in psychotherapy	98
Doctoral student	14	Individual	95
Psychotherapist	9	Group	65
Nurse	7	Individual and group	63
Sales	5	In therapy at time of study	84
Business and industry	5	Mean time in therapy (years)	6.4
Postdoctoral fellow	2	Ever in sex therapy	5
Disabled	2	In sex therapy at time of study	0

TABLE 2

Demographic Data on the Interview Participants

N = 10

Age	%	Sexual Preference	%
25–29 years	20	Lesbian	40
30–39 years	60	Heterosexual	30
40–49 years	20	Celibate	10
Mean age (years)	34.9	Undecided	10
		Bisexual	10
Race			
White	80	*Relationship Status*	
Hispanic	20	Living with life partner	50
		Significant involvement	
Religion		at time of study	20
None	40	No significant involvement	
Jewish	20	at time of study	20
Catholic	20	None	10
Protestant	10		
Other	10	*Children*	
		No	60
Years of Education		Yes	40
High school	10	Mean number of children	2
Some college	10	Mean age of children (years)	13.9
Bachelor's degree	40		
Master's degree	40	*Therapy*	
		Ever in psychotherapy	100
Occupation		Individual	100
Media and the arts	30	Group	60
Counseling and education	30	Individual and group	60
Doctoral student	20	In therapy at time of study	80
Secretarial	10	Mean time in therapy (years)	7
Business and industry	10	Ever in sex therapy	0
		In sex therapy at time of study	0
Socioeconomic Status			
Middle class	70		
Working class	30		

TABLE 3

Family Background on the Questionnaire Participants

N = 43

Socioeconomic Status of Childhood Family

	%
Middle class	54
Working class	37
Upper class	9

Occupation of Childhood Breadwinner

	%
White collar	43
Blue collar	30
Law and medicine	20
Military service	7

Religious Affiliation of Childhood Family

	%
Protestant	37
Catholic	35
Jewish	21
None	7

Number of Children in Childhood Family

	%
One child	7
2–3 children	40
4–5 children	37
6–9 children	16
Mean number of children per family	3.8

Birth Position in Childhood Family

	%
Middle child	40
Youngest child	30
Eldest child	23
Only child	7
Eldest or only daughter	60

TABLE 4

Incest Background on the Questionnaire Participants
N = 43

Siblings Incestuously Abused

	%
Yes	63
Younger sibling(s)	56
Older sibling(s)	28
Both younger and older	16
Female sibling(s)	85
Male sibling(s)	15
Don't know	30
No	7

Age During Incest

When incest began:	1–14 years
Mean age:	5.2 years
When incest ended:	5–20 years
Mean age:	13.4 years
Mean number of years incest lasted:	8.4

Identity of the Offender

	%
Father	59
Older brother	13
Grandfather	11.5
Uncle	10
Mother	6.5

Number of Incest Offenders

	%
One offender	68
Two offenders	21
Three offenders	9
Four offenders	2
Total number of offenders	63

TABLE 5

Incest Experience of the Questionnaire Participants

N = 43

Coercion Used by the Offender (Percentage = respondents who experienced)	%
Threat of force	63
Force	58
Pressure	58
Threat of loss of love	49
Bribery	42
Threat of consequences to others	33
Administration of drugs and/or alcohol	9

Nature of the Sexual Activity (Percentage = respondents who experienced)	
Activity not involving direct physical contact	56
Kissing and/or fondling	95
Manipulation of male and/or female genitalia	84
Oral-genital contact	70
Simulated intercourse	37
Vaginal intercourse	49
Anal intercourse	12
Vaginal and anal penetration with objects	7
Vaginal, anal, breast and/or buttock "exams"	7
Administration of douches and/or enemas	2
Sexual activity involving sadism	21
Group sexual activity	7
Sexual activity involving animals	5
Impregnation by the offender	5

Frequency of the Sexual Activity	
Daily	16
Weekly	26
Monthly	19
Several times a year	23
Once or twice	16

Reason Incest Ended	
Puberty attained	38
Physical separation from offender	30
Refusal to continue/threat to disclose	15
Disclosure	5
Not known	12

TABLE 6

Family Background on the Interview Participants

N = 10

Socioeconomic Status of Childhood Family

	%
Working class	50
Middle class	30
Upper class	20

Occupation of Childhood Breadwinner

	%
Blue collar	40
White collar	30
Medicine	20
Military service	10

Religious Affiliation of Childhood Family

	%
Protestant	30
Catholic	30
Jewish	30
None	10

Number of Children in Childhood Family

	%
2–3 children	40
4–5 children	50
6–9 children	10
Mean number of children per family	3.7

Birth Position in Childhood Family

	%
Middle child	50
Youngest child	40
Eldest child	10
Eldest or only daughter	50

TABLES

TABLE 7

Incest Background on the Interview Participants

N = 10

Siblings Incestuously Abused

	%
Yes	70
Younger sibling(s)	43
Older sibling(s)	43
Both younger and older	14
Female sibling(s)	83
Male sibling(s)	17
Don't know	20
No	10

Age During Incest

When incest began:	1–11 years
Mean age:	5.6 years
When incest ended:	6–19 years
Mean age:	13.8 years
Mean number of years incest lasted:	8.2

Identity of the Offender

	%
Father	44
Older brother	17
Grandfather	11
Uncle	11
Mother	11
Grandmother	6

Number of Incest Offenders

	%
One offender	40
Two offenders	50
Four offenders	10
Total number of offenders	18

TABLE 8

Incest Experience of the Interview Participants

N = 10

Coercion Used by the Offender (Percentage = participants who experienced)	%
Threat of force	50
Force	20
Pressure	30
Threat of loss of love	30
Bribery	30
Threat of consequences to others	10
Administration of drugs and/or alcohol	10

Nature of the Sexual Activity (Percentage = participants who experienced)	
Activity not involving direct physical contact	70
Kissing and/or fondling	80
Manipulation of male and/or female genitalia	80
Oral-genital contact	70
Simulated intercourse	60
Vaginal intercourse	50
Anal intercourse	10
Vaginal, anal, breast, and/or buttock "exams"	30
Administration of douches and/or enemas	10
Sexual activity involving sadism	20
Impregnation by the offender	10

Frequency of the Sexual Activity	
Daily	30
Weekly	50
Monthly	10
Several times a year	10
Once or twice (with a secondary offender)	30

Reason Incest Ended	
Puberty attained	20
Physical separation from offender	50
Refusal to continue/threat to disclose	10
Not known	20

TABLE 9

Themes from the Interviews

N = 10

Themes in order of significance	Total # of women influenced	Aspects of sexuality influenced	In how many women
Fear *subtheme:* boundaries	10	functioning "lifestyle" reproduction preference body perception	9 of 10 8 of 10 6 of 10 2 of 10 1 of 10
Control	10	functioning "lifestyle" body perception reproduction preference	10 of 10 6 of 10 5 of 10 3 of 10 1 of 10
Power *subtheme:* entrapment	10	functioning "lifestyle" reproduction body perception	8 of 10 6 of 10 3 of 10 3 of 10
Shame	9	body perception functioning "lifestyle" reproduction	8 of 9 7 of 9 4 of 9 2 of 9
Trust *subthemes:* betrayal abandonmen	9	functioning "lifestyle" reproduction	8 of 9 5 of 9 2 of 9
Self-esteem	9	"lifestyle" functioning	7 of 9 4 of 9
Anger	5	functioning "lifestyle" reproduction body perception	3 of 5 3 of 5 2 of 5 2 of 5
Guilt	5	functioning "lifestyle"	4 of 5 2 of 5
Confusion	4	"lifestyle" preference gender identity	2 of 4 2 of 4 2 of 4

APPENDIX F

Treatment and
Self-Help Resources

Survivor and Partner Education

Bass, E., & Davis, L. (1988). *The courage to heal: A guide for women survivors of child sexual abuse.* New York: Harper & Row.

Bear, E., & Dimock, P. (1988). *Adults molested as children: A survivor's manual for women and men.* (Available from Safer Society Press, Shoreham Depot Road, Orwell, VT 05760.)

Davis, L. (1991). *Allies in healing: When the person you love was sexually abused as a child.* New York: Harper Perennial.

Maltz, W. (1988). *Partners in healing: Couples overcoming the sexual repercussions of incest* [video]. (Available from Independent Video Services, 401 East 10th Avenue, Suite 160, Eugene, OR 97401.)

Maltz, W. (1991). *The sexual healing journey: A guide for survivors of sexual abuse.* New York: Harper Collins.

Maltz, W., & Holman, B. (1987). *Incest and sexuality: A guide to understanding and healing.* Lexington, MA: Lexington Books.

Westerlund, E. (1987). *Incest: What to think, what to say, what to do.* (Available from Incest Resources, Inc., 46 Pleasant Street, Cambridge, MA 02139.)

Westerlund, E. (1989). *Starting from scratch: The I.R.* group model.* [A manual that can be used to organize a survivors' group or a partners' group.] (Available from Incest Resources, Inc., 46 Pleasant Street, Cambridge, MA 02139).

Cognitively Based Self-Help

Burns, D. (1980). *Feeling good: The new mood therapy.* New York: Signet.

Emery, G. (1981). *A new beginning.* New York: Simon & Schuster.

Emery, G., & Campbell, J. (1986). *Rapid relief from emotional distress.* New York: Rawson.

Physically Based Self-Help

I.R.* obics Program Packet. (Available from Incest Resources, Inc., 46 Pleasant Street, Cambridge, MA 02139.)

Inside Out Program Packet. (Available from Incest Resources, Inc., 46 Pleasant Street, Cambridge, MA 02139).

Picture This! Program Packet. (Available from Incest Resources, Inc., 46 Pleasant Street, Cambridge, MA 02139.)

Reclaiming Your Body Program. [Dance/movement/imagery work for survivors]. (Workshops, classes, and individual consultation/instruction available from Marcie Mitler, M.Ed., 2 Newport Road, Cambridge, MA 02140.)

Child Sexuality

Calderone, M., & Johnson, E. (1983). *The family book about sexuality*. New York: Bantam.

Calderone, M., & Ramey, J. (1982). *Talking with your child about sex*. New York: Ballantine.

"Normalcy" and Appreciation: Body

Boston Women's Health Book Collective (1984). *The new our bodies, our selves*. New York: Simon & Schuster.

Freedman, R. (1988). *Bodylove*. New York: Harper & Row.

Henderson, J. (1986). *The lover within*. Barrytown, NY: Station Hill Press.

Hutchinson, M. (1985). *Transforming body image: Learning to love the body you have*. Trumansberg, NY: Crossing.

Rush, A. (1973). *Getting clear: Body work for women*. New York: Random House.

"Normalcy" and Appreciation: Sexual Feelings and Behaviors

Barbach, L., & Levine, L. (1980). *Shared intimacies: Women's sexual experiences*. New York: Bantam.

Friday, N. (1973). *My secret garden*. New York: Pocket Books.

Friday, N. (1975). *Forbidden flowers*. New York: Pocket Books.

Hite, S. (1976). *The Hite report: A nationwide study of female sexuality*. New York: Macmillan.

Kitzinger, S. (1985). *Woman's experience of sex*. New York: Penguin.

Self-Help Guides: General

Loulan, J. (1984). *Lesbian sex*. San Francisco: Spinsters/Aunt Lute.

Loulan, J. (1987). *Lesbian passion*. San Francisco: Spinsters/Aunt Lute.

Raley, P. (1980). *Making love: How to be your own sex therapist*. New York: Avon.

Raley, P. (1985). *Making love better: Have an affair with your partner*. New York: St. Martin's.

Self-Help Guides: Masturbation and Orgasm

Barbach, L. (1975). *For yourself: The fulfillment of female sexuality.* New York: Signet.
Dodson, B. (1987). *Sex for one: The joy of self-loving.* (Available from The Sexuality Library, 1210 Valencia Street, San Francisco, CA 94110.)
Graber, B., & Graber, G. (1975). *Woman's orgasm.* New York: Warner.
Heiman, J., & LoPiccolo, J. (1988). *Becoming orgasmic: A sexual and personal growth program for women.* New York: Prentice-Hall.

Sexual Materials

Books/Tapes/Erotica:

The Sexuality Library
1210 Valencia Street
San Francisco, CA 94110

Vibrators (at best prices):

Prelude Products
Windmere Corporation
4920 N.W. 165th Street
Hialeah, FL 33014

Vibrators/Sex Toys/Erotica:

Eve's Garden, Ltd.
119 West 57th Street
Suite 1406
New York, NY 10019

Open Enterprises, Inc. (Good Vibrations)
1210 Valencia Street
San Francisco, CA 94110

Vaginal Dilators:

E.F. Young & Company
1350 Old Skokie Road
Highland Park, IL 60035

APPENDIX G

Deep Muscle Relaxation Guide

Session I

1. Dangle arms at sides and note tingling/numbness/warmth.
2. Regulate breathing and relax on each exhale.
3. Note sensations of relaxation.
4. Grip arm of chair and note tightening in forearm.
5. Release, release further, and recapture sensations from step 3.
6. Pull arm of chair toward self (elbow bent) and note contraction of bicep. Pull arm of chair toward self (elbow straightened) and note contraction of tricep.
7. Release. Release further.
8. Shrug shoulders and release fully.
9. Pull shoulders back and release fully.
10. Hug self and release fully.

Session II

1. Raise forehead up and release in increments.
2. Frown and wrinkle nose and release fully.
3. Smile and release fully.
4. Purse lips and release fully.
5. Push tongue into roof of mouth and release fully.
6. Clench teeth and release fully.
7. Press chin to chest and release fully.

Session III

1. Tense stomach (anticipate punch) and release fully.
2. Tighten buttocks (raise self off chair) and release fully.
3. Lift legs, turn toes in, tighten, and release fully.
4. Lower legs, turn toes in, tighten, and release fully. Turn toes out, tighten, and release fully.
5. Curl toes in and release fully.

Session IV (No muscle tightening employed)

1. Place hands on lap (seated) and close eyes.
2. Regulate breathing and relax on each exhale.
3. Imagine tension draining out of muscles and flowing out of body—feel heaviness, feel calm as each muscle group is relaxed.
4. Visualize self in place of safety, beauty, and peace.

REFERENCES

Bain, J.A. (1928). *Thought control in everyday life.* New York: Funk & Wagnalls.

Baisden, M. (1971). *The world of rosaphrenia: The sexual psychology of the female.* Sacramento, CA: Allied Research Society.

Beck, A. (1976). *Cognitive therapy and the emotional disorders.* New York: International Universities Press.

Becker, J., Skinner, L., Abel, G., Axelrod, R., & Cichon, J. (1984). Sexual problems of sexual assault survivors. *Women and Health, 9,* 5–20.

Becker, J., Skinner, L., Abel, G., & Cichon, J. (1986). Level of post-assault sexual functioning in rape and incest victims. *Archives of Sexual Behavior, 15,* 37–49.

Becker, J., Skinner, L., Abel, G., & Treacy, E. (1982). Incidence and types of sexual dysfunctions in rape and incest victims. *Journal of Sex and Marital Therapy, 8,* 65–74.

Belmonte, F., & Boyer, J. (1983). NCAN statement on incest. *NCAN News, 13,* 2.

Bender, L., & Blau, A. (1937). The reaction of children to sexual relations with adults. *American Journal of Orthopsychiatry, 7,* 500–518.

Bender, L., & Grugett, A. (1952). A follow-up report on children who had atypical sexual experience. *American Journal of Orthopsychiatry, 22,* 825–837.

Berry, G. (1975). Incest: Some clinical variations on a classical theme. *Journal of the American Academy of Psychoanalysis, 3,* 151–161.

Bess, B., & Janssen, Y. (1982). Incest: A pilot study. *Hillside Journal of Clinical Psychiatry, 4,* 39–52.

Boekelheide, P. (1978). Sexual adjustment in college women who experienced incestuous relationships. *Journal of the American College Health Association, 26,* 327–330.

Butler, S., (1978). *Conspiracy of silence: The trauma of incest.* New York: Bantam Books.

Caldirola, D., Gemperle, M., Guzinski, G., Gross, R., & Doerr, H. (1983). Incest and pelvic pain: The social worker as part of a research team. *Health and Social Work, 8,* 309–319.

Coid, J., Allolio, B., & Rees, L. (1983). Raised plasma metenkephalin in patients who habitually mutilate themselves. *Lancet, 2,* 545–546.

Courtois, C. (1979a). Characteristics of a volunteer sample of adult women who experienced incest in childhood or adolescence. *Dissertation Abstracts International, 40,* 3194A-3195A. (University Microfilms No. 0117)

Courtois, C. (1979b). The incest experience and its aftermath. *Victimology, 4,* 337–347.

Courtois, C. (1980). Studying and counseling women with past incest experience. *Victimology, 5,* 322–334.

Courtois, C., & Watts, D. (1982). Counseling adult women who experienced incest in childhood or adolescence. *Personnel and Guidance Journal, 60,* 275–279.

Ellis, A. (1962). *Reason and emotion in psychotherapy.* New York: Lyle Stuart.

Faria, G., & Belohlavek, N. (1984). Treating female adult survivors of childhood incest. *Social Casework: Journal of Contemporary Social Work, 65,* 465–471.

Finkelhor, D. (1979). *Sexually victimized children.* New York: Free Press.

Finkelhor, D. (1980). Sex among siblings: A survey on prevalence, variety, and effects. *Archives of Sexual Behavior, 9,* 171–194.

Flannery, R. (1987). From victim to survivor: A stress management approach in the treatment of learned helplessness. In B. Van der Kolk (Ed.), *Psychological trauma* (pp. 217–232). Washington, DC: American Psychiatric Press.

Fortune, M. (1983). *Sexual violence: The unmentionable sin: An ethical and pastoral perspective.* New York: Pilgrim Press.

Fritz, G., Stoll, K., & Wagner, N. (1981). A comparison of males and females who were sexually molested as children. *Journal of Sex and Marital Therapy, 7,* 54–59.

Gagnon, J. (1965). Female child victims of sex offenses. *Social Problems, 13,* 176–192.

Giorgi, A. (1970). *Psychology as a human science: A phenomenologically based approach.* New York: Harper & Row.

Gligor, A. (1966). Incest and sexual delinquency: A comparative analysis of two forms of sexual behavior in minor females. *Dissertation Abstracts International, 27,* 3671B. (University Microfilms No. 4588)

Gordon, L. (1955). Incest as revenge against the preoedipal mother. *Psychoanalytic Review, 42,* 284–292.

Greenland, C. (1958). Incest. *British Journal of Delinquency, 9,* 62–65.

Greenwald, H. (1958). *The callgirl: A social and psychoanalytic study.* New York: Ballantine.

Gundlach, R. (1977). Sexual molestation and rape reported by homosexual and heterosexual women. *Journal of Homosexuality, 2,* 367–384.

Gundlach, R., & Riess, B. (1967). Birth order and sex of siblings in a sample of lesbians and nonlesbians. *Psychological Reports, 20,* 61–62.

Heims, L., & Kaufman, I. (1963). Variations on a theme of incest. *American Journal of Orthopsychiatry, 33,* 311–312.

Henderson, D. (1975). Incest. In A. Freedman, H. Kaplan, & B. Sadock (Eds.). *Comprehensive textbook of psychiatry* (2nd ed.) (pp. 1530–1539). Baltimore: Williams & Wilkins.

Herman, J. (1981). *Father-daughter incest.* Cambridge: Harvard University Press.

Herman, J., & Hirschman, L. (1977). Father-daugher incest. *Signs: Journal of Women in Culture and Society, 2,* 735–756.

Hersko, M., Halleck, S., Rosenberg, M., & Pacht, A. (1961). Incest: A three way process. *Journal of Social Therapy, 7,* 22–31.

Hirschman, L. (1980). Incest and seduction: A comparison of two client groups. *Dissertation Abstracts International, 40*, 4485B-4486B. (University Microfilms No. 0851)

Hite, S. (1976). *The Hite report: A nationwide study of female sexuality.* New York: Macmillan.

Howard, H. (1959). Incest—The revenge motive. *Delaware State Medical Journal, 31,* 223-225.

Jacobson, E. (1938). *Progressive relaxation.* Chicago: University of Chicago Press.

James, J., & Meyerding, J. (1977a). Early sexual experience and prostitution. *The American Journal of Psychiatry, 134,* 1381-1385.

James, J., & Meyerding, J. (1977b). Early sexual experience as a factor in prostitution. *Archives of Sexual Behavior, 7,* 31-42.

Jehu, D. (1988). *Beyond sexual abuse: Therapy with women who were childhood victims.* New York: John Wiley & Sons.

Jehu, D., Klassen, C., & Gazan, M. (1985-1986). Cognitive restructuring of distorted beliefs associated with childhood sexual abuse. *Journal of Social work and Human Sexuality, 4,* 1-35.

Kaplan, H. (1974). *The new sex therapy.* New York: Brunner/Mazel.

Kaufman, I., Peck, A., & Tagiuri, C. (1954). The family constellation and overt incestuous relations between father and daughter. *American Journal of Orthopsychiatry, 24,* 266-277.

Kinsey, A., Pomeroy, W., Martin, C., & Gebhand, P. (1953). *Sexual behavior in the human female.* Philadelphia: Saunders.

Kubo, S. (1959). Researches and studies on incest in Japan. *Hiroshima Journal of Medical Sciences, 8,* 99-159.

Landis, C. (1940). *Sex in development.* New York: Harper & Brothers.

Landis, J. (1956). Experiences of 500 children with adult sexual deviation. *Psychiatric Quarterly Supplement, 30,* 91-109.

Langmade, C. (1983). The impact of pre- and postpubertal onset of incest experiences in adult women as measured by sex anxiety, sex guilt, sexual satisfaction and sexual behavior. *Dissertation Abstracts International, 44,* 917B. (University Microfilms No. 3592)

Lazarus, A. (1971). *Behavior therapy and beyond.* New York: McGraw-Hill.

Lofland, J. (1971). *Analyzing social settings.* Belmont, CA: Wadsworth.

LoPiccolo, J., & LoPiccolo, L. (1978). *Handbook of sex therapy.* New York: Plenum.

Lukianowicz, N. (1972). Incest. *British Journal of Psychiatry, 120,* 301-313.

MacFarlane, K., & Waterman, J., Eds. (1986). *Sexual abuse of young children.* New York: Guilford.

Magal, V., & Winnick, H. (1968). Role of incest in family structure. *Israel Annals of Psychiatry and Related Disciplines, 6,* 173-189.

Maisch, H. (1972). *Incest* (C. Bearne, Trans.). New York: Stein & Day.

Maltz, W. (1991). *The sexual healing journey: A guide for survivors of sexual abuse.* New York: Harper Collins.

Maltz, W., & Holman, B. (1987). *Incest and sexuality: A guide to understanding and healing.* Lexington, MA: Lexington Books.

Masters, W., & Johnson, V. (1970). *Human sexual inadequacy.* Boston: Little, Brown.

Mayer, R., & Greenwood, E. (1980). *The design of social policy research.* Englewood Cliffs, NJ: Prentice-Hall.

REFERENCES

McGuire, L., & Wagner, N. (1978). Sexual dysfunction in women who were molested as children: One response pattern and suggestions for treatment. *Journal of Sex and Marital Therapy, 4*, 11–15

Medlicott, R. (1967). Parent-child incest. *Australian and New Zealand Journal of Psychiatry, 1*, 180–187.

Meiselman, K. (1978). *Incest: A psychological study of causes and effects with treatment recommendations.* San Francisco: Jossey-Bass.

Meiselman, K. (1980). Personality characteristics of incest history psychotherapy patients: A research note. *Archives of Sexual Behavior, 9*, 195–197.

Molnar, G., & Cameron, P. (1975). Incest syndromes: Observations in a general hospital psychiatric unit. *Canadian Psychiatric Association Journal, 20*, 373–377.

Patton, M. (1980). *Qualitative evaluation methods.* Beverly Hills, CA: Sage.

Rascovsky, M., & Rascovsky, A. (1950). On consummated incest. *International Journal of Psychoanalysis, 31*, 42–47.

Rasmussen, A. (1934). The role of sex crimes against children under 14 in the development of mental illnesses and character disorders. *Acta Psychiatrica et Neurologica, 9*, 351–434.

Richardson, J., & Zaleski, W. (1983). Naloxone and self-mutilation. *Biological Psychiatry, 18*, 99–101.

Rosenfeld, A. (1979). Incidence of a history of incest among 18 female psychiatric patients. *American Journal of Psychiatry, 136*, 791–795.

Rush, F. (1980). *The best kept secret: The sexual abuse of children.* Englewood Cliffs, NJ: Prentice-Hall.

Russell, D. (1983). The incidence and prevalence of intrafamilial and extrafamilial sexual abuse of female children. *Child Abuse and Neglect: The International Journal, 7*, 133–146.

Russell, D. (1986). *The secret trauma: Incest in the lives of girls and women.* New York: Basic Books.

Silbert, M., & Pines, A. (1981). Sexual child abuse as an antecedent to prostitution. *Child Abuse and Neglect: The International Journal, 5*, 407–411.

Silbert, M., & Pines, A. (1983). Early sexual exploitation as an influence in prostitution. *Social Work, 28*, 285–289.

Simari, C., & Baskin, D. (1982). Incestuous experiences within homosexual populations: A preliminary study. *Archives of Sexual Behavior, 11*, 329–344.

Sjoberg, G., & Nett, R. (1968). *A methodology for social research.* New York: Harper & Row.

Sloane, P., & Karpinski, E. (1942). Effects of incest on the participants. *American Journal of Orthopsychiatry, 12*, 666–673.

Sprei, J., & Courtois, C. (1988). The treatment of women's sexual dysfunctions arising from sexual assault. In J. R. Field & R. A. Brown (Eds.). *Advances in the understanding and treatment of sexual problems: Compendium for the individual and marital therapist.* New York: Spectrum.

Taylor, S., & Bogdan, R. (1984). *Introduction to qualitative research methods: The search for meanings* (2nd ed.). New York: John Wiley & Sons.

Tsai, M., Feldman-Summers, S., & Edgar, M. (1979). Childhood molestation: Variables related to differential impacts on psychosexual functioning in adult women. *Journal of Abnormal Psychology, 88*, 407–417.

Tsai, M., & Wagner, N. (1978). Therapy groups for women sexually molested as children. *Archives of Sexual Behavior, 7*, 417–427.

Van der Kolk, B., & Greenberg, M. (1987). The psychobiology of the trauma

WOMEN'S SEXUALITY AFTER CHILDHOOD INCEST

response: Hyperarousal, constriction, and addiction to traumatic reexposure. In B. Van der Kolk (Ed.), *Psychological Trauma* (pp. 63–87). Washington, DC: American Psychiatric Press.

Verebey, K., Volavka, J., & Clouet, D. (1978). Endorphins in psychiatry. *Archives of General Psychiatry, 35,* 877–888.

Vitaliano, P., & James, J. (1977). Multivariate analysis of the relationship between prostitution and initial sexual activity. (Research Report No. MH-29968). Rockville, MD: National Institute of Mental Health.

Weinberg, S. (1955). *Incest behavior.* New York: Citadel.

Westerlund, E. (1983). Counseling women with histories of incest. *Women and Therapy, 2,* 17–31.

Westerlund, E. (1986). Freud on sexual trauma: An historical review of seduction and betrayal. *Psychology of Women Quarterly, 10,* 297–310.

Wolpe, J. (1973). *The practice of behavior therapy.* New York: Pergamon Press.

Wolpe, J., & Lazarus, A. (1966). *Behavior therapy techniques.* New York: Pergamon Press.

Woodbury, J., & Schwartz, E. (1971). *The silent sin.* New York: Signet.

Wyatt, G. (1985). The sexual abuse of Afro-American and white American women in childhood. *Child Abuse and Neglect: The International Journal, 9,* 507–519.

INDEX

abandonment, 50, 134, 139, 146, 223
Abel, G., 3, 17, 20
abortion, 57, 89–90, 120, 128, 141
abuse, physical, 50, 89, 115, 134, 140
age:
  during incest, 39, 42
  of participants, 31, 34
alcohol abuse, 44, 45, 47, 50, 53, 60, 116, 140
Alcoholics Anonymous, 140, 145
Allen, Dr. Murray, 163
anger, 101, 123, 146, 223
  and body, 46, 53, 89, 119, 126, 136, 140
  interrupting the displacement of, 150–51,
    165
  and reproduction, 58, 128, 141
  and sexual functioning, 82–83, 93–94, 117–
    18
  and sexual "lifestyle," 65, 66–67, 68–69,
    111, 116–17, 121, 144
arousal, 19, 80–83
  and control, 94, 100, 113, 122
  and detaching/disconnecting/leaving body,
    81–82, 91, 113, 134, 144
  during incest, 46, 53–54, 83, 113, 121, 135
  and fear, 122, 138, 139, 145
  and guilt, 122, 134, 138
  interference with, 80, 107, 113–14, 117,
    134, 145
  and numbing, 81–82, 94, 101, 121
  previous study findings, 19
  "the split" and, 84–85
  and trust, 91, 100, 122

aversion, 65
  see also sexual functioning; sexual "life-
    style"
Axelrod, R., 17

Baisden, M., 4
Baskin, D., 14, 16, 22
Beck, A., 150
Becker, J., 3, 4, 17, 18, 19, 20, 21, 22, 23, 86
Belmonte, F., 4, 19
Belohlavek, N., 3, 20
Bender, L., 8, 13
Berry, G., 8
Bess, B., 3, 4, 5, 18, 22, 23
betrayal, 50, 67, 71, 85, 90, 122, 133, 146, 223
  by body, 53–54, 55, 56, 58, 59, 136
birth position, in childhood family, 38, 42
bisexuality, 15, 16, 23, 27, 61, 72, 96–99, 110
  see also sexual preference
Blau, A., 8
body perception, 20, 24, 26, 52–56, 59–60
  as being "ugly," 56, 96, 115
  body control, 53–54, 58, 81–82, 83–84, 89,
    109, 119, 127, 134, 136, 140, 141, 162
  body estrangement, 54, 115, 126, 135–36,
    140, 162, 164
  body hatred, 53, 58, 89, 119, 126, 135, 140,
    161, 164
  body "ownership," 53, 116, 128, 135, 140,
    162, 164
  changing one's, 91, 102, 161–62
  fitness and positive, 54, 89, 91, 119–20, 140

body perception (*continued*)
  gender and, 55–56, 104–6, 127
  illness and, 55, 89, 140–41
  influences on, summary of, 177
  negative and distorted, 52, 96–97, 105, 114,
    126, 135–36
  physical appearance and, 56
  promiscuity and, 68
  prostitution and, 70
  self-hatred and, 89, 134, 141
  weight and, 55–56, 105, 108–9, 126–27, 136
Boekelheide, P., 3, 11, 22, 72
boundaries, 50, 79, 106, 107, 113, 117, 123,
  138, 145, 164, 223
Boyer, J., 4, 19
Butler, S., 35

Caldirola, D., 86
Cambridge Women's Center, 25
Cameron, P., 9, 10, 13
celibacy, 16, 23, 27, 61, 62, 67, 68, 69, 72, 90,
  99–100, 110, 130–31, 135, 137–38
children:
  fears about having, 56–57, 90, 109, 115,
    128, 141–42
  number in childhood family, 38, 42
  of participants, 33, 35, 91, 103, 108, 135
  parenting of, 49
  sexual impulses toward, 71
Cichon, J., 3, 17, 20
clothes and dressing, 55, 97, 104, 109, 114–
  15, 121, 136, 142
Clouet, D., 162
cognitive techniques, 102
  see also treatment, cognitive component
commitment:
  loss of power and, 71, 84, 112
  loss of sexual feeling and, 70–71, 84–85,
    122
compulsion, 66–67
  see also sexual functioning; sexual "life-
    style"
confusion, 146, 223
  and gender identity, 55, 92, 105–6, 146
  and limits and boundaries, 50
  and pregnancy, 56
  and sexual functioning, 76, 78, 82
  and sexual "lifestyle," 65, 67, 117, 118, 138
  and sexual preference, 63–64, 71–72, 106,
    128–30, 137
control, 123, 145, 223
  and body, 53–54, 58, 81–82, 83–84, 89, 109,
    119, 127, 134, 136, 140, 141, 162
  and reproduction, 56, 58, 109, 128, 136–
    37, 141
  and sexual functioning, 76, 78–79, 81–82,

    83–84, 94, 100, 101, 109, 113, 117, 122,
    138, 142, 143
  and sexual "lifestyle," 66, 67, 68, 93, 100,
    111–12, 116, 121, 138
  and sexual preference, 62, 137
coping mechanisms, 46–47
Courtois, C., 3, 5, 17, 18, 21, 23, 86, 160*n*

déjà vu, feelings of, 82, 135, 137
desire, 18, 77–80
  and control, 113, 138, 142
  difficulty acting on, 90, 100, 113, 117, 138,
    142
  loss of, 77, 79, 90, 93, 100, 110, 122, 131,
    143
  previous study findings, 18
  "the split" and, 84
dissociation, 46, 47, 81–82, 94, 142, 144
Doerr, H., 86
drug abuse, 45, 47, 50, 53, 60, 69, 140
dyspareunia, 20, 86, 179

Edgar, M., 3, 11
education, of participants, 32, 34
Ellis, A., 150
endorphins (opioids), 162–63
entrapment, 84, 89, 94, 109, 112, 122, 128,
  223
exercise:
  as antidote to the incest, 54, 127
  compulsive, 119–20
  positive body perception and, 54, 89, 91,
    119–20, 140
  see also fitness
exhibitionism, by offender, 4, 40, 43
extrafamilial abuse, 17, 22, 26

fantasy, 74–76
  confusion and, 76
  control and, 76, 100, 143
  guilt/shame and, 76
  inhibition in, 74–76, 90, 133, 138
  magical thinking and, 75, 76, 133–34
  sadomasochistic, 76, 118, 138–39
Faria, G., 3, 20
fear, 123, 145, 223
  and body, 55, 89, 92, 105, 126
  and reproduction, 56–57, 58, 59, 89, 92,
    109, 128, 136–37, 141–42
  and sexual functioning, 78, 79, 81, 82, 83,
    84–85, 94, 100, 113, 117, 122, 133, 137,
    138, 139, 145
  and sexual "lifestyle," 65, 67, 68, 69, 71, 92–
    93, 99, 107, 111–12, 117, 118, 122, 132–
    33
  and sexual preference, 62, 64, 129–30, 137

Feldman-Summers, S., 3, 11
feminism:
  and prescriptivism, 64
  societal attitudes toward incest and, 8
Finkelhor, D., 3, 4, 10, 11, 15, 16, 17, 19, 21, 22, 72, 73
Fiske, 28
fitness, body perception and, 54, 89, 91, 119–20, 140
flashbacks, 20, 80, 85, 152–53, 158–60
food abuse, 45, 47, 50, 53, 60, 126–27, 140
"frigidity," 7–8, 135
Fritz, G., 3, 17, 21, 22, 23

Gagnon, J., 17
Gazan, M., 160n
Gebhand, P., 4
Gemperle, M., 86
gender identity, 123, 146
  body perception and, 55–56, 104–6, 127
  confusion about, 92, 106, 146
Gligor, A., 9, 13
Gordon, L., 7
Greenberg, M., 162
Greenland, C., 8
Greenwald, H., 7, 12
Gross, R., 86
Grugett, A., 8, 13
guilt, 101, 124, 146–47, 223
  and body, 53, 121, 126, 136
  and sexual functioning, 75, 76, 77, 80–81, 113, 122, 133–34, 138
  and sexual "lifestyle," 65, 66, 68, 69, 121, 122, 131–32
  interrupting interference from, 151
  reducing guilt and self-blame, 101, 167–68
Gundlach, R., 14, 15
Guzinski, G., 86

Halleck, S., 7
health, 48, 55
  see also body perception; exercise; fitness
Heims, L., 13
Henderson, D., 4
Herman, J., 3, 5, 7, 10, 15, 16, 17, 18, 19, 20, 23, 72, 73, 86
Hersko, M., 7, 8, 13
heterosexuality, 15, 16, 23, 27, 61
  see also sexual preference
Hirschman, L., 3, 5, 7, 18, 23
Hite, S., 19
Holman, B., 158, 168
homosexuality, 13–16
  see also sexual preference
Howard, H., 7, 8, 10

incest:
  definition used for study, 26
  disclosure of, 44–45
  influence on sexuality, previous studies, 3
  incidence and prevalence among U.S. females, 4, 5
  memories of, 47, 82, 126
  perceived effects of, 47–51
  reasons incest ended, 40–41, 43
  responses to, 46–47
  types of sexual activity involved, 26
Incest Resources, Inc., x, xii, 24–25, 28, 166, 176
inhibition, 65–66
  see also sexual functioning; sexual "lifestyle"
Inside Out, Therapeutic Bodywork for Incest Survivors, 164–65
interviews, 28–29, 211–13
  analysis of, 29, 185
  "focused," 28–29
  objective of, 29
intimacy, 50–51, 70, 84–85, 99, 111–12, 117, 132–33
intrafamilial abuse, 17, 22, 26
I.R.* obics, Therapeutic Aerobics for Incest Survivors, 162–64

Jacobson, E., 154
James, J., 12, 13
Janssen, V., 3, 4, 5, 18, 22, 23
Jehu, D., 160n
Johnson, V., 5, 19, 157

Kaplan, H., 5
Karpinski, E., 7, 8, 10, 12, 13
Kaufman, I., 7, 8, 9, 13
Kendall, 28
Kinsey, A., 4, 17, 19
Klassen, C., 160n
Kubo, S., 7, 8, 9, 10, 13

Landis, C., 4, 8, 17, 19
Landis, J., 4, 8, 17, 19
Langmade, C., 3, 11, 15, 18, 21, 23, 72, 73
Lazarus, A., 150, 154
lesbianism, 72, 97
  difficulties in coming out, 64, 90, 120, 178
  stigma and, 120, 129–30, 137
  see also sexual preference
Lofland, J., 28
LoPiccolo, J., 5
Lukianowicz, N., 7, 8, 9, 10, 12, 13

MacFarlane, K., 17
McGuire, L., 3, 4, 18, 19, 20, 22, 87, 158

Magal, V., 8, 13
"magical thinking," 75, 76, 133–34, 169–70
Maisch, H., 7, 9, 10, 13
Maltz, W., 149n, 158n, 168n
Martin, C., 4
masochism. see sadomasochism
Masters, W., 5, 19, 157
masturbation, 40, 66, 67, 83, 175
    inhibition in, 90, 133, 139, 143
    versus sex with partner, 100, 113, 118, 122
    see also sexual functioning
Medlicott, R., 7, 10, 14
Meiselman, K., 3, 5, 9, 10, 15, 17, 18, 19, 20,
    23, 71, 72, 86
memories. see incest
men:
    contempt for, 67, 68, 70, 111, 121, 144
    fear of, 62, 64, 65, 66, 107, 129, 130, 136,
    137
    exclusion of men from the study, 26
men, gay, attraction to, 78, 106–7
menstruation, fears about, 56, 89
miscarriage, 57, 120
Merton, 28
Meyerding, J., 12
Molnar, G., 9, 10, 13
Mosher Forced Choice Sex Guilt Subscale,
    18

Nett, R., 28
nonresponsiveness, previous studies, 7–8

occupations:
    of childhood family breadwinner, 38, 41
    of participants, 32, 34, 88, 91, 96, 103, 108,
    114, 119, 125, 135, 139
offenders:
    coercion used by, 39, 42–43
    fathers as, 4, 96, 103, 108, 114, 125, 135,
    139
    grandparents as, 91, 139
    mothers as, 114, 118, 119
    number of, 39, 42
    profile of, 45
    siblings as, 88–89, 91, 125
    stepfathers as, 4, 139
    stepgrandfathers as, 4
    uncles as, 119, 139
orgasm, 7–8, 19–20, 83–84
    and control, 94, 101, 107
    during incest, 46, 53, 81, 83, 134, 139
    gratifying, 107–8
    and guilt, 122, 134
    nongratifying, 95, 134, 139
    painful, 126, 139
    previous study findings, 7–8, 19–20

self-help guides to, 168, 226
sense of abandonment after, 134, 139
"the split" and, 85
and trust, 91, 100, 107
Overeaters Anonymous, 140

Pacht, A., 7
parenting:
    effects on, 49
    fear of, 56–57, 90, 109, 115, 128, 141–42
    single or adoptive, 57, 110
    see also children; reproduction
participants in the study, 24–36
    age of, 27, 31
    comparison of, 44
    criteria used for inclusion, 26–27
    family portraits of, 45–46
    demographics of, 31–35
    histories of, 37–43
    perceived effects of the incest on, 47–51
    profile of, 44–45
    race of, 27
    religion of, 50, 88, 91, 96, 103, 108, 114,
    119, 125, 135, 139
    responses to the incest, 46–47
    socioeconomic status of, 27
    the study sample, 24–26
partners:
    choosing appropriate partners, 153–54
    considering partner issues, 170–75
    repulsion to during pregnancy, 58, 128
Peck, A., 7
personality, effects on, 47–48
physical violence, 44, 45, 46, 89, 115, 134,
    140
Picture This!, Rage Release for Incest Survi-
    vors, 165–66
Pines, A., 13, 14–15, 18, 19, 22
Pomeroy, W., 4
pornography, 3, 6, 40, 69, 118, 156–57
power, 123, 145, 223
    and body, 54, 59, 141, 162
    and reproduction, 56, 109, 141
    and sexual functioning, 78–80, 82, 85, 138
    and sexual "lifestyle," 67, 68, 69, 70, 71,
    111–12, 121, 131, 132, 138, 144
pregnancy, 56, 57–58, 128
    by offender, 40, 43, 120
    confusion about, 56
    entrapment and, 109, 128
    fears about, 92, 109, 128
    issue of control and, 109, 128, 141
prevalence and incidence of incest, among
    U.S. females, 4, 5
promiscuity, 6, 7–8, 9–11, 27, 123, 146
    affection-seeking and, 100, 117, 131, 143

as an expression of anger, 68, 111, 116–17,
    123, 146
issues of power/control and, 111, 116, 117,
    121, 132
negative self-perception and, 100, 111, 116,
    121, 131, 142–43
sexual "lifestyle" and, 68–69
prostitution, 6, 7–8, 12–13, 27, 123, 146
as an expression of anger, 121, 123, 144,
    146
issues of power/control and, 131, 144
negative self-perception and, 121, 131–32,
    144
sexual "lifestyle" and, 69–70
protectors, 45–46
psychic "numbing," during incest, 46, 47
psychotherapy, 33, 35

questionnaire:
    analysis of, 28, 184–85
    areas covered in, 27–28
    demographic information, 27, 31–33
    histories of participants, 37–41
    return rate of, 25, 27, 31

race and ethnicity of participants, 31, 34
rape:
    as content of fantasies, 76
    incidence of sexual problems following, 4,
        17
    relation to previous incest, 50, 96, 135, 140,
        146
Rascovsky, A., 7, 8, 10
Rascovsky, M., 7, 8, 10
Rasmussen, A., 13
religion:
    influence of incest on, 50
    of participants, 27, 31, 34, 41, 88, 91, 96,
        103, 108, 114, 119, 125, 135, 139
repression, 4, 47
reproduction, 24, 26, 27, 56–59, 60
    birth, 58, 92, 136
    birth control, 106
    development of reproductive capacity, 56,
        89, 105, 135
    fears about pregnancy, 92, 109, 128
    fears about reproductive capacity, 55, 89,
        92
    gynecological dysfunction/disorder, 48,
        126, 175
    influences on, summary of, 178
    nursing, 58–59, 106, 136–37
    obstetrical and gynecological care, 60, 126,
        142
    pregnancy, 56, 57–58, 92, 109, 115, 120,
        128

reproductive decision-making, 56–57, 89–
    90, 106, 109–10, 120, 128
reproductive dysfunction/disorder, 56, 60,
    175
research:
    assumptions, 29–30
    bias, 22, 36
    general research questions, 30
    problems of prior studies, 22
    study methodology, 24–29, 181–87
responsiveness, previous studies, 7–8
revictimization, 50, 96, 135, 140, 146
    biochemical changes and, 162–63
Richardson, J., 163
Riess, B., 14
Rosenberg, M., 7
Rosenfeld, A., 4
runaway behavior, 13
Rush, F., 7
Russell, D., 3, 4, 5, 17, 19

sadomasochism, 20, 27, 71, 118
    as content of fantasies, 75–76, 118, 138–39
Schwartz, E., 4
self-blame, 21, 141, 146
    factors involved in, 21
    reducing guilt and self-blame, 101, 167–68
self-esteem, 48, 123, 146, 223
    difficulty with self-protection and, 50, 96,
        116, 131, 135, 140
    overachieving and, 49
    promiscuity and, 66, 100, 111, 116, 121,
        131, 142–43
    self-neglect and, 140
self-hatred, 77, 89, 134, 141, 146
self-help, xi, 154, 157, 161, 166, 176, 180
    books and materials, 224–26
    discussion groups, 176
    guides to masturbation and orgasm, 168,
        226
    recommendations, xi, 148–76
    resources, 224–26
self-medication, 47
self-mutilation, 47, 162–63
self-respect:
    lack of, 96, 116
    see also self-esteem
sexual activity:
    changes in during pregnancy/nursing, 58,
        59
    frequency of incestuous, 40, 43
    impact of incest on later, 10–11
    nature of incestuous, 39–40, 43
    see also sexual functioning; sexual "life-
        style"
sexual adjustment, 21–22

sexual exploitation:
  leading to prostitution, 12–13
  risk of, following incest, 3
  in therapy, 50
sexual functioning, 3–5, 7–8, 16–20, 24, 26,
  27, 74–87
  aversion and, 18, 107, 135, 143–44
  arousal and, *see* arousal
  compulsion and, 175
  desire and, *see* desire
  fantasy and, *see* fantasy
  influences on, summary of, 179
  inhibition and, 90, 94, 101, 107–8, 113–14,
    117–18, 122, 133–34, 138–39, 143, 144,
    145
  orgasm and, *see* orgasm
  satisfaction/dissatisfaction, 17–18, 26, 85–
    86
  "the split" and, 50–51, 84–85, 179
sexual "lifestyle," 24, 26, 27, 29, 64–71, 72–73
  alternation between promiscuity and celi-
    bacy, 69
  aversion and, 65, 107, 138, 143
  celibacy and, 67–68, 69, 90, 99–100, 110,
    130–31, 137
  changes in, 64–65, 73, 90, 99–100, 110–13,
    116–18, 121–22, 131–33, 143–44
  compulsion and, 66–67, 99, 100, 110–11,
    116, 121, 131–33, 143
  influences on, summary of, 178–79
  inhibition and, 65–66, 90, 93, 99, 100, 107,
    113, 116, 117–18, 122, 131, 133, 138, 143
  monogamy/nonmonogamy, 70, 99, 111,
    117, 133
  pornography and, 69
  promiscuity and, 68–69
  prostitution and, 69–70
  "the split" and, 70–71, 99, 111–12, 132–33,
    178
sexual orientation, 71
sexual preference, 13–16, 23, 24, 25, 26, 27,
    61–64, 71–72
  associations with incest, 62
  assumptions and, 64
  certainty about, 61–62
  changes in, 90, 99, 110, 115–16, 120, 128–
    30, 137
  confusion about, 63–64, 71–72, 106, 128–
    30, 137
  dissatisfaction with, 63
  influences on, summary of, 178
  of participants, 32, 35, 61–62
  satisfaction with, 61–62
shame, 124, 145, 223
  and body, 46, 48, 53, 54, 104, 109, 114, 126,
    135–36

and reproduction, 57, 58, 136–37
and sexual functioning, 75, 77, 80–81, 83,
  90, 113–14, 121, 133–34
and sexual "lifestyle," 65, 66, 67–68, 113,
  122, 142, 144
reducing shame, 54, 56, 114, 161–65, 167–
  69
siblings:
  abuse by, 88–89, 91
  also incestuously abused, 38, 41, 42
Silbert, M., 13, 14–15, 18, 22
Simari, C., 14, 16, 22
Simon Fraser University, 163
Sjoberg, G., 28
Skinner, L., 3, 17, 20
Sloane, P., 7, 8, 10, 12, 13
societal attitudes toward incest, 8
socioeconomic status:
  of participants, 32, 34, 37, 41
"split, the," the nonintegration of emotional
  and sexual intimacy, 50–51, 70–71, 84–
  85, 111–12, 132–33, 178, 179
Sprei, J., 160*n*
Starting from Scratch: The I.R. Group
  Model*, 176
Stoll, K., 3, 17
Study, The, 24–36
  criteria for inclusion in, 26–27
  general research questions, 29–30
  intent of, x, 23, 177
  participants, 33–35
  interviews, 28–29, 211–13
  limitations of, 35–36
  participant sample, 24–26, 27
  purpose of, 24
  participant demographics, 31–33
  the questionnaire, 27–28, 188–210
  researcher bias, 36
suicide attempts and feelings, 47, 48, 145

Tagiuri, C., 7
thematic analysis:
  of interviews, 29, 185
  of questionnaires, 28, 184–85
touch:
  fear of with children, 49, 57, 137
  sensitivity to, 117, 134, 137, 143
Treacy, E., 3, 17
treatment, behavioral component, 154–60
  altering associations, 159–60
  clinical implications of study findings,
    179–80
  progressive exercises, sensate focus, 157–
    58
  relaxation, 154–56, 227–28
  sensual and sexual self-pleasuring, 157

systematic desensitization, 154, 156
triggers that elicit incest memories and
    flashbacks, 158–60
use of erotica versus pornography, 156–57
treatment, cognitive component, 150–54
    clinical implications of study findings,
        179–80
    corrective cognitive statements, 150–52
    image-altering techniques, 152
    image-stopping techniques, 152
    interrupting displacement of anger, 150–
        51
    interrupting interference from guilt, 151
    managing flashbacks, 152–53
    reparenting and nuturing child parts of
        self, 153
    role of partner, 151, 152–54
    separation of past and present, 150, 153,
        154
treatment, educational component, 166–76
    clinical implications of study findings,
        179–80
    considering partner issues, 170–75
    correcting "magical thinking," 169–70
    establishing a sense of normalcy and
        appreciation, 168–69
    objectives of, 166
    providing reassurance, 175–76
    reducing guilt and self-blame, 167–68
treatment, physical component, 161–66
    clinical implications of study findings,
        179–80
    Inside Out, Therapeutic Bodywork for
        Incest Survivors, 164–65
    I.R.* obics, Therapeutic Aerobics for
        Incest Survivors, 162–64
    Picture This!, Rage Release for Incest
        Survivors, 165–66
treatment, recommendations for sex thera-
    pists, 149–50
treatment, self-help recommendations and,
    xi, 148–76
treatment, self-help resources and, 224–26

trust, 146, 223
    and body, 54, 59, 98
    and reproduction, 57, 109, 128
    and sexual functioning, 83, 91, 100, 107,
        122
    and sexual "lifestyle," 66, 69, 99, 100, 118
Tsai, M., 3, 5, 11, 17, 18, 19, 21, 22, 23, 72,
    86, 87

vaginal:
    closure, 80
    infections, 126
    pain, 80, 83, 126
vaginismus, 20, 86, 179
Van der Kolk, B., 162
Verebey, K., 162
Vitaliano, P., 13
Volavka, J., 162

Wagner, N., 3, 4, 5, 17, 18, 19, 20, 22, 86, 87,
    158
Waterman, J., 17
Watts, D., 3, 5, 18
Weinberg, S., 7, 8, 9, 10, 12, 13
Westerlund, E., 3, 5, 7, 11, 17, 18, 19, 20, 52,
    87
Westerlund Incest Survivors Questionnaire,
    27–28, 188–210
Winnick, H., 8, 13
Wolpe, J., 154
women:
    mistrust of, 154
    numbers of, with incest histories, 4, 5
    as offenders, 45
    as protectors, 45–46
    see also participants in the study
Woodbury, J., 4
work:
    problems of participants, 48–49
    see also occupations
Wyatt, G., 4, 17

Zaleski, W., 163